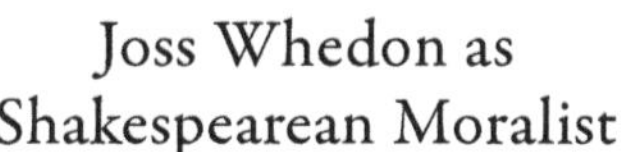

Joss Whedon as
Shakespearean Moralist

Joss Whedon as Shakespearean Moralist

Narrative Ethics of the Bard and the Buffyverse

J. Douglas Rabb *and*
J. Michael Richardson

Foreword by Kim Fedderson

McFarland & Company, Inc., Publishers
Jefferson, North Carolina

ALSO OF INTEREST

Indian from the Inside: Native American Philosophy and Cultural Renewal, 2d ed., by Dennis H. McPherson and J. Douglas Rabb (McFarland, 2011)

The Existential Joss Whedon: Evil and Human Freedom in Buffy the Vampire Slayer, Angel, Firefly *and* Serenity, by J. Michael Richardson and J. Douglas Rabb (McFarland, 2007)

LIBRARY OF CONGRESS CATALOGUING-IN-PUBLICATION DATA

Rabb, J. Douglas.
    Joss Whedon as Shakespearean moralist : narrative ethics of the Bard and the Buffyverse / J. Douglas Rabb and J. Michael Richardson ; foreword by Kim Fedderson.
        p.   cm.
    Includes bibliographical references and index.

    ISBN 978-0-7864-7440-0 (softcover : acid free paper) ∞
    ISBN 978-1-4766-1786-2 (ebook)

    1. Whedon, Joss, 1964– —Criticism and interpretation.
2. Shakespeare, William, 1564–1616—Ethics.   3. Narration (Rhetoric)—Moral and ethical aspects.   I. Richardson, J. Michael   II. Title.

PN1992.4.W49R525 2015
791.4302'33092—dc23   2014035486

BRITISH LIBRARY CATALOGUING DATA ARE AVAILABLE

On the cover: *Whedon as Shakespeare* by Mark Nisenholt, professor of visual arts, Lakehead University, Thunder Bay, Ontario

Printed in the United States of America

McFarland & Company, Inc., Publishers
    Box 611, Jefferson, North Carolina 28640
        www.mcfarlandpub.com

Acknowledgments

We are grateful to Kim Fedderson for the kind words of the foreword, and to Mark Nisenholt for his cover art *Whedon as Shakespeare*. Both, in their own way, capture rather well the main themes of the book.

We want to thank Rhonda W. Wilcox, co-editor of *Slayage: The Journal of the Whedon Studies Association*, for encouraging us in our studies of Whedon. As we will show, the very fact that there is a Whedon Studies Association supports our contention that Whedon is the Shakespeare of our time.

We also thank Rhonda for permission to use, as we have, our 2009 *Slayage* paper, "Myth, Metaphor, Morality and Monsters: The Espenson Factor and Cognitive Science in Joss Whedon's Narrative Love Ethic," *Slayage: The Online International Journal of Buffy* Studies, 7.4 (28) 2009, and her own "'Let It Simmer': Tone in 'Pangs,'" *Slayage: The Journal of the Whedon Studies Association*, 9.1 (33) 2011.

Contents

Foreword
by Kim Fedderson

"Joss Whedon is the Shakespeare of our time." The authors make a bold claim, one that their intended readers, who, depending upon their perspectives on the tensions between popular and high culture, contemporary and traditional dramatic forms, innovation and adaptation (not to mention the level of their interest in vampires, werewolves, and apocalyptic science fiction), will variously celebrate, deride, but, most certainly, debate.

What does Whedon's being "Shakespeare" entail? J. Douglas Rabb, a philosopher with a long-standing interest in the moral imagination and the co-author of the influential *Indian from the Inside: Native American Philosophy and Cultural Renewal* (with Dennis H. McPherson, 2d ed., McFarland, 2011), and J. Michael Richardson, a colleague of mine at Lakehead University with whom I have collaborated extensively on Shakespeare in popular culture, are in an excellent position to address this question. They are perhaps best known for *The Existential Joss Whedon: Evil and Human Freedom in* Buffy the Vampire Slayer, Angel, Firefly *and* Serenity (McFarland, 2007), one of the earliest book-length scholarly engagements with Whedon's work.

In this new book, they argue that, like Shakespeare, Whedon is a writer whose works are highly imaginative, dramatically innovative, intellectually stimulating, and, despite, or because of, these features, have found a wide audience. Shakespeare continues to be the most widely produced writer of all time, and Whedon's audience continues to expand: his recent film, *The Avengers,* is one the highest grossing pictures of all time. Rabb and Richardson present a rich catalogue of Whedon's direct borrowings from Shakespeare: bits of dialogue, characters (inclusive of a claim that Beatrice from *Much Ado About Nothing* is Buffy's precursor), plot motifs, and allusions to *The Merchant of Venice, Othello, Macbeth, Measure for Measure*, and *The Tempest*. The affinities between the two extend beyond mere borrowings. Whedon, they contend, is

Shakespeare-like in his manner as well as his matter. Both have a significant impact on their respective cultures. Like Shakespeare, Whedon coins new words (his penchant for "-y" suffixes, as in "angsty," or "-age" suffixes, as in "slayage"), and these are finding their way into the language. Both establish themselves in emergent genres, embraced by popular audiences but frequently held in less regard by contemporary cultural arbiters. While auteurs, both are comfortable with the collaborative contributions of others. Both rely upon companies of actors whose roles in previous performances seep into new roles. Both employ meta-theatrical turns, inviting audiences to glimpse the ethical meanings beneath the surface of the texts.

This concern for ethics and the role the imagination plays in ethical decision-making is the central focus of this book. Rabb and Richardson claim that Whedon, like Shakespeare, is "a great ethicist." They contend both Whedon and Shakespeare compose narratives which provide what Kenneth Burke called "equipment for living." The dramatized stories they tell have the potential to inform our ethical decision-making, influencing the choices we make as we try to secure a good life. Drawing on cognitive science, in particular the work of Lakoff and Johnson, Rabb and Richardson argue that metaphor (e.g., life as a journey) can capture the complexity of our experience and so inform our moral choices better than a series of abstract ethical precepts (the Ten Commandments) or principles (Mill's utilitarian "the greatest good for the greatest number," or Kant's rationalist "categorical imperative"). They argue that the desire to establish transcendental universal ethical principles, good for all places and all times, is frustrated by the embodied nature of human experience. As brains with bodies, we engage in ethical decision-making always already situated in particularly concrete circumstances complexly determined by our geographical, historical, societal, and cultural locations. The imagination, which through metaphor and narrative is able to wed abstract tenor (e.g., justice) and vehicle (e.g., scales) eclipses reason in its ability to represent the complexity of embodied human experience; and in this respect, is better able to inform ethical-decision making than reason's abstractions which purchase their universality by the shucking off the particularity of worldly experience.

As an early modern, Shakespeare's moral imagination presents us with worlds pushed out of joint, often as a consequence of excessive adherence to or willful transgression of societal codes and cultural customs, creating complex ethical dilemmas the implications of which frequently exceed the promise or hope of resolution afforded by comedy's marriages and tragedy's funerals. Whedon, situated in a postmodernity in which there is little or no consensus over what constitutes a world in or out of joint, makes TV shows and movies out of popular genres (e.g., teen horror, science fiction, comic book action heroes) which capture the irony and anxiety suitable to what some claim are these indeterminate, pre-apocalyptic or post-apocalyptic times.

Far more than an appreciation for either Whedon or Shakespeare, what's really at stake here—pun fully intended—is the extent to which the works produced by these writers provide their respective readers—Shakespeare's early modern readers and Whedon's postmodern readers—with narrative frames which assist them in making moral choices in rather different historical moments. The questions that Rabb and Richardson raise about the relation of the literary imagination to the moral imagination, about the role of precept and narrative in ethical decision-making, are timely, urgent, and necessary.

Kim Fedderson is a professor of English at Lakehead University, Thunder Bay, Ontario, and dean and vice-provost of the University's Orillia campus.

Introduction

There's been a paradigm shift in the mythos.
—"New Rules, Part One"

This is a study in narrative ethics drawing on the works of Shakespeare and Whedon. William Shakespeare needs no introduction. He is regarded as the greatest writer in the English-speaking world, and perhaps the greatest writer the world has ever seen. We will argue that he is also one of the world's greatest ethicists. Joss Whedon, we will argue, is the Shakespeare of our time. He is a third generation television writer. David Lavery, in *Joss Whedon, A Creative Portrait: From* Buffy the Vampire Slayer *to* Marvel's The Avengers (31–37), provides a detailed account of the achievements of Whedon's grandfather and father. His grandfather, John Ogden Whedon (1904–1991), wrote for *Lux Video Theatre* (1951–1955), *Kraft Television Theatre* (1956), *The Alcoa Hour* (1957), *Leave It to Beaver* (1958–1959), *The Donna Reed Show* (1961), *The Dick Van Dyke Show* (1962–1964), and *The Andy Griffith Show* (1963–1964). His father, Tom Whedon (b. 1932), wrote for *Captain Kangaroo* (1962–1965), *The Dick Cavett Show* (1971), *The Electric Company* (1972–1977), *Alice* (1977–1980), *United States* (1980), *Benson* (1980–1981), *It's a Living* and *The Golden Girls* (1989–1991).

Joss Whedon himself is best known for *Buffy the Vampire Slayer* (1997–2003), *Angel* (1999–2004), *Firefly* (2002), *Dollhouse* (2009–2010), and *Marvel's Agents of S.H.I.EL.D.* (debuted in 2013), as well as the movies *Buffy the Vampire Slayer* (1992), the *Firefly* spinoff *Serenity* (2005), *The Cabin in the Woods* (released in 2012), *Marvel's The Avengers* (released in 2012), and his black-and-white film version of Shakespeare's *Much Ado About Nothing* (released in 2013). Lavery also points out that musical inclination and talent are evident in John, Tom, and Joss Whedon: in 1950 John Whedon co-wrote a musical entitled *Texas, Lil' Darlin,* which had a "good run (283 performances) on Broadway" (32); in the 1960s Tom Whedon co-wrote a musical entitled *Money* and "author[ed] at least 50 songs for *The Electric Company*" (33); and Joss Whedon himself penned a musical episode of *Buffy* entitled "Once More with Feeling," as well as the Internet show *Dr. Horrible's Sing-Along Blog*. Joss Whedon's work has attracted the attention of numerous scholars, as witnessed by the large number of books and articles on his works. See our Works Cited for a sample of this scholarship and the online Whedon bibliography on the *Slayage* website (http://slayageonline.com/). Critical work on Whedon has become so extensive that it has actually been referred to as a "vast scholarly canon" (Nancy Holder, "Preface" to Lavery 2014). Much of this work deals with philosophical and ethical issues in the Whedonverses. We will show how Whedon, like Shakespeare, can and should be read as a form of narrative ethics.

We should indicate where our interest in narrative ethics is coming from. For the past fifteen plus years we have been working with the Centre for Health Care Ethics (CHCE) at our university. One of us is a founding member of CHCE and still serves as a volunteer on the Executive Board. We both somewhat regularly participate in CHCE's major educational program, "Encounters in Bioethics," which during the regular academic year from September through April sponsors monthly presentations on ethical issues in health care. The sessions are available on-site and via videoconference to all organizations connected to the Ontario Telemedicine Network. We have been speakers at these sessions and have served as panel discussants responding to other speakers. In fact we opened the 2007 academic year with a presentation entitled "Myth, Metaphor, Morality and Medicine: Finding the Care in Health Care Ethics," in which we raised the following questions: "Is our moral thinking driven by Myths and Metaphors or Reason and Principles?" "Can a popular TV series like *Buffy the Vampire Slayer* say something significant about our moral life?" "Do stories we tell each other help our understanding of alternative moral views?" "Could empirical science be used to decide between ethical theories?" and "What is the relation between Cognitive Science and Ethical Theory?" (Rabb and Richardson 2007).

The Encounters in Bioethics Series has been particularly useful in our own research, which is more theoretical, dealing with the philosophy of literature, cross-cultural values, and the nature of ethical thinking itself. Our training is in philosophy and literature, not health care, and the opportunity to engage with front line health care professionals has been invaluable. One thing we have observed as audience members is that while most presentations on bioethics mention the standard bioethical principles of beneficence, nonmaleficence, autonomy, and justice, the presenters seem not to know quite what to do with these principles (see Beauchamp and Childress 2008). They often pay only lip service to the principles, explaining for example that "beneficence" means doing some good, "nonmaleficence" demands we do no harm, and "autonomy" means at the very least getting informed consent. The speakers then, it seems, just go on to discuss the particular "case studies" they present as if they had never mentioned these principles. Their "case studies" are usually one or two short paragraphs illustrating the particular ethical issue they wish to discuss. The discussions themselves are often both interesting and challenging, but, as we said, hardly ever draw on the principles introduced at the beginning of the talk. This is not in any way a criticism of the presentations; rather, we suggest such principles are actually of little use in dealing with real life problems in medical ethics, those that health care professionals must face every working day. Speaking of such principles, philosopher Mark Johnson observes in *Moral Imagination: Implications of Cognitive Science for Ethics*, that "they 'work' for the prototypical cases—the nonproblematic ones—about which there is widespread agreement within moral traditions. What moral laws we have are precisely those that are formulated to fit the prototypical cases" (1993, 190). Over the years we have observed that many of the problems in medical ethics discussed in the Encounters in Bioethics Series arise out of developments in medical technology not even conceivable when these ethical principles were formulated. Johnson confirms: "The emergence of new technologies, such as recent reproductive technologies, has created new moral problems and situations that neither existed nor were even imagined when certain 'standards' of sexual, familial, and biomedical practice were gradually formulated in our moral tradition ... events such as the development of in vitro fertilization and genetic engineering have confronted us with possibilities that might actually require us to revise our concepts of personhood and our assumptions about what is 'natural' in the reproductive process" (106). For these reasons, a growing number of ethicists, like D. Micah Hester, for example, argue that we should "move away from the language and use of principles altogether" (2001, 28). Hester would, we believe, approve of the kind of specific-problem discussions we have in our Encounters in Bioethics Series because he argues, "ethical and clinical decisions begin with particular individuals" (28). He can't understand why so many ethicists in this day and age "insist on justifying all activity from the level of abstract principles and not through reflection on specific problems" (26). We have grown to agree with him. "Principles lose touch with individuals and their specific values and interests. They do not account for differences among individuals and situations" (Hester 28). It is for these reasons that we decided we should undertake a major study of narrative ethics, not limited to bioethics, but more broadly based, relating to all forms of applied ethics, as well as to moral theory itself. This book is the result. We hope it will contribute to the narrative turn in moral philosophy.

We chose to concentrate on the works of Shakespeare and Whedon because Shakespeare is writing *before* the influence of the modern moral philosophers of the 17th and 18th centuries, while Whedon is writing in the *post*modern period. Most contemporary theories of ethics can be traced back to the 17th and 18th centuries. Consequentialism is based on the utilitarian philosophers Jeremy Bentham (1748–1832) and John Stuart Mill (1806–1873). Contractualism has its foundation in philosophers like John Locke (1632–1704). And finally Kantian Ethics with its Categorical Imperative or Supreme Principle of Morality is due, of course, to the German philosopher Immanuel Kant (1724–1804). In Chapter Eight we explain and discuss these moral theories with specific reference to the works of Joss Whedon. Whedon has attracted so much attention from moral philosophers that consequentialists, contractualists, and Kantians have each interpreted Whedon's work using their own pet theory. While we find this an interesting and entertaining way of teaching these modern moral theories to undergraduates, we are not convinced that it casts much light on the works of Whedon, illuminating the theories more than the works of Whedon. Whedon, as we said, is writing in a *post*modern era. We argue that he has more in common with the *early* modern Shakespeare than with these modern theories of ethics. Though he is writing in postmodern times, Whedon is not an ethical relativist like so many postmodern authors. As Gregory Stevenson argues in *Televised Morality: The Case of* Buffy the Vampire Slayer: "*Buffy*'s perspective on good and evil is not a relativistic one in which the categories of good and evil are constantly redefined based on current circumstances, but neither is it an absolute one in which good and evil are always clearly defined" (73). This shows the sophistication of Whedon's narrative in recognizing that the opposite of ethical relativism is not ethical absolutism. It is possible to reject both absolutism and relativism, provided you can offer some viable justification for moral choice. We will argue that moral choice can best be explained through narrative, and, as we will show, is usually grounded in metaphorical thought rather than in absolute ethical principles or abstract universal moral rules. As Stevenson puts it, "*Buffy*'s worldview is absolute in its conception of good and evil in the sense that both are categories that exist unequivocally ... the real problem is differentiating between the two" (73–74). Whedon's narratives are dedicated to showing how this is possible. The arguments they present are all metaphorical arguments about slaying our personal and social demons. As Stevenson rightly points out, our demons "can be overcome by the power of love, community, and forgiveness" (236) and by rejecting the simplistic binary logic implicit in "demons bad, people good.... Something wrong with that theorem?" (4.19 "New Moon Rising"). What is wrong with that theorem becomes apparent through narratives about vampires with souls who fight on the side of good and the story of the vampire slayer Faith who goes bad.

Shakespeare too gives us complex, fully-rounded characters, placed in complicated, highly-nuanced situations in which they must struggle with both their own natures and with ethical conundrums and quagmires that are not reducible to the kind of question that can be answered by a simple appeal to a universal principle, consequentialist or otherwise. These characters frequently find that the moral principles they can and do adduce are just not adequate to the ambiguities and ambivalences within the problems they are facing.

The major portion of our study is a detailed discussion of representative works of Shakespeare and Whedon, showing how they can and should be read as narrative arguments supporting a narrative ethics.

We are under no illusion that our study of narrative ethics will change the world. We would be content if it encouraged a few moral philosophers to go back to Shakespeare. We would be happy if ethicists and moral philosophers started binge-watching *Buffy* as well as other works of Joss Whedon. And that—that really might change the world.

ONE

Joss Whedon, the Shakespeare for Our Time

*Right, because "Buffy the Vampire Slayer" is
downright Shakespearean—"New Rules, Part One"*

"Joss Whedon and Shakespeare Are a Match Made in Heaven"—these words appear on the screen in large letters near the end of the trailer for Joss Whedon's 2012 black-and-white movie adaptation of Shakespeare's *Much Ado About Nothing*. Whedon's movie, the first production of Bellwether Pictures, a company started by Joss Whedon and his wife Kai Cole, premiered at the Toronto International Film Festival in September 2012, to rave reviews. For example, Lou Lumenick of the *New York Post* says that "this is the funniest Shakespeare film I … recall seeing … this may not be a 'Much Ado' for purists, but it will be enjoyed by many who wouldn't normally dream of watching a Shakespeare adaptation" (September 11, 2012). On the other side of the ocean, *The Guardian's* Catherine Shoard proclaims, "Joss Whedon's impact on youth culture is already hard to overestimate. Now he's made the first great contemporary Shakespeare since Baz Luhrmann's *Romeo and Juliet*.... Whedon's key coup is in simply directing a very good version of the play. He's got a keen ear for comedy, a no-nonsense approach to ditching the gags that don't work, a deft hand for slapstick and an eagerness to use it. Just as with this summer's surprise smash (*The Avengers*), he assembled a crack squad of a cast, then dispatched them with purpose" (September 13, 2012). This "crack squad of a cast" contains many "regulars" which Whedon draws from his previous television shows and movies. We count at least a dozen. Lou Lumenick speaks of the "Bard's glorious dialogue delivered with gusto (and precise diction) by a stock company drawn almost entirely from the ranks of his various TV shows" (September 11, 2012).

Similarly, Shakespeare's acting company, the Lord Chamberlain's Men, which came to be called the King's Men, re-used many actors for several plays. This is alluded to, rather amusingly, in the film *Shakespeare in Love*, when Ned Alleyn (Ben Affleck) marches into the theater and demands imperiously, "What is the play and what is my part?" It is worth noting that Edward (Ned) Alleyn (1566–1626) was, historically, the principal actor of the Lord Admiral's Men (the chief rival of the Lord Chamberlain's Men). *Shakespeare in Love* is being speculative at best by having Alleyn play Mercutio in *Romeo and Juliet*, or any other Shakespeare play for that matter. Alleyn was well connected, being the son-in-law of Philip Henslowe, and won acclaim and admiration for performances as Christopher Marlowe's Tamburlaine, Doctor Faustus, and Barabas, the title character in *The Jew of Malta*. These parts may well have been written specifically for him. It is thought by some that he also played Orlando in Robert Greene's *Orlando Furioso*, and perhaps Hieronymo in *The Spanish Tragedy* by Thomas Kyd. He eventually became very wealthy and owned a number of playhouses (including the Rose and the Fortune), as well as bearpits, and brothels. The Lord Admiral's Men occupied the Fortune, which was built the year after the Globe Theater. Alleyn was also the founder of Dulwich College. His main rival for pre-eminence as an actor was Richard Burbage (1567–1619), of the Lord Chamberlain's Men. Burbage was in fact the first theatrical embodiment of many of Shakespeare's most celebrated characters, including *Hamlet, Othello, Richard III* (for which he was especially renowned), and *King Lear*. He also appeared in the plays of many of the great contemporary writers, such as Ben Jonson (the titular *Volpone*, and Subtle in *The Alchemist*), John Marston (*The Malcontent*), John Webster (*The Duchess of Malfi*) and Beaumont and Fletcher (*The Maid's Tragedy*). An anonymous elegy, which exists in several versions, confirms that Burbage is well remembered for his many roles in Shakespeare's tragedies:

> He's gone, and with him what a world are dead,
> Friends, every one, and what a blank instead!
> Take him for all in all, he was a man
> Not to be match'd, and no age ever can.
> No more young Hamlet, though but scant of breath,
> Shall cry "Revenge!" for his dear father's death.
> Poor Romeo never more shall tears beget
> For Juliet's love and cruel Capulet:
> Harry shall not be seen as king or prince,
> They died with thee, dear Dick, [and not long since]
> Not to revive again....
> Tyrant Macbeth, with unwash'd, bloody hand,
> We vainly now may hope to understand.
> Brutus and Marcius henceforth must be dumb,
> For ne'er thy like upon the stage shall come,

> To charm the faculty of ears and eyes,
> Unless we could command the dead to rise....
> What a wide world was in that little space,
> Thyself a world the Globe thy fittest place!
> [quoted in Mabillard 2000].

This version of the elegy associates Burbage with an enormous number and range of plays, and even if we question the accuracy of the list, it speaks worlds about the impression Burbage made on the public's mind.

Noted comic actors also appeared frequently in several of Shakespeare's plays, many of which were probably written with their specific talents and attributes in mind. For example, William Kempe (c. 1560–c. 1603) was a shareholder in the Lord Chamberlain's Men along with Richard Burbage and Shakespeare himself, but left the company in 1599, before the building of the Globe Theater. It is known for certain that he played Dogberry in *Much Ado About Nothing* and Peter in *Romeo and Juliet* and quite probably Bottom in *A Midsummer Night's Dream*, Costard in *Love's Labours Lost*, and Launcelot Gobbo in *The Merchant of Venice*. He may have been the original Falstaff as well, although the character Falstaff, while retaining some of the rustic clown features of the other roles, is a different and much more complex comic role than Kempe is usually associated with. In any case, Falstaff does not appear in Shakespeare after Kempe's departure from the Lord Chamberlain's Men. Kempe was succeeded by, or perhaps replaced by, Robert Armin (1568–1615), in the Lord Chamberlain's Men. Armin was the leading actor in Shakespearean comedy. He inherited the role of Dogberry from Kempe. We can imagine Elizabethan patrons comparing Kempe's Dogberry to that of Armin. Armin built his professional reputation on developing and playing intelligent and philosophical clown/fool roles such as Touchstone in *As You Like It*, Feste in *Twelfth Night*, and the Fool in *King Lear*. He possibly also played Lavatch in *All's Well That Ends Well*, Thersites in *Troilus and Cressida*, and the Porter in *Macbeth*. Armin was named as one of the principal actors in the First Folio (1623). As noted above, both Kempe and Armin played Dogberrry in *Much Ado About Nothing*, a role humorously filled by Nathan Fillion in Joss Whedon's adaptation. Just as Kempe, Armin, and Burbage were "regulars" in Shakespeare, so Nathan Fillion has been in Whedon, having played, in addition to Dogberry, Caleb in *Buffy the Vampire Slayer*, Captain Malcolm Reynolds in *Firefly/Serenity*, and Captain Hammer, corporate tool, in *Dr. Horrible's Sing-Along Blog*. From a product placement standpoint, it's a pity that Robert Armin isn't alive today to play Whedon's Captain Hammer; in ages yet to come scholars could have compared the Fillion Hammer with the Armin Hammer.

If Shakespeare were alive today, he would likely be writing for film, television, and perhaps even the Internet, if a way is found to monetize the blogosphere. In *30 Great Myths About Shakespeare* ("Myth 19: If Shakespeare were writing now, he'd be writing for Hollywood"), Laurie Maguire and Emma Smith note that both the Renaissance theater business and the Hollywood film industry "reach a wide audience and are commercially as well as aesthetically, successful, making some of their key players rich (including Shakespeare, a share-holder in the Lord Chamberlain's Men)" (125). Interestingly enough, Maguire and Smith ultimately reject the idea that Shakespeare would write for Hollywood, on the grounds that Hollywood plays up the visual and the spectacular at the expense of the script and the verbal. However, they do not mention the possibility of independent film, which quite often relies more heavily on the script, and in general they seem to assume that all film is like Hollywood, an assumption which is patently false, but encouraged by the phrasing chosen for this myth. But most surprising of all is that they do not consider television as a likely venue for Shakespeare. Granted, the episodic nature of much television makes a parallel with Dickens more tempting, but channels like HBO and sometimes the BBC do multipart, but definitely finite, dramas—*House of Cards*; *Prime Suspect*; *Downton Abbey*; *I Claudius*; *Upstairs, Downstairs*; *Fawlty Towers*, etc. The Masterpiece Theater approach allows for shows that are heavily script-centered, whether they are adapting an old text or creating a new fiction altogether. Whedon's *Much Ado About Nothing* is, of course, a paradigmatic example of a script-centered indie film, and is based on a Shakespeare script. Agreeing that everyone in the cast of his *Much Ado* makes "Shakespeare appear effortless," Whedon says that "If it doesn't sound contemporary, then the distance between it and the audience is going to be insurmountable. And the fact is, the language is fun to say. It is lovely to speak it, and to hear it said. I think, nobody was better than Kenneth Branagh at taking this endless paragraph that you read as a kid, and then speaking it as though it was the next thing he was speaking and you understood it perfectly. That's what you need, and all of these actors are so facile with it, and it comes so naturally to them ... because they've done it a million times. Nathan Fillion's done some at our house for readings, and that was it. He was a nervous kitten. But you can't tell that he hasn't been speaking it all the time. And that has to do with my knowing of their precision with their instrument. I mean, not to sound like a pretentious guy, but there are actors I love whose control over their voices is not so specific. And you really need that" (Whedon 2012a).

In addition to Nathan Fillion, other Whedon "regulars" appearing in his *Much Ado* include Amy Acker (Beatrice), who played Fred/Illyria in *Angel*, Dr. Claire Saunders and Whiskey in *Dollhouse*, and Wendy Lin in *The Cabin in the Woods*; Alexis Denisof (Benedick), who played Wesley Wyndham-Pryce in *Buffy* and *Angel*, Senator Daniel Perrin in *Dollhouse*, and The Other in *Marvel's The Avengers*; Clark Gregg (Leonato), who played Phil Coulson in

Marvel's The Avengers and *Agents of S.H.I.E.L.D.*; Reed Diamond (Don Pedro), who played Laurence Dominic in *Dollhouse*; Fran Kranz (Claudio), who played Topher Brink in *Dollhouse* and Marty in *The Cabin in the Woods*; Sean Maher (Don John), who played Simon Tam in *Firefly/Serenity*; Riki Lindhome (Conrade), who played Cheryl in "Him" (*Buffy the Vampire Slayer* 7.6); Ashley Johnson (Margaret), who played a waitress in *The Avengers*; Tom Lenk (Verges), played Andrew Wells in *Buffy* and *Angel* as well as a minion of Harmony and later of Glory, and Ronald the intern in *The Cabin in the Woods*; Romy Rosemont (The Sexton), played Shawna Lynde in *The Avengers*; and Jillian Morgese (Hero), who has an uncredited role as a woman in a restaurant in *The Avengers*. Whedon fans seem to enjoy seeing familiar actors in new roles.

Alyson Buckman, in her featured presentation at the fifth biennial *Slayage* Conference at the University of British Columbia, refers to this phenomenon as "hyperdiegetic casting." She defines hyperdiegetic casting as "the way in which meaning is created through the use and reuse of actors solely and specifically within a particular, cohesive narrative space, in this case the Whedonverse, although such use and reuse may have referents outside of the Whedonverse as well and thus then bring in the more general term 'intertextuality of casting.' Whedon has built a collective, specialized fund of knowledge available specifically to those who have watched (and rewatched) his fictions, although certainly one may bring additional subtext" (Buckman 2012, 1).

Buckman notes that the term "intertextuality of casting" was coined by Jeffrey Bussolini in his *Slayage 3* conference paper. An expanded version of this paper has since appeared as an article in the *Slayage* journal itself. Bussolini defines intertextuality of casting as follows: "the often intentional crossover of actors and actresses between and among different shows, and the way in which bringing along recognizable faces and styles serves to cross-pollinate televisual texts and create a larger televisual intertext ... this casting serves in important ways to shape the 'Verses' of the artworks at hand and ... the conscious choice of such casting offers an artistic tool in creating a televisual text" (par. 3). We found that our old friend Topher as Marty enhanced our enjoyment of *The Cabin in the Woods*. Buckman also draws attention to the fact that Fran Kranz played both Topher and Marty and seems equally intrigued with the result: "Kranz's Marty in *Cabin in the Woods* is a delightful nod to the fan of *Dollhouse*: to hear Marty talking about the 'puppetmasters' when Kranz also played Topher, a puppetmaster par excellence, provided me a great deal of pleasure" (8). As the elegy for Richard Burbage we cited above strongly indicates, Shakespeare's audience would have had similar experiences with hyperdiegetic casting, seeing, for example, their favorite hyperactive villain, Richard III, playing Hamlet paralyzed by indecision.

Rhonda Wilcox also sees parallels between Whedon and Shakespeare.

In her *Slayage* article, "In 'The Demon Section of the Card Catalog': *Buffy* Studies and Television Studies," referring to the "power of language," she notes that "people quote lines of *Buffy* (often Whedon) the way they quote Shakespeare, making the text a part of the way to see life. *Buffy* has at its command not only the power of language but of image and of music…. Nowadays, people sometimes learn history in order to better enjoy Shakespeare's plays—not the other way around. We love the language, we love the characters, we love the struggle of the characters—or their comedic play. The same is true for *Buffy*" (par. 24). In citing Shakespeare, we sometimes find ourselves quoting original contributions to the English language. The Oxford English Dictionary credits Shakespeare for introducing nearly 3,000 words into the English Language and many of them are still commonly used today (Listphoria). Whedon is also credited with creating new words. Michael Adams's book, *Slayer Slang: A Buffy the Vampire Slayer Lexicon*, discusses many of them, explaining the various techniques used in their construction. Many of these techniques are also the ones that Shakespeare used in his creation of an often unique vocabulary; for example, changing nouns into verbs, verbs into adjectives, adding prefixes and suffixes, and conjoining familiar words in unfamiliar ways. The phrase "witching time of night" may sound like it comes from *Buffy* given the show's dense population of witches, poltergeists, vampires, demons, and sundry other supernatural creatures, but it does in fact originate in *Hamlet*, when the melancholy Dane says, "'Tis now is the very witching time of night, / When churchyards yawn and hell itself [breathes] out / Contagion to this world. Now could I drink hot blood, / And do such [bitter business as the] day / Would quake to look on" (3.2. 388–392). In *Buffy* season four Spike even heats up a cup of blood in the microwave. Much of Whedon does not sound unlike Shakespeare; for example, in "Welcome to the Hellmouth" (*Buffy* 1.1), the Master's servant Luke, in a deliberately archaic-sounding passage, except perhaps for the final sentence, intones: "And like a plague of boils, the race of man covered the Earth. But on the third day of the newest light would come the Harvest. And the blood of men will flow as wine. When the Master will walk among them once more! The Earth will belong to the old ones. And Hell itself will come to town. Amen!" The term "witchy," however, is a real Whedon creation, as in "Willow's witchy-power" (*Buffy* 4.21 "Primeval"). Buffy's friend, Willow Rosenberg, eventually develops her "witchy" powers to such an extent that she is capable of destroying the world, and very nearly does, though most of the time she uses her powers to aid Buffy in the fight against evil. Just adding the suffix "-y" to a noun is a common Whedon technique for creating novel words. Michael Adams, in his classic text, *Slayer Slang*, notes that "-y has become the ultimate slayer slang suffix" because it is "more flexible than *-ness*, more interesting, and ultimately more disruptive, than *-age*" (67). Here are some of his examples: "Angely, angsty, avoidy, bitey, bookwormy, brainwashy, Bronzey, broody, cardboardy, cartoony, checky, chickeny, commandery, couply, crayon-breaky, depressedy, developmenty, diggy, discipliny, ... dusty, eaty, fangy, fevery, fighty, fortressy, frowny, ... griefy, groiny, hackery, haunty, heart of darnessy, huntery, judgy, kitteny, knifey, lizardy, matchy, ... metaphory, melty, murdery, necklacey, ... demony, out-of-the-loopy, passiony, pointy, pokey, posty, punctury, rampagey, ranty, researchy, revealy, rinsey, roby, rumbly, rushy, samey, secret agenty, shrimpy, skulky, slippy, snoozey, stammery, stay iny, stompy, stiff upper-lippy, stakey, stretchy, strippy, surfacey, topicy, trancey, twelve-steppy, twitchy, unbendy, unminiony, unmixy, unwindy, vampiry, vampy, veiny, wakey-girl, whispery, wicca-y, wiggy, witchy, wolfy, and wrathy" (67 n.11). Whedon's "groiny" for the sex act is not as memorable as Shakespeare's "making the beast with two backs." Still, both are original, apt in their context, and striking in their own ways. In *Othello*, Iago torments Desdemona's father Brabantio by telling him, "I am one, sir, that comes to tell you your daughter and the Moor are now making the beast with two backs (1.1. 115–117), deliberately lowering the loving sex life of these newlyweds to the level of the coupling of animals, in effect continuing the image with which he first approached Brabantio: "Your heart is burst, you have lost half your soul;/Even now, now, very now, an old black ram/Is tupping your white ewe" (1.1. 87–89). Whedon's use of the cacophonous term "groiny" does not appear in a positive context either. Cordelia is worried that Angel and Buffy are about to get back together and unwittingly reactivate the gypsy curse that will remove Angel's human soul if he experiences a moment of true happiness, thus releasing the evil vampire Angelus upon the world, again. As she confesses her worries to Doyle, "Let me explain the lore here, okay? They suffer, they fight. That's business as usual. They get groiny with each other, the world as we know it falls apart" (*Angel* 1.8 "I Will Remember You"). Cordelia here is once again speaking the unvarnished truth, much like her Shakespearean namesake from *King Lear*. Given that *Buffy* and *Angel* are written by a team of authors under Whedon's close supervision, Michael Adams argues that "raw numbers suggest that -*y* is less characteristic of Whedon's style than the styles of the other writers: within the materials collected here, Noxon employs the suffix 11 times, with Petrie on her heels at 10; Espenson follows with 9, Kirshner with 8, Fury with 7, and Whedon with a mere 6, roughly half the number of forms created by Noxon" (43–44). What Adams fails to note is that Whedon is known for going over the scripts, adding his own flourishes and occasional jokes, and sometimes making major revisions. In an interview with a number of the authors, they admit to learning Slayer Slang from Whedon who seems to speak this way naturally. David Fury states that "the language of *Buffy* is really the language of Joss Whedon." Jane Espenson adds, "A lot of it is the way Joss naturally speaks ... absorbed by all of us and put into the speeches," or as Fury puts it, "channeling Joss" ("*Buffy* Speak' featurette"). Adams's methodology of simply counting the number of "-y" suffixes in a script attributed to a specific writer leaves much to be desired, is sort of suspecty. However, Adams is very thorough in his discussion of Whedon's language. For example, he gives the following list of words created using the "-age" suffix, with his customary dedication to extreme completage: "agreeage, AIMage, appearage, blood-coughage, breakage, Christian Baleage, clearage, clueage, Dewage, downage, drinkage, droppage, Ewanage, flingage, Jossage, kickage, kissage, linkage, lurkage, meetage, missage, moveage, pluggage, poofage, postage, poundage, punnage, quotage, saveage, scorage, scrollage, sighage, signage, slayage, slayerage, sliceage, slowage, sparkage, spoilage, spoilerage, stakage, stealage, suckage, swappage, taggage, thuddage, topicage, vibage, viewage, VIPage, visitage, watchage, weirdage, whuppage, and wiggage" (63 n8). "Slayage" is a term which should be around for a long time, since it is part of the title of the online refereed journal *Slayage: The Journal of the Whedon Studies Association*. The fact that there is a Whedon Studies Association suggests at the very least that Joss Whedon is no ordinary author. The term "slayage" also refers to Buffy's calling, the art and science of slaying vampires, demons, and other supernatural threats. It denotes the results of such activity as well. However, vampires themselves, unlike for example werewolves and most demons, do not become corpses. Whedon introduces something new into vampire lore in that his vampires explode into a cloud of dust immediately upon having a wooden stake plunged into their heart; hence, terms like "dusted," "staked," and their cognates, having of course nothing to do with either housework or gardening. Whedon often extends the meanings of such ordinary terms thus creating new meanings and new contexts, specifically here the *Buffy*verse. The term "*Buffy*verse" is a new addition to the English language, required once academics started writing about Whedon's newer works each with its own universe, such as *Firefly, Serenity, Dollhouse, The Cabin in the Woods*, and so forth. The suffix "-verse" seems to be derived from *Firefly*, where "'verse" is constantly used as a contraction of "universe." We now use the term "Whedonverse" when discussing the commonalities in Whedon's work. For example, all of Whedon's works, and we argue, all of Shakespeare's too, contain underlying messages, often conveyed metaphorically or even allegorically. These usually do not so much reflect as cast new light on our own world and our ordinary lives, helping us see ourselves in extraordinary ways.

The original title of the Whedon Studies journal was *Slayage: The Online International Journal of* Buffy *Studies*. Thus far most of the terms Whedon has introduced are "teenage" slang terms originating in *Buffy*, as is evident from Adams's book *Slayer Slang*. However, neologizing can be found in all of his work. For example, *Firefly/Serenity* gives us both new colloquialisms which extend the meanings of already extant terms, such as "shiny" (good or valuable) and new technical terminologies such the "rim" (on the outer edge) and "core" (central) planets in this new 'verse, and "wave" (an audio-visual or holographic message transmitted through the "cortex" among such planets). In *Serenity* Whedon appropriates the Shakespearean name "Miranda" (Prospero's daughter in *The Tempest*) as the name for an isolated planet whose very existence the Alliance tries to efface. The television series *Dollhouse* introduces such extended terms as "dollhouse," "active," "doll," and "attic." In this context they all become technical terms employed by the Rossum Corporation. The name "Rossum" is derived from Karel Čapek's 1921 play *R.U.R.,* which stands for *Rossum's Universal Robots* (see Koontz 2010). This play first introduced the word "robot," from the Czech "robota," denoting serfdom. In Whedon's narrative the dolls or actives are not much better than robots. They are human beings with their proper identities neurologically "wiped" and reprogrammed by Rossum's technicians to their customers' specifications. *Buffy the Vampire Slayer* introduced a variation of the term "robot" with Spike's Buffybot built by Warren Mears, based on the technology he used to make his robot girlfriend April. Xander refers to April as a "sexbot," exclaiming, "I mean what guy doesn't dream about that?" (5.15 "I Was Made to Love You").

The PBS site on Slayer Slang suggests: "*Buffy* has introduced new slang terms and phrases in nearly every episode.... Undoubtedly, most slayer slang will prove ephemeral, not that there's anything wrong with that; indeed, short-lived terms and tendencies are often significant in their time and can influence the course of American English.... Some items of slayer slang, however, steadily intrude on everyday speech and may be here to stay, not only as slang, but as standard American English" (MacNeil/Lehrer Productions). We think it is fair to say that both Shakespeare and Whedon have contributed original words, phrases, and expressions to the English language. Shakespeare is of course the more towering figure of the two, well worthy of Bardolatry. However, we think that Joss Whedon too is kind of Bardy.

Stating that "Whedon is probably the closest thing to Shakespeare that we have around these days," Wilcox draws on the parallel between theater and television, and reminds us that, like Shakespeare, "Joss Whedon worked with a company of artistic collaborators" (2006 par. 24). In *Why* Buffy *Matters*, Wilcox argues: "Part of Joss Whedon's genius is his ability to bring out the best in those he works with. I would posit this as a necessity for a great television artist. It struck me only recently that one of the great themes of the show—the importance of community, trust, friendship—is found not only in the episodes but also in their creation. The cast and crew of *Buffy* were extraordinary, and Joss Whedon set the tone for their collaboration" (6).

The two main points Wilcox makes here about the "Whedon Company" are (1) that Whedon "brings out the best" in his actors, which can be seen in the variety and range of roles in which he casts them, as in the list above for instance, and (2) the intimacy that is suggested by "community, trust, friendship." These two points are also central to the smooth functioning of the Lord Chamberlain's Men. Peter Thomson, in *Shakespeare's Theatre*, when describing the formation of the Lord Chamberlain's Men during a plague year, notes that "it was an inauspicious time to form a new company of players, but what is extraordinary about the group that assembled in 1594 under the patronage of the Lord Chamberlain, Henry Carey, Lord Hunsdon, is the familiarity of its names. This was not a random collection of individuals, but a re-union of friends. Loyalty and genuine affection play a part in the subsequent history of the Chamberlain's Men in a way that we can neither ignore nor adequately measure. Even among some of the hired men, there is evidence of a commitment beyond the normal limits of a working relationship" (8). The Lord Chamberlain's Men, like Whedon, required their actors to have considerable range and versatility, since they would be required to play multiple roles, often in the same play, as Thomson notes: "Against [T.W. Baldwin's] assumption that each actor developed a consistent line (irascible old man; low and high comedian; strong-minded lady; pert maid; benevolent old man, etc.) must be set the stronger alternative of the necessary versatility of a small number of actors in a company familiar with large cast-lists and the prudent paring down of pay-rolls. The playing of four, three, or two parts was much more a rule than an exception. John Sincler (Sincklo or Sinklo) played five in *The Seven Deadly Sins*, and may well have done the same for the Chamberlain's Men, whom he joined as a hired man in 1594" (9). It is even possible that William Kempe left the company because he became too closely associated with too narrow a range of roles. Thomson notes that "since we know that Kempe created the role of Dogberry, it is tempting to believe that he specialised in such parts" and he even appears as a character in an anonymous Cambridge play in which he "instructs an undergraduate in the playing of 'a foolish mayor or a foolish justice of peace'" (11).

While the common expression "created the role of" does not necessarily imply that the actor contributed lines or plot ideas to the playwright, it also does not exclude that possibility. What it does imply is that the actor creates the material, physical embodiment of the character, which in the script exists only as words which can be delivered in all sorts of ways, and that this embodiment is largely how the character will be remembered by the paying public: see, for example, the way Peter Falk created Columbo (whoever did the actual writing most of us neither know nor much care), Tony Shaloub created Mr. Monk, Alyson Hannigan created Willow, etc. When several actors in some form of succession play the same part, we still associate the part with the actors and regard the specific incarnation as his, not as the writer's—hence we have, e.g., Sean Connery's James Bond, Daniel Craig's, Timothy Dalton's, etc. When we are asked who our favorite Bond is, how often do we bother to compare them to Ian Fleming's Bond? The words in the script, whether for the early modern stage or for the 21st-century screen, are in some ways a series of prompts and hints to directors and actors, setting boundaries and limits to what can legitimately be done, far more than a "sacred object" necessitating a single interpretation by actors and directors. Since the paying public will link the character to a specific actor, and have their own favorite actors, the playwright or screenwriter would be well-advised to write to the strengths of the actors in his company, whether those strengths lie in specific character types or in great versatility and ability to play numerous and varied characters, like Meryl Streep, for example. Even if there is not full-fledged collaboration, in the sense of working together on a script, there has to be considerable cooperation among the writers and the actors for a play to be brought to the stage or a script to the screen in a way that will be aesthetically appealing and commercially viable. Neither playwrights nor screenwriters can afford to forget the "bums in seats" principle.

Thomson, in his study of Elizabethan acting practices, *Shakespeare's Theatre,* notes that the character Dogberry in *Much Ado* was written "with Kempe in mind" while Feste in *Twelfth Night* was written for Armin. *As You Like It*'s "Touchstone might just have been played by both, but with divergent emphases. Dogberry, like Kempe, demands attention and the centre of the stage. Feste is content in the corners" (35). Kempe's Touchstone would be a very different character than Armin's even though the words in the script would be the same. As Thomson notes, "There was more prestige in being an actor—provided you were a successful actor—than in being a playwright.... The possession of good stories was more important to an Elizabethan theatre company than the spreading of fine literature. The fact that Shakespeare ... provided both cannot be used to defend a claim that the Chamberlain's Men *demanded* both. The more immediate reason was the tempting profitability of dramatic writing, sufficient to attract men who might otherwise have applied their genius only to epic, lyric, or satiric poetry. If you were writing for money, plays brought quicker rewards" (61). The parallel with writing a weekly television series is obvious. Thomson concludes his survey of Elizabethan stage practices with the following cogent reminder: "It has been often enough said, but not often enough understood, that Shakespeare was a member of a theatre company. Nothing demands compromises and the cutting of corners more persistently than the staging of a play; and the number of compromises increases in proportion to the number of plays being presented within a given period" (81).

In her study, *Why* Buffy *Matters*, Rhonda Wilcox admits the fact that "television as creation by committee" leads "some people to doubt that television can be art" (1). Wilcox, however, argues that "*Buffy* is art, and art of the highest order" (1). In Shakespeare's day, drama was similarly despised by those who fancied themselves as having elevated tastes. For example, "in 1612, Sir Thomas Bodley grouped plays with almanacs and proclamations among the 'idle books, and riff-raffs' which he reproached the keeper of his library for cataloguing, admitting that 'Haply some plays may be worth the keeping: but hardly one in forty" (Thomson 58). The reference here is, of course, to the Bodleian Library in Oxford University. Wilcox notes in her defense of serial drama in television: "a fictional form which is popular is often not respected for quite some time. Ben Jonson had to battle for serious consideration of Elizabethan drama—not only his own, but that of his contemporary the actor/author Shakespeare. Non-dramatic poetry was considered the higher art form in that period.... The form of art most suited to an age will produce both its best work and its most work—so by statistical likelihood, many bad works will be produced in that form ... and even great work is not always immediately appreciated" (2). Wilcox is arguing, of course, that both Shakespeare and Whedon stand out from the "idle books and riff-raffs" of their contemporaries. On a personal note, Wilcox suggests "as a teacher of literature, I see *Buffy* as part of a long cultural stream" (2).

This "long cultural stream" from Shakespeare to Whedon takes us through the rise of the novel in the late 18th and early 19th centuries. At this time, novels were not considered great literature any more than the theater was in Shakespeare's time. In fact, both were frowned upon as contributing to immorality, just as some people today still believe that movies, television shows, and video games contribute to juvenile delinquency. The Elizabethan theater was regarded as scarcely more wholesome entertainment than were bear-baiting and houses of prostitution. As we noted above, Edward Alleyn profited from all three (lived off the avails of all three). In *The Anatomie of Abuses* (1583), Philip Stubbes characterizes the theater's threat to public morality in vivid and unambiguous terms: "You say there are good examples to be learned in them [plays], truly so there are, if you will learn falsehood; if you will learn cozenage [duplicity]; if you will learn to deceive; if you will learn to play the hypocrite ... to lie and falsify; if you will learn to jest, laugh and fleer [sneer], to grin, to nod ... if you will learn to play the vice, to swear, tear, and blaspheme both heaven and earth; if you will learn to become a bawd [madam], unclean and to divirginate maids, to deflower honest wives; if you will learn to murder, slay, kill, pick, steal, rob, and rove: if you will learn to rebel against princes, to commit treasons, to consume treasures..." (quoted by Maguire and Smith, 126). In the early days of Hollywood a similar moral panic was more than evident and culminated in the Hays Code, which was "imposed on Hollywood from 1930 onwards" and "aimed to ensure that 'no picture shall be produced which will lower the moral standards of those who see it' and took as a governing precept that films 'affect the moral standards of those who, through the screen, take in these ideas and ideals'" (Maguire and Smith, 125–126).

Rhonda Wilcox in *Why* Buffy *Matters*, argues that just as the theater and the novel have now become high literature, so television series like Whedon's *Buffy the Vampire Slayer* should be regarded with similar esteem. We are arguing that we should extend Wilcox's insight to include the use of such literary texts as a form of narrative ethics that will lead people to make responsible ethical decisions. Wilcox argues that "a fictional form which is popular is often not respected for quite some time" (2005, 2). As we argued above, concerning the theater, she notes, "Ben Jonson had to battle for serious consideration of Elizabethan drama" (2). With respect to the rise of the novel, Wilcox, who wrote her Ph.D. dissertation on Charles Dickens, indicates that "when Dickens published his novels in serialized 'shilling numbers,' [not unlike a serialized television narrative today] they were widely enjoyed but condescended to." She goes on to say, "that the historian Thomas Carlyle, Dickens's friend, considered most novels worthless but magnanimously told an acquaintance that Dickens was worth a penny" (2). What Wilcox does not mention is that Carlyle himself authored at least one novel, *Sartor Resartus*, and was criticized for it by his friend, the philosopher John Stuart Mill in much the way Carlyle condescended to Dickens's novels. In a letter the philosopher wrote to Carlyle, Mill says, "It has frequently occurred to me of late to ask of myself and of you, whether that mode of writing between sarcasm or irony and earnest, be really deserving of so much honour as you give it by making use of it so frequently; ... are there many things, worth saying, and capable of being said in that manner which cannot be as well or better said in a more direct way" (quoted in Baker, 224). This is an instance of the classic battle between philosophy and literature, or "ciuill [civil] war among the muses" as Sir Philip Sidney puts it in his *An Apologie for Poetrie*, first published in 1595 (1961, 2). In this work, Sidney addresses the question of whether morality is better taught by the philosopher or by the poet, and begins the discussion with a mocking description of the approach of the philosophers: "These men casting larges[s] as they goe of Definitions, Diuisions, and Distinctions, with a scornefull interrogative doe soberly aske whether it bee possible to finde any path so ready to leade man to vertue as that which teacheth what vertue is, and teacheth it not onely by deliuering forth his very being, his causes, and effects, but also by making known his enemie vice, which must be destroyed, and his cumbersome seruant Passion, which must be maistered, by shewing the generalities that contayneth it, and the specialities that are deriued from it, lastly, by playne setting downe, how it extendeth it selfe out of the limits of a mans own little world to the government of families, and maintayning of publique societies" (14). And a few pages later, Sidney concludes that "the Philosopher teacheth, but he teacheth obscurely, so as the learned onely can vnderstande him, that is to say that he teacheth them that are already taught; but the Poet is the food for the tenderest stomacks, the Poet is indeed the right Popular Philosopher" (19) and further, the poet "beginneth not with obscure definitions, which must blur the margent with interpretations, and load the memory with doubtfulesse; but hee commeth to you with words set in delightfull proportion ... and with a tale forsooth he commeth unto you, with a tale which holdeth children from play, and old men from the chimney corner. And, pretending no more, doth intende the winning of the mind from wickednesse to vertue: euen as the childe is often brought to take most wholsom things by hiding them in such other as haue a pleasant tast.... So it is in men (most of which are childish in the best things, till they bee cradled in their graues): glad they will be to heare the tales of *Hercules, Achilles, Cyrus,* and *Aeneas*; and, hearing them, must needs heare the right description of wisdom, valure, and iustice; which, if they had been barely, that is to say, Philosophically, set out, they would sweare they bee brought to schoole againe" (25–26). As Robert E. Stillman explains in "The Scope of Sidney's Defence of Poesy: The New Hermeneutic and Early Modern Poetics": "Readers do not merely identify with virtuous characters. Instead, they are metamorphosed by love of those virtues pictured by such characters ... they are taught fictions that heighten understanding about their natures and that move them by reason of such knowledge to virtuous action" (382).

Carlyle echoes Sidney in the face of Mill's criticism through his own defense of literature over and above philosophy. This in spite of the fact that Carlyle is in part responsible for introducing Immanuel Kant and German transcendental philosophy to the English speaking world. In his discussion of the literary man in *Heroes and Hero-worship,* drawing on one of Kant's German followers, Johann Gottlieb Fichte, Carlyle says, "Fichte calls the Man of Letters ... a Prophet, or as he prefers to phrase it, a Priest, continually unfolding the Godlike to men: Men of Letters are a perpetual Priesthood, from age to age, teaching all men that a God is still present in their life, that all 'Appearance,' whatsoever we see in the world, is but a vesture for the 'Divine Idea of the World,' for 'that which lies at the bottom of Appearance.' In the true Literary Man there is thus ever, acknowledged or not by the world, a sacredness: he is the light of the world; the world's Priest;—guiding it, like a sacred Pillar of Fire, in its dark pilgrimage through the waste of Time" (Carlyle, Vol. 1 380). We note in passing that the phrase "wastes of time" is from Shakespeare's Sonnet 12. In referring to the literary man as a priest or prophet, Carlyle seems to be suggesting that literature can lead its readers to the supreme principle of morality, what Kant called the Categorical Imperative. Priests are called "father" because like God-the-father they are a symbol of patriarchal moral authority. We discuss Kant's Categorical Imperative as a form of Strict Father Family Morality in Chapter 8. Fichte had argued that we should be able to discover the Kantian Categorical Imperative through philosophical reason alone. However, in his *Critique of All Revelation* (*Kritik aller Offenbarung*), he also allowed that "mankind can fall so deep into moral corruption that it can be brought back to morality in no other way than by religion, and to religion in no other way than by the senses. A religion that is to affect such men can be based on nothing but direct divine authority" (111). Fichte defines "revelation" (*Offenbarung*) as "an appearance effected in the sensuous world by the causality of God, through which he proclaims himself as moral law-giver" (96). Through Biblical revelation, then, the parables and other narratives of the Bible, we can discover the moral law. Carlyle seems to be suggesting that it is not just Biblical literature, but all great literature, which helps us to see how the world ought to be. This gives literature an advantage over the sterile logic of mere philosophy. As L.C.R. Baker argues in his paper "The Open Secret of *Sartor Resartus*: Carlyle's Method of Converting his Reader": "*Sartor* manifests a new form of persuasion—a form required because traditional rhetoric is inappropriate and inadequate for Carlyle's purposes.... Typical rhetoric is logical and linear; Carlyle's message is complex and multidimensional. In addition, the kind of persuasion Carlyle wants does not force the reader, does not conquer or convince him. Instead, he wants the reader to be allowed to discover the Open Secret of the Clothes Philosophy for himself.... He does not tell us exactly what we should see. Instead, his pervasive ironic play with the meaning of symbols 'guides' the reader, as Carlyle says, to a stage of enlightenment whereby he begins to see the Open Secret of the Clothes Philosophy" (222). Carlyle's ironic metaphor of the Clothes Philosophy is, of course, suggesting that great literature can show how God, the moral law-giver, can be revealed through the natural world in its sartorial splendor seen as the garments of God. Though there is still some controversy about the matter, there is good evidence that Carlyle's Clothes Philosophy is inspired by Fichte's interpretation of Kant (Rabb 76ff). In *Heroes and Hero-Worship*, Carlyle argues, "Fichte, in conformity with the Transcendental Philosophy, of which he was a distinguished teacher, declares first: that all things which we see or work with in this earth, especially we ourselves and all persons, are as a kind of vesture or sensuous Appearance: that under all there lies, as the essence of them, what he calls the 'Divine Idea of the World.'... To the mass of men no such Divine Idea is recognizable in the world; they live merely, says Fichte, among the superficialities, practicalities, and shows of the world, not dreaming that there is anything divine under them" (Carlyle, Vol. 1 379).

Carlyle thus is arguing that great literature can help the reader get beyond the "superficialities, practicalities, and shows of the world." Carlyle evidently did not believe that Dickens's novels were instances of great literature, claiming that "Dickens had not written anything which would be found of much use in solving the problems of life. But he was worth something; he was worth a penny to read of an evening before going to bed, which was about what a reading of him cost you" (Collins 210). Great literature, in Carlyle's time, would more likely have included the Bible and Shakespeare, and Carlyle might well have added his own *Sartor Resartus*. It at least takes the reader beyond the confines of mundane reality and brings about a deeper religious insight. Today, novels are regarded as perfectly capable of being great literature. Wilcox broadens the field to also include television narratives. We are extending Wilcox's argument by maintaining that outstanding works of televisual and cinematic storytelling, specifically those of Joss Whedon, function not only as what Carlyle called great literature but also as a valid form of narrative ethics, showing how the world ought to be. Occasionally, Whedon's dialogue comments on the show itself, indicating the ethical subtext. For example in *Angel* 4.1 ("Deep Down"), Angel explains to his alienated teenage son, Connor, in one such metafictional moment, "Nothing in the world is the way it ought to be. It's harsh, and cruel. But that's why there's us. Champions. It doesn't matter where we come from, what we've done or suffered, or even if we make a difference. We live as though the world was what it should be, to show it what it can be."

Of course, as is well known, "Shakespeare revels in meta-theater in many of his plays, frequently making comparisons of life and the stage" (Sinclair). All the world is a stage, after all. Shakespeare's tragedies show that evil, though triumphant for a while, is ultimately defeated. For example, although Macbeth was able to seize the throne of Scotland via regicide, his kingly robes sit ill upon him, he feels forced into further homicides in a self-defeating attempt to feel secure in his power, and is finally vanquished by Macduff. At the end of the play, Macduff enters carrying Macbeth's severed head, saying, "Behold, where stands/The usurper's cursed head" (5.9.20–21). While the most immediate addressees for these lines are Malcolm and members of his invading English army, the actor can make them metatheatrical by turning and displaying the head to the theater audience, thus underlining for them the political moral pertaining to the fate of treasonous tyrants. This is hardly the unambiguous triumph of good over evil, however, since in a sense it repeats the regicide committed by Macbeth, with the addition of an invading foreign army.

In the Whedonverse as well, the distinction between good and evil is not always clear. Vampires and demons are the embodiments of evil, but not all vampires and demons are evil, Angel the vampire with a soul, for example, or the demons Whistler and Clem. This complicates the fight against evil, which is, in a sense, what the Whedonverse is all about. It will be remembered that in the *Buffy*verse closing the Hellmouth is almost literally preventing evil from entering the world. In the Whedonverse, the "Hellmouth," the source from which evil emerges, takes various forms. For example, in *The Avengers* it is a portal in the sky out of which pour the invading forces until the team of heroes and scientists cooperate to shut it down; in *Dollhouse*, it is the Rossum Corporation; in *Firefly/Serenity* it turns out to be the planet Miranda, from which the Reavers come; and in *The Cabin in the Woods* it is the subterranean Old Ones held in check only by the evil of human sacrifice. Thus both Shakespeare and Whedon seem to have a metanarrative ethical subtext running through their works, and in neither, just as in real life, are ethical matters simple, clear, or unambiguous.

Whedon himself admits, sometimes with tongue in cheek, that there is a parallel between his work and that of Shakespeare. At the panel discussion of Whedon's *Much Ado* at WonderCon Anaheim on March 31, 2013, it was noted that, even with the modern setting, "*Much Ado* seems to work very well, and feels very Whedon, despite the story being told in Shakespeare's words" (Schwartz). Whedon whimsically suggested that that's because "they both use confusing language in their most famous works. 'I think a lot of [our words] don't make any sense and they're in the wrong order and you've got to look shit up,' Whedon said. 'I'm just like Shakespeare.' Immediately after those words came out of his mouth, Whedon added, 'That quote will get tweeted and everyone will hate me.' Hilariously, one fan shouted, 'It's already tweeted'" (Schwartz).

Two

Shakespeare's Brain and Whedon's Brains: Cognitive Theory in Narrative and Ethics

In her book *Shakespeare's Brain*, Mary Thomas Crane challenges Michel Foucault's "deconstruction of the author" by introducing a cognitive reading of Shakespeare's plays, emphasizing embodiment. She admits, however, that a "Foucauldian theory, along with a new emphasis on the collaborative nature of play production in early modern England, has led Shakespearean scholars to form a more complex and qualified notion of Shakespearean authorship. A focus on Shakespeare's brain allows us to attend to Shakespeare as author without losing the complexity offered by contemporary theory" (3). As we noted in our last chapter, Joss Whedon's works, like those of most contemporary television productions, are usually the result of a fast-working team of writers. Some of the more notable members of this creative team are Joss' brothers Jed and Zack Whedon, Maurissa Tancharoen, Steven S. DeKnight, David Fury, Drew Goddard, Drew Greenberg, David Greenwalt, Rebecca Rand Kirshner, Marti Noxon, Doug Petrie, Tim Minear, Ben Edlund, and Jane Espenson. In our next chapter, "Joss Whedon's 'Big Brain': The Espenson Authorship Controversy," we discuss in detail Espenson's contributions to this team, including episodes for which she is credited as the principal author. We still feel comfortable discussing "the works of Joss Whedon," despite the contributions of his creative teams.

Mary Thomas Crane argues that "cognitive theory may provide some help in getting around the current critical impasse between those who assume an author with conscious control over the text he produces and those who assume that cultural construction leaves little or no room for authorial agency." She goes on to suggest that "the cognitive sciences do seem to offer more theoretical orientations that assume some combination of the two" (16). Drawing primarily on the work of cognitive scientist George Lakoff and philosopher of cognitive science Mark Johnson, Crane argues that "cognitive theory offers new and more sophisticated ways to conceive of authorship and therefore offers new ways to read texts as products of a thinking author engaged with a physical environment and a culture" (4). She goes on to argue that "from a cognitive perspective, meaning is anchored (although ambiguously and insecurely) by a three-way tether: brain, culture, discourse" (24). We are going one step beyond Crane's interest in *authorial* agency by emphasizing *moral* agency (of both characters and readers/viewers) through a kind of narrative ethics in the works of both Shakespeare and Whedon.

In our earlier book, *The Existential Joss Whedon*, we noted that one of the first scholars to discuss Whedon in the context of the cognitive work of Lakoff and Johnson was Gregory Stevenson in his classic book *Televised Morality: The Case of* Buffy the Vampire Slayer. "Stevenson is the only scholar/commentator who has dealt with Whedon's exploration of metaphor and morality in anything like the detail it deserves ... citing George Lakoff and Mark Johnson's *Metaphors We Live By*, Stevenson argues that we are in fact justified in seeing and analyzing the metaphorical structure of a television series like *Buffy the Vampire Slayer* because 'metaphors belong as much to the province of thought as to that of words' (32)" (Richardson and Rabb 151). We actually criticized Stevenson for not drawing on Lakoff and Johnson's 1999 book *Philosophy in the Flesh: The Embodied Mind and Its Challenge to Western Thought*. "There Lakoff and Johnson distinguish between 'basic experiential morality,' such as 'health is good,' 'everyone ought to be protected from physical harm,' and more abstract universal moral concepts such as 'justice,' 'rights,' 'nurturance,' etc., all of which must be defined metaphorically" (151). Lakoff and Johnson's groundbreaking insight is that "there is no ethical system that is not metaphorical" (Lakoff and Johnson 1999, 325). If they are correct, and we believe this study of Shakespeare and Whedon provides corroborating evidence that they are in actual fact correct, it follows that moral reasoning is based more on moral imagination and emotion than it is on reason and moral principles.

Citing George Lakoff's *Women, Fire, and Dangerous Things*, Crane notes that "according to Lakoff, all thought is fundamentally 'imaginative, in that those concepts which are not directly grounded in experience employ metaphor, metonymy, and mental imagery—all of which go beyond the literal mirroring, or *representation*, of external reality.' ... According to such a model, metaphor becomes not an aberration from or exception to primarily logical processes of meaning but a basic component of thought and language" (9).

Crane uses Shakespeare's *The Tempest* to illustrate how cognition naturally occurs independently of "primarily logical processes." She seizes on Shakespeare's use of a set of terms that are linked chiefly by sound rather than logical sense: "*pinch*, *pitch*, *pity*, *pen*, and *pine* (and its cognate *pain*)" (180). She draws attention to the fact that "these words are also linked by their association with inarticulate human or animal cries of pain. They form the center of a group of images that explore the way human subjects exist in a body and within a natural environment ... and attempt to gain control over it" (180). Prospero in reprimanding Caliban tells him,

> For this, be sure, to-night thou shalt have cramps,
> Side-stitches, that shall pen thy breath up; urchins
> Shall, for that vast of night that they may work,
> All exercise on thee; thou shalt be pinch'd
> As thick as honeycomb, each pinch more stinging
> Than bees that made 'em.
>
> [1.2.325–330].

Crane notes that this passage brings together "animals, pinches and cramps" as well as, most importantly, both "confinement" and "pain" (186). Urchins (goblins in the form of hedgehogs) and bees are known for pinching and hence causing pain. "Pen thy breath up" connotes confinement and discomfort. The passage can be taken as a metaphor for Prospero's confinement on a desert island, along with his daughter Miranda. He is here projecting his painful confinement onto Caliban. Both Prospero and Miranda are confining, in the sense of enslaving, Caliban, the "monstrous savage" they have found there. Confinement in fact permeates this play. Prospero has liberated the spirit Ariel from confinement in a cloven pine, but has made him his servant in recompense. Ariel feels this confinement strongly and yearns for the freedom Prospero eventually grants him at the end. By means of the tempest causing a shipwreck, raised by his magic and enacted through the agency of Ariel, Prospero has, in effect, imprisoned his enemies, that is, his brother Antonio, Alonso the King of Naples, and the rest of their party, on this island where he has them at his mercy. The crew of the ship remains confined aboard in a deep sleep until near the play's end. Colin McGinn, in *Shakespeare's Philosophy*, notes that "the tempest" in the play is created by the spell of Prospero's words and that the play itself, *The Tempest*, is in fact a tempest of Shakespeare's words (136). These words limit, confine, or even imprison the actors who speak them. They feel confined or penned to the stage and in the epilogue ask the audience to release them with their applause. This epilogue is voiced by Prospero, though at times the actor playing Prospero lets his mask slip and speaks in his own voice:

> Now my charms are all o'erthrown,
> And what strength I have's mine own,
> Which is most faint. Now 'tis true,
> I must be here confin'd by you,

> Or sent to Naples. Let me not,
> Since I have my dukedom got,
> And pardon'd the deceiver, dwell
> In this bare island by your spell,
> But release me from my bands
> With the help of your good hands.
> Gentle breath of yours my sails
> Must fill, or else my project fails,
> Which was to please. Now I want
> Spirits to enforce, art to enchant,
> And my ending is despair,
> Unless I be reliev'd by prayer,
> Which pierces so, that it assaults
> Mercy itself, and frees all faults.
> As you from crimes would pardon'd be,
> Let your indulgence set me free.

The epilogue begins with a triple reference. "Now my charms are all o'erthrown," can refer to Prospero's having relinquished his magic, or the actor's stepping outside the role of Prospero, or finally Shakespeare the author's talking about the play that has just been performed, thus breaking the spell of words that has held the audience entranced. Prospero in relinquishing his magic has set his prisoners free and admitted that it was he who had caused the tempest that drove the ship upon the island and placed his brother Antonio and his other enemies at his mercy. This emphasizes the fact that Prospero has forgiven Antonio for usurping his place as the Duke of Milan and expelling him and his infant daughter Miranda. During another storm, Prospero and Miranda were set adrift "some leagues to sea" (1.2.145) in an open boat with neither "tackle, sail, nor mast" (1.2.147). By "Providence divine" (1.2.159) they were cast ashore on the island created by the words of this play on the bare stage where the presenter of the epilogue is now standing. This is creation by the word, consistent with the biblical-sounding language in the epilogue cited above. Prospero in magically creating the tempest that casts Antonio and company onto his island is therefore visiting upon his enemies a version of the very punishment they had inflicted upon him. The actor in stepping outside his role is, like Prospero, giving up the magic represented by the tempest of words he has been given to speak. These words have allowed him to keep the audience enthralled just as his character has enslaved Caliban, Ariel, and Antonio and company. The actor is now in the hands of, at the mercy of, the audience: "Now 'tis true, / I must be here confin'd by you.... But release me from my bands / With the help of your good hands." When he says, "Gentle breath of yours my sails / Must fill, or else my project fails, / Which was to please" the speaker of the epilogue is both continuing the motif of Prospero sailing away from the island, and addressing the audience indicating that at least one of Shakespeare's projects is to please them. The breath refers to the air being moved by their applauding hands. However, Shakespeare's project is not just to please. It is also to instruct through metaphor, allegory, or in a word, narrative. As David Lowenthal in his study *Shakespeare and the Good Life* notes, "the playwright is ... in the service of the audience, a slave to the audience, which must be pleased if it is to confer its approbation.... But he ceases to be a slave when he can exert a power of his own—a power that comes from ... his art. By the poet's or playwright's art, he turns the tables on the audience, and gets it in *his* power; with it in his power, he need not simply please, but can please, influence, and instruct all at once" (61). Although McGinn in *Shakespeare's Philosophy* says that "Shakespeare is not in general an allegorical writer," he goes on to admit "but in *The Tempest* the impression of allegory is strong: the characters 'stand' for something" (143). For McGinn Prospero is "Shakespeare's representative ... intended to stand for the idea of the artist" (143). McGinn identifies three components of the artist's identity: "his creative spirit [Ariel], his animal self [Caliban], and his internal audience—his critical self-consciousness [Miranda] ... the play then is an allegory of the solitary artist's mind and its inner architecture" (147). Shakespeare is being self-critical in his portrait of the artist, for his Prospero is intoxicated with power, "the power to make things happen as he imagines them" (McGinn 2006, 144). As McGinn goes on to explain, "this is not an idealized portrait of the artist, as a soft hearted sensitive, but as someone who dabbles in what Prospero calls his 'rough magic'—an apt enough description of Shakespeare's own tough and penetrating style. There is something lacking in Prospero in the kindness department (despite his late forgiveness of his enemies), and I think this is part of Shakespeare's picture of an artist. For Prospero can be touchy and insecure, as well as proud of his own prowess—the very essence of an artist, one might say" (144). In Whedon's *Buffy the Vampire Slayer* Willow Rosenberg seems to become as intoxicated with magic as Prospero in *The Tempest*. But unlike Prospero, she is unable to control her addiction, becoming the dark Willow and nearly destroying the world (Season Six). The fact that Prospero does not go so far suggests to scholars like John Vyvyan that *The Tempest* is a reverse tragedy. In *The Shakespearean Ethic*, Vyvyan argues: "*The Tempest* ... shows us the regeneration sequence set out completely as the tragic pattern reversed.... It is one of Shakespeare's fundamental propositions that tragedy begets tragedy, for ever and ever, until someone has the strength, the courage and the understanding to say, Enough!" (161–163). Of all Shakespeare's heroes, Prospero is one of the few who does have the courage, strength, and understanding to do just this. As we noted above, Prospero, through his magical tempest, has his enemies under his control, but chooses, albeit reluctantly, to forgive them, to show them mercy rather than to enact further revenge. This is an ethical choice freely taken on Prospero's part, which heads off an otherwise tragic ending. As Vyvyan points out, "everything now hangs on the hero's decision, which is not forced upon him by outward circumstances, but is a moral action.... If he turns to the right, a conclusive victory is possible; if he turns to the left, everything may yet go wrong. At such moments in Shakespearean drama, fate seems to be waiting, like a huge machine, for the hero to put it into motion; it does not compel him" (163). Insofar as tragic heroes are concerned, Vyvyan's basic position is "that no Shakespearean hero is compelled to follow his fate; there is always a spiritual quality in him which, if it is asserted as it ought to be, is superior to fate" (8). The tragic hero always confronts such a moral crossroads, and makes the wrong decision. For example, Macbeth chooses to listen to and follow his interpretation of the witches as well as the sexual and political pressures exerted by Lady Macbeth. He thus embarks on a tragic career of regicide followed by other murders in a hopeless and self-contradictory attempt to make his position secure. Hamlet, already ill-disposed towards his uncle Claudius, chooses to accept the direction of a dubious ghost, to reject the concerns and the love of his girlfriend Ophelia, and to ignore the promptings of his nobler self, represented at least in part allegorically by Ophelia, in order to proceed with a plan for revenge that litters the stage with corpses and stains Hamlet's own soul.

Prospero turns in the other direction, due in part to the love and compassion shown and demonstrated by his daughter Miranda, who can be seen allegorically as part of his better self. Prospero is conscious of and grateful for Miranda's influence on him, and says to her in gratitude, "O, a cherubin / Thou wast that did preserve me. Thou didst smile / Infused with a fortitude from heaven" (1.2.152–154).

Despite his genuine love of and gratitude toward Miranda, Prospero asserts considerable patriarchal authority over her and, in effect, colonizes her as much as she and he both colonize Caliban. In her article, "'The Dark Backward and Abysm of Time': *The Tempest* and Memory," Evelyn B. Tribble points out that in the second scene of *The Tempest*, when Prospero is explaining to Miranda how they came to be on the island, he becomes agitated at her vague but happy memory of some women tending to her when she was three years old. As Sarah Beckwith argues at length in her book *Shakespeare and the Grammar of Forgiveness*, this shows that Miranda "cannot be the blank slate that Prospero imagines she is" (161). Prospero repeatedly tries to assure himself that Miranda is "attending" to *his* narration rather than to *her* own childhood memories, "the rivalrous spectre of the attending women" (Tribble 158): "Dost thou attend me?" (1.2.78), "Thou attendst not! ... I pray thee mark me" (87–88) and "Dost thou hear?" (106). Tribble explains that "Prospero demands more of Miranda than her attention: he also demands and attempts to shape her affect" (158). He is so successful that Miranda ventriloquizes "the language of [her] father" thoroughly and convincingly enough that directors and editors often assign some of her lines in this scene to Prospero (Tribble 160). Prospero begins his lecture to Miranda by ordering her to "sit down /… ope thine ear. / Obey, and be attentive" (1.2.32–38). Prospero has said, "'Tis time / I should inform thee farther" (1.2.22–23). Tribble stresses the colonizing implication of these lines, noting that "'inform' here clearly impl[ies] its root meaning of 'shape' or 'imprint.'… Prospero demands a bodily comportment that will produce her as a suitable attendant upon her father's stories" (158).

In *Decolonizing Feminisms: Race, Gender, & Empire Building*, Laura Donaldson has named this phenomenon the "Miranda Complex," and explains that in this social formation Miranda is simultaneously the colonizer (of Caliban) and the colonized (by Prospero), although Miranda is entirely unaware that either Caliban or she herself are in fact oppressed. She is both conflicted and complicit but is blissfully ignorant of her state. Donaldson's acute observation not only illuminates Shakespeare's *The Tempest*, but also has helped us to clarify Joss Whedon's use of "Miranda" in the movie *Serenity* (Rabb and Richardson 2008a, 136–137). This mysterious word is first uttered in a bar when River Tam says "Miranda" "when she is triggered by a subliminal code on a public television screen into an attack on the patrons of the bar" (Rabb and Richardson 2008a, 134). We eventually discover that "Miranda" was the name "of a remote planet that the Alliance has removed from navigation charts and official histories" (Rabb and Richardson 2008a, 134). The planet Miranda has been wiped from history and geography, from cultural memory, by the totalitarian government of the day (the ultimate oppressor), the sinister Alliance, even more thoroughly than Prospero has manipulated and supplanted Miranda's happy childhood memories of ladies in waiting and her earlier life in Milan.

In our contribution to Rhonda Wilcox and Tanya Cochran's *Investigating Firefly and* Serenity, chapter 10, "Reavers and Redskins: Creating the Frontier Savage," we argue that "the Reavers represent 'blood-thirsty Savage Redskins' in Joss Whedon's futuristic Cowboy-and-Indian narratives, *Firefly* and its movie sequel *Serenity*" (127). We maintain that Whedon is deconstructing the negative stereotypes of "Red Indians" perpetuated by Hollywood "B-Westerns." Agnes Curry in her article "'We Don't Say Indian': On the Paradoxical Construction of the Reavers" criticizes us for taking this stance, arguing that "by the time a possibly deconstructive moment takes place—late in the climax of *Serenity*—previous scenes have inculcated the savage stereotype so effectively at the subliminal level that one possibly revisionary scene could hardly trouble it" (par. 3). The "deconstructive moment" late in the climax of the movie that

Curry is referring to takes place on the planet Miranda after the crew of the Firefly-class spaceship Serenity have traveled there at great risk to their lives. They discover a planet littered with corpses, even more than in a Shakespearean tragedy. The entire population seems to have just given up living and allowed themselves to die. Many of the planets and moons in this solar system had been terraformed in the attempt to give them an earth-like environment to support humankind after they fled Earth-That-Was because it could no longer support human life. On Miranda something in the terraforming process had gone horribly wrong. As the holographic recording on an abandoned Alliance research vessel explains, "It's the Pax, the G-32 Paxilon Hydrochlorate that we added to the air processors. It ... was supposed to calm the population, weed out aggression ... it worked. The people here stopped fighting. And they stopped everything else ... breeding ... talking ... eating.... There's thirty million people here and they all just let themselves die" (*Serenity*). It turns out that not everyone died. The Paxilon Hydrochlorate transformed 0.1 percent of the population into cannibalistic savages, the so-called mythical monsters that the Alliance has named the Reavers. As the Alliance scientist Dr. Caron on the holographic recording goes on to explain, "Their aggressor response increased ... beyond madness. They've become ... they've killed most of us ... not just killed, they've done ... things" (*Serenity*). At this point, her report is interrupted as a Reaver breaks into her research vessel and attacks her: "She screams continuously as the Reaver tops her, biting at her clothes, at her skin" (*Serenity: The Official Visual Companion*, 129). The revelation that the Reavers were created as a result of Alliance experimentation is the occasion for what Curry calls "the possibly deconstructive moment" of the movie. One of the crew of Serenity says in a horrified whisper, "Reavers ... they made them." River seems unable to cope with this revelation: "River falls to her knees vomiting" (*Serenity: The Official Visual Companion*, 130). River was raised and educated under the Alliance and was being trained as an operative in an Alliance secret facility where her natural psychic abilities were being enhanced through cognitive experimentation. The movie previously showed "a 16-year-old RIVER sitting in a metal chair, needles stuck in her skull ... being adjusted by a technician. A second monitors her brain patterns. The lab is cold, blue, steel. Insidiously clean" (*Serenity: The Official Visual Companion*, 43). Near the beginning of the movie, we are introduced to an approximately 10-year-old River as a schoolgirl telling her teacher that what she thinks is wrong with the Alliance is that "we meddle.... People don't like to be meddled with. We tell them what to do, what to think, don't run don't walk we're in their homes and in their heads and we haven't the right. We're meddlesome" (*Serenity, Serenity: The Official Visual Companion*, 43).

Curry's criticism is aimed primarily at our claim that "just as the young

River told her teacher what is wrong with the Alliance is that 'we meddle ... we're meddlesome' so, though she probably could never articulate it, River has now come to realize that '*we* made them.' Her reaction is due in part to cultural guilt, a concept ... Whedon explores in depth in [the *Buffy* episode] 'Pangs'" (Rabb and Richardson 2008, 135). Curry contends that "previous scenes have inculcated the savage stereotype so effectively at the subliminal level that one possibly revisionary scene could hardly trouble it" (par. 3). We argue on the contrary that this powerful exposure to the savage stereotype is in fact necessary in order to increase the emotional impact of the sudden revelation that "*we* made them." River has obviously up to this time identified herself with her upbringing in a privileged family under the Alliance. She was rescued from the Alliance training facility by her brother Simon and has been pursued ever since because of the fear that she had been exposed to the secrets of Miranda through her psychic abilities while in the training facility. Her claim at the beginning of the movie that "we" are meddlesome indicates both her identity with and criticism of the Alliance and increases the impact of the vomiting scene upon learning the true horrors of the Alliance. Rhonda Wilcox's reading of this scene seems to confirm our own in that River is expelling that part of herself associated with the Alliance and regains her true self. Following Susan Swinford, Wilcox argues that "the moment when River vomits on learning the truth represents 'externalizing the truth'; it is an ugly truth, and she expels it from within her, thus reclaiming her own health and self" (Wilcox 2008, 161). Wilcox goes on to note that the movie seems "to endorse the view underlying much psychoanalysis: that knowing the truth about the past can help you reclaim yourself, your own consciousness, your story" (161).

In *The Tempest* Prospero seems to accept Caliban as part of his story in that Caliban both represents Prospero's dark side and the "savage other" whom he further colonizes by teaching him English. This in turn gives Prospero mastery over Caliban: Prospero can direct his behavior through orders and threats, which he could not do until he had first given him the linguistic and cognitive means to understand what Prospero was saying. Caliban had earlier attempted to take charge of the narrative by asserting that the island is his "by Sycorax my mother" (1.2.331), but this assertion and attempt at autonomy are possible only through the language that Prospero has taught him and used to colonize him. As Tribble argues, "Caliban takes possession of his own narrative, though as writers on *The Tempest*'s colonial themes would remind us, only through the language that he has been taught. The power Prospero deploys here is somatic: the threat to 'rack thee with old cramps,' [1.2.369] a threat which of course only works through its [verbal] *reminder* of bodily pain" (160). In a sense, Prospero has created Caliban as a savage just as the Alliance made the Reavers. As Crane notes: "Despite his own claims to attempt to teach and civilize Caliban, Prospero's tortures are relentlessly imagined as turning him into a beast—even while that beastlike nature is the justification for the torments" (188). Prospero himself admits as much when he says, "This thing of darkness I / Acknowledge mine" (5.1.275–276). This is clearly reminiscent of Whedon's implication that "*we* made them." The planet Miranda, along with the unburied corpses of its innocent settler population, has been abandoned by the Alliance and erased from all records, both astronomical and historical. In Shakespeare's *The Tempest*, Miranda is a symbol of innocence. She and her father were abandoned to the mercies of the raging sea by Prospero's brother Antonio, who has since given no further thought to them. As we have seen above, Prospero credits Miranda with saving him and preserving his life. Essentially, she gives Prospero a reason for living that transcends the merely self-centered. He has to redirect much of his energies, otherwise spent in resentful brooding over his mistreatment by Antonio, to caring for his daughter. The discoveries that the crew of Serenity make on the planet Miranda similarly give them a new and larger purpose and focus in life. They use the knowledge of the events on the planet Miranda to offer a measure of freedom to all the people subject to the Alliance and its covert activities. Pity and compassion for the victims on Miranda prompts the crew of Serenity and their captain Malcolm Reynolds (Mal) to "broadwave" the holographic recording concerning the origin of the Reavers and the death of the settlers "to every screen for thirty worlds" (*Serenity*). This while pursued by and fighting against both Alliance operatives and Reavers, a typically Whedonesque moment of self-sacrifice. Their action, exposing one of the Alliance's darker secrets, frees, at least in part, its subjects, including those on the central planets, who are complacently living comfortable lives unaware of the covert activities of their government. Mal addresses his crew about the revelations on Miranda: "This report is maybe twelve years old. Parliament buried it, and it stayed buried 'til River dug it up. This is what they feared she knew. And they were right to fear, 'cause there's a universe of folk that are gonna know it too. They're gonna see it. Somebody has to speak for these people.... You all got on this boat for different reasons, but you all come to the same place. So now I'm asking more of you than I have before. Maybe all. 'Cause as sure as I know anything I know this: They will try again. Maybe on another world, maybe on this very ground, swept clean. A year from now, ten, they'll swing back to the belief that they can make people ... better. And I do not hold to that. So no more running. I aim to misbehave" (*Serenity*). Mal has been flying under Alliance radar, but now, from the point of view of the Alliance, he "aims to misbehave," showing the ironic significance of his first name, Mal, which is derived from the Latin term for "bad."

We catch a glimpse of life on the central planets from a visit the crew of

Serenity makes to the planet Ariel. Its name obviously takes us back to Shakespeare's *The Tempest* and the spirit Ariel, who is obliged to serve his master Prospero. Shortly after his arrival on the island, Prospero had freed Ariel from the cloven pine in which the witch Sycorax had imprisoned him: "she did confine thee, / By help of her more potent ministers, / And in her most unmitigable rage, / Into a cloven pine, within which rift / Imprison'd, thou didst painfully remain / A dozen years; within which space she died, / And left thee there.... It was mine art, / ... that made gape / The pine, and let thee out" (1.2. 274–293). In effect then, Ariel has spent twelve years imprisoned by Sycorax, and the next twelve in forced service to Prospero as payment for relieving him of the first torment. Ariel is, however, set free at the end of the play, just as the citizens of the planet Ariel, like those of all the other central planets, are granted a measure of freedom via the knowledge broadwaved to them about the darker side of their government's covert activities on Miranda. It is no coincidence that the Alliance Parliament had buried the story of the catastrophe on Miranda for the past twelve years, as Mal says above. The number twelve takes us back to *The Tempest*. The newly acquired knowledge broadwaved by Mal should serve to jolt the citizens of the core planets out of their complacency and to make them aware of their own servitude to the Alliance. We see more of the Alliance government's covert activities during the visit of Mal and his crew to the planet Ariel. Though the planet appears to have first-rate restaurants, museums, and medical facilities, enjoyed by a relatively happy, or at least content, population, we are shown that senior government agents are free to kill citizens without charges, arrest, or trial. On Ariel it appears that citizens don't even have Miranda rights! In this context, Mercedes Lackey's article "*Serenity* and Bobby McGee: Freedom and the Illusion of Freedom in Joss Whedon's *Firefly*" is often quoted by Whedon scholars because it aptly pinpoints a parallel between Whedon's futuristic world and our own current reality: "The dystopian society in which the crew of *Serenity* operates feels *real*.... It resonates because the rules by which this dystopia operates are familiar.... The Alliance uses a lot of the same psychological weapons on its own people that all the major governments of the world ... are ... using today" (63–64). The people on Ariel, and the other central Alliance planets, wittingly or unwittingly, have given up a good measure of their personal freedom and civil rights in exchange for security and material comfort. A member of Serenity's crew explains her reluctance to so much as set foot on Ariel, even for something as innocuous as feeding the pigeons: "Probably get the firing squad for littering.... It's a Core planet, it's spotless. It's got sensors, and where there ain't sensors, there's feds. All Central planets are the same" ("Ariel"). However, Dr. Simon Tam, River's brother, would like to sneak his sister into a hospital on Ariel in order to run a series of diagnostic tests so that he can determine exactly what the scientists in the Alliance academy had been doing to her. Since Simon received his medical training in an Alliance hospital, he is familiar with the layout of such facilities. Thus he is able to devise an elaborate plan not only to sneak his sister in, but also to show the crew of Serenity how to access medical supplies which they could steal and sell on the frontier planets for considerable profit: "Government run facility. They'd be restocked in a matter of hours ... stealing from the rich, selling to the poor" ("Ariel"). Simon needs the crew's assistance in order to help his sister. Since he and his sister are wanted fugitives, his plan involves the "Romeo and Juliet" ploy of administering a drug that would simulate their deaths so that they can be wheeled in through the front door in coffins. (Spoiler alert! It works better than in *Romeo and Juliet* because they both survive.) Simon has to train crew members to act as paramedics bringing the "bodies" into the hospital morgue after resuscitation attempts apparently failed. He coaches them in the medical jargon to use to get by the front desk. They are not exactly fast learners, which leads to a series of Shakespearean-like malapropisms. For example,

> MAL: The patients were cynical and not responding and we couldn't bring them back.
>
> SIMON: They were cyanotic.
>
> MAL: They were *cyanotic* and not responding—
>
> SIMON (WITH MAL): Not responsive.
>
> MAL: *Responsive....*
>
> MAL: Pupils were fixed and dilapidated—
>
> SIMON: Dilated....
>
> MAL: We got there and the patients were cyanotic... Not responding... Non responsive... And we tried to reviv... Resuscitate them... And, despite our best efforts... Ah, they kicked... Despite our best efforts. Ah, they...

Fans of *Firefly* should enjoy constable Dogberry in Whedon's version of *Much Ado About Nothing*, since hyperdiegetic casting has Nathan Fillion playing the roles of both Malcolm Reynolds and the malapropistic Dogberry. Some of Dogberry's more notable and amusing verbal slip-ups include "vigitant" for "vigilant" ("be vigitant" [3.3.94]); "confidence" for "conference" and "decerns" for "concerns" ("I would have confidence with you that decerns you nearly" [3.5.2–3]); "odorous" for "odious" ("comparisons are odorous" [3.5.16]); "comprehended" for "apprehended" and "aspicious" for "suspicious" ("Our watch, sir, have comprehended two aspicious persons" [3.5.46]); "dissembly" for "assembly" ("Is our whole dissembly appeared?" [4.2.1]); "suspect" for "respect" ("Dost thou not suspect my place? dost thou not suspect my years?" [4.2.74–75]); and "redemption" for its opposite "damnation" ("thou wilt be condemn'd into everlasting redemption for this" [4.2.56–57]). It is obvious from these examples why Whedon chose his old friend Nathan Fillion (Mal) to play Dogberry.

Not only do the crew of Serenity obtain paramedic uniforms and fake IDs from Ariel's black market, but they also build a functional replica of an official flying ambulance from materials found in the planet's junkyards: "Big hospitals mean big waste, so we shouldn't have any trouble finding what we're looking for" ("Ariel"). They are able to pilot their ambulance right up to the front door of the hospital and wheel the coffins containing Simon and River past security guards to the front desk, where Mal tells the receiving doctor, "Got a couple of DOAs, by the time we got there..." ("Ariel"). Interrupting, the completely uninterested doctor tells him to take them down to the morgue. All their rehearsing with medical jargon and so forth was unneeded. They are able to get to the morgue without incident, where they awaken Simon and River Tam by injecting an antidote to their death-simulating drug. The Tams are left under the protection of one of the crew members, Jayne Cobb, to make their way to the 3-D imaging suite, while Mal and his second-in-command, Zoe, head off with the caskets to "pick up," i.e., steal, medical supplies. Mal and Zoe successfully complete their mission and return to the ambulance with only a few minor incidents to keep up the tension. Jayne accompanies the Tams to 3-D imaging.

Jayne Cobb is the muscle of the crew. He is the kind of guy who names his guns and has many of them. Unfortunately, he is a deeply flawed character, the only sense in which he is deep. He has arranged to sell out the Tams for a large reward, the price on their heads offered by the Alliance. Once Simon has completed the imaging of his sister's brain, Jayne tells them there has been a change of plans and leads them to a back exit where they are arrested by uniformed federal agents: "Federal Marshals! Don't move! River and Simon Tam, by the authority of the Union of Allied Planets, you are hereby bound by law" ("Ariel"). When Jayne surreptitiously asks for his reward, he discovers that he too is under arrest for harboring fugitives, and that the federal agent fully expects to collect the reward for himself. After processing, two guards escort them to the holding cells. On the way, Jayne, with Simon's help, overcomes the two guards despite the fact that he and Simon are both handcuffed. Jayne retrieves the key from the guard he has killed and removes the handcuffs from himself and the Tams.

Meanwhile, back in the processing area, two plain-clothed senior federal agents wearing ominous blue gloves approach and are told by the chief of the uniformed agents: "The prisoners'll be out in a minute. Let me get the paperwork together for you.... The men were tight lipped. And the girl was just spewing gibberish. We got it all down" ("Ariel"). It is here that we learn something about the more ominous nature of the Alliance and its federal police.

The blue-gloved agents are obviously concerned about the government secrets that might be buried somewhere in River's psyche. One of the blue-gloved agents says indignantly, "You spoke to the prisoners?" and the other asks, "Did your men also speak with them?" ("Ariel"). We discover that the uniformed agents are not permitted to go on living for fear that they might have gained some knowledge of government secrets from the prisoners, particularly River. One of the blue-gloved agents pulls a small rod-like device from his suit pocket. It springs open, revealing two short aerials extending from either end. The high-pitched sonic waves emanating from this device cause the uniformed agent's nose, mouth, and eyes to bleed profusely. We also see blood oozing from his fingernails. He dies in obvious agony. The same fate falls upon the other uniformed agents under his command, anyone who had any contact with the prisoners. The blue-gloved agents will obviously go to any lengths to protect Alliance secrets. Fortunately, the blue-gloved agents do not catch up with Jayne and the Tams, who run into Mal coming in through a back door of the hospital, looking for them. Jayne had wanted to exit via the front door, the way they had been brought into the security substation, which would now require fighting their way through an estimated six federal agents. He is driven to follow Simon and River toward a possible back exit by the sheer horror of the screams emanating from the dying federal agents at the hands of the blue-gloved operatives. River has obviously sensed the arrival of these two operatives as she mutters over and over "two by two, hands of blue" ("Ariel"). Her psychic abilities, however, are not always reliable as she often utters sheer nonsense, "spewing gibberish" as her captor had reported. Sitting with Simon and Jayne in the prisoner processing area, she had said such things as, "They took Christmas away.... Came down the stairs for the shiny presents, but they took the tree and the stockings. Nothing left but coal.... And don't look in the closet either. That's greedy. It's not in the spirit of the holiday" ("Ariel"). River's brain had been damaged by the experiments conducted on her as a teenager at the Alliance training facility. When Simon looks at the 3-D scans in the hospital, he begins to realize just how extensive the intrusion has been: "That's a scalpel scar. They opened up her skull ... and then they cut into her brain.... The only reason to make an incision into someone's brain is to lobotomize them—you go in to remove damaged tissue. Why someone would cut into a healthy brain ... they did it over and over ... they stripped her amygdala" ("Ariel"). Simon goes on to explain the function of the amygdala to a confused and perturbed Jayne: "You know how ... you get scared. Or worried, or nervous. And you don't want to be scared or worried or nervous, so you push it to the back of your mind. You try not to think about it. The amygdala is what lets you do that—it's like a filter in your brain that keeps your feelings in check ... they took that filter out of River. She feels everything. She can't not" ("Ariel"). Not only does this help us understand River's character a little more, but it also reveals something about the oppressive nature of the Alliance, that they would actually experiment on the brain of an innocent teenage girl, in an attempt to control and enhance her natural psychic abilities. We don't learn the full extent of the Alliance's willingness to experiment on its population until we arrive at the planet Miranda near the end of the movie *Serenity*—some 30 million dead and around 30 thousand turned into cannibalistic monsters, the Reavers, the Calibans of this 'verse.

Our comparison of Whedon's *Firefly/Serenity* and Shakespeare's *The Tempest* presupposes a postcolonial reading of *The Tempest*. Actually, we don't like the term "postcolonial," partly because we teach at a university that has a large number of Native students. Native scholars, both students and faculty, have told us, in no uncertain terms, that *they* will let us know when we are in a *post*colonial era. A number of Shakespearean scholars question a colonial or postcolonial reading of *The Tempest*. For example, Charles H. Frey in both "*The Tempest* and the New World" and "Embodying the Play" argues that "while it is true that the text of *The Tempest* contains references to the Bermuda islands, to the brave new world, to dead Indians, and to a god 'Setebos' worshipped, in fact, by sixteenth-century natives of South America, Prospero's island is narratively placed in the Mediterranean. Caliban's mother was 'blue-eyed' and Caliban was a 'freckled' infant (I.ii.269, 283), so that any attempt to image Caliban as a native American or as a black or negroid slave is distinctly problematic" ("Embodying the Play" 76).

It is generally agreed that Shakespeare based his description of the island on pamphlets describing Bermuda. He was obviously familiar with the practice of displaying "Red Indians" on the streets of London. Coming upon Caliban, and trying to determine whether he has encountered a fish, a monster, or a man, Trinculo, one of the ship's survivors, says: "Were I in England now (as I once was) and had but this fish painted, not a holiday fool there but would give a piece of silver. There would this monster make a man; any strange beast there makes a man. When they will not give a doit [half a farthing] to relieve a lame beggar, they will lay out ten to see a dead Indian" (2.2.27–33). Such displays would have been on a cultural par with bear-baiting, whoring, and theater-going. As for the freckled son of a blue-eyed mother, the context is more likely to be that of English colonial oppression of the Irish, which was practiced well before the English exploitation of North America. And in terms of the geography implied by the play's story, we agree with Frey that Prospero's island must be in the Mediterranean, since Antonio and company end up there when returning to Italy from Tunis. We also agree with Frey that concentrating exclusively on a colonial reading of *The Tempest* is to miss something important about the play.

Frey, however, does closely examine a number of possible New World related sources Shakespeare might have used. He cites Caliban offering to gather food for the island's new arrivals:

> I prithee let me bring thee where crabs grow;
> And I with my long nails will dig thee pig-nuts,
> Show thee a jay's nest, and instruct thee how
> To snare the nimble marmazet. I'll bring thee
> To clust'ring filberts, and sometimes I'll get thee
> Young scamels from the rock
>
> [2.2.167–172].

What are "scamels?" Arguing that "we must go 'outside' the play to apprehend and create meanings for words and passages within it," Frey suggests that they may be "small fish described as '*fort scameux*' and '*squame*' [as recounted in French and Italian accounts of the voyages of Magellan and El Cano]. The possibility that Shakespeare, in referring to 'scamels,' is adapting a foreign word like '*squamelle*' (that is, furnished with little scales) would seem worth investigating" ("*The Tempest* and the New World" 33). Caliban had previously shown similar hospitality when Prospero and Miranda first landed on the island: "I lov'd thee / And show'd thee all the qualities o' th' isle, / The fresh springs, brine-pits, barren place and fertile" (1.2.336–338). An analogue to this can be found in Francis Fletcher's account of Sir Francis Drake's meetings with the Patagonians: "Herewith the General with some of his company went on shore where the giant men and women with their children repaired to them showing themselves not only harmless, but also most ready to do us any good and pleasure. Yea they showed us more kindness than many Christians would have done" (quoted in Frey "*The Tempest* and the New World" 35). Frey points out that "Fletcher goes on to say that the natives brought them such food 'as their country yielded in most kind and familiar sort'" (35). Frey suggests that "we will never settle how much of this material was indigenous to the Western Hemisphere and how much was imported in the minds of men who came from Europe" ("*The Tempest* and the New World" 37). Actually, Christopher Columbus seems to have had similar positive encounters with Natives as those of Drake. He says of them, "They are so ... free with all they have, that no one would believe it who has not seen it; of anything that they possess, if it be asked of them, they never say no; on the contrary, they invite you to share it and show as much love as if their hearts went with it" (quoted in Morison, 231). Almost 150 years after Columbus we find similar accounts in the *Jesuit Relations* concerning the Huron: "We see shining among them some rather noble moral virtues.... Their hospitality towards all sorts of strangers is remarkable; they present to them in their feasts, the best of what they have prepared, and as I have already said, I do not know if anything similar, in this regard, is to be found anywhere. They never close the door upon a Stranger, and once having received him into their houses, they share with him the best they have; they never send him away, and when he goes away of his own accord, he repays them with a simple 'thank you'" (Mealing 45). Just as Prospero treats Caliban as a savage despite his originally helpful demeanor, so the settlers in the New World similarly treated its Indigenous inhabitants. This is the very point we were making about the origin of the Reavers in *Firefly/Serenity*: Whedon literalizes the "we made them." Both Whedon's story of the origin of the Reavers on the planet Miranda and Shakespeare's *The Tempest* are wondrous tales indeed.

In his "*The Tempest* and the New World," Frey actually implies that one possible origin of the name "Miranda" is the title of the 1590 Latin translation of Thomas Harriott's *Brief and True Report on Virginia*, which begins *Admiranda narratio*, a narrative to be wondered at. Frey (39) draws our attention to this title when discussing the response of Ferdinand, son of Alonso the King of Naples, upon first learning her name: "Admir'd Miranda, / Indeed the top of admiration!" (3.1.37–38). The phonetic resemblance between *admiranda* and "admir'd Miranda" is startling and too much of a coincidence to be ignored. As Frey has argued in "Embodying the Play," the "temptation to link Prospero and Caliban in some respects with interactions in the New World between natives and Europeans may become barely resistible" (76). Frey, however, thinks we should resist because otherwise we may lose the immediate embodied impact of the play upon the audience: "I want to expose and contest the myopic dominance of social constructions—such as the colonialist Shakespeare—which fail to allow for ways in which the play's thick texture and deep structure implicate many other significant issues" (76). Frey argues that audience "'response' has always suggested a species of interaction with literature much more immediate, emotional, visceral, and, yes, relatively 'independent' of intellectual/social contexts than other forms of interpretation or of criticism. (And nearly all forms of 'reader-response' criticism remain mired in schemes of analytical or social psychology that deny significance to literally immediate, direct, or embodied response.) ... I come at the difference partly in terms of the 'distinction between thinking *about* a play and thinking the play directly'" (74). Frey's experiential approach to Shakespeare "dares to suggest ... that the body is much, much larger than culture, that 'much of the mind works in the body,' that 'corporeal and medical issues are invoked' in the study of Shakespeare" (78). He goes on to explain that the play "consists of signs which we apprehend and process with our various senses. Seeing or hearing such signs leads, for example, to manifold responses within our bodies, responses which may weakly be termed 'images' or 'percepts' for some limited purposes but which actually include all the complex sensations that may produce thoughts, feelings, and even externally observable behaviour such as laughter, crying, changes in heartbeat and breath rates, muscle tension or relaxation, postural shifts, exclamations, and so on" (80–81).

Of course a play can make an audience laugh, or cry, or feel concerned for the fate of endangered characters. *The Tempest*, indeed, opens with just such a moment and just such an intent. According to the initial stage direction, the audience first experiences "a tempestuous noise of thunder and lightning" and then sees a team of desperate sailors fighting to save their ship, their passengers, and their own lives. We quite naturally and spontaneously are fearful for them and wish their safety, for we as yet do not know that the storm is a result of magic and the sailors and passengers are not in fact at risk. And, in case we have missed the point, the second scene opens with Miranda, as the ideal audience, observing this storm and responding in the way we ourselves should, with pity and fear viscerally felt and expressed:

> O! I have suffered
> With those that I saw suffer. A brave vessel
> (Who had, no doubt, some noble creature in her)
> Dash'd all to pieces!), the cry did knock
> Against my very heart
>
> [1.2.5–9].

Neither Miranda nor the audience know that the storm is a product of Prospero's magic and that he is protecting those on the foundering ship. The audience, like Miranda, is already on edge, so when the Boatswain shouts, "Heigh, my hearts! ... yare, yare! Take in the topsail" (1.1.5–6), the audience, like the crew, jump to attention. As Frey points out, when an actor in a play shouts, "Heigh!" (Hey!) to another character, we know what it means and respond appropriately, "because we can consult, through memory or recall, experiences of being roused in our attention and readiness for action by 'Hey!' We have learned to respond to this particular sound to alert ourselves and others to demands of effort, and such alertness only has meaning because we have felt and can still consult or recall the physiological coordinates of tensing muscles, straightening posture, widening eyes, and the like that tell us what an arousing 'Hey!' is for" (81). Frey is stressing that "literary or dramatic intake is not disembodied ... but is instead embodied, attuned to, and exercising many registers of distinctly somatic feeling" (81). Frey believes "that Shakespeare does display a uniquely 'materializing imagination,' one that relentlessly connects abstractions, ideas, and ideals to material and bodily worlds" (92). Frey stands in opposition to what he regards as "a kind of false intellectualism that employs only the thinnest slice imaginable of cerebral cortex to abstract from a fully resonant text one or two exemplifications of ideological or other theory ...

students often learn to produce verbal abstractions concerning texts studied without learning to observe or respond to more concrete dimensions of the texts" (94). Citing Kristin Linklater's *Free Shakespeare's Voice*, Frey argues, "The *way* you speak Shakespeare's words will determine the *depth* at which you plumb his meaning.... Time and again I have seen, heard, and felt Shakespeare's words enter and restore power to a boy or a girl, a woman or a man, whose sense of worth has been obliterated by childhood abuse, social inequality or racial bigotry. This happens *not when they read Shakespeare, not when they hear Shakespeare, but when they speak the words themselves*" (95, emphasis in the original). When we speak Shakespeare's words, we are in fact truly embodying them.

Though Frey does not mention cognitive science, his view of embodiment ties in very nicely with Lakoff and Johnson's embodied metaphors emphasized by Mary Thomas Crane in her book, *Shakespeare's Brain*. We are arguing that a narrative ethics employing metaphor and the moral imagination can and should draw upon the emotional and aesthetic response to narrative explored by Frey. We realize that some would argue that such aesthetic evaluations have no relevance to ethical judgments. Many philosophers and ethicists insist on a strict distinction between ethics and aesthetics. They would argue that ethical judgments are based on reason. The faculty of pure practical reason is thought to provide moral principles, which can be used to suppress our emotions, to keep our feelings, emotions, and desires in line. Frey's aesthetic reading of Shakespeare actually supports our contention that a narrative ethics can be found in literature and story. Like Crane, we support our contention by drawing upon second-generation cognitive science, which argues against this kind of compartmentalization of ethics over and against aesthetics. One of the most prominent thinkers to use the findings of cognitive science to discuss ethics is University of Oregon philosopher, Mark Johnson, whom we discussed above in relation to Crane's cognitive reading of Shakespeare. In his 1993 groundbreaking study, *Moral Imagination: Implications of Cognitive Science for Ethics*, Johnson argues that "the rigid separation of the aesthetic from the moral is rooted in the.... Enlightenment view of cognition that we have inherited..." from 17th- and 18th-century science and philosophy (207). What Johnson calls the "Enlightenment folk theory of Faculty Psychology" was used to support the view that "our mental acts can be broken down into separate and distinct forms of judgment" (207). A "folk theory" is, of course, one that is usually widely believed, but not based on science. Such folk theories can in fact be very misleading. In the case of the "Enlightenment folk theory of Faculty Psychology" it was believed that we have epistemic or theoretical judgments based on reason, dealing with the way the world is; moral judgments based on ethical principles, dealing with the way things ought to be and how we ought to behave; and, thirdly, aesthetic judgments "based on *feelings* and *imagination*, expressing our feeling response to certain perceptible forms of natural and artificial objects. It was regarded as crucial not to confuse moral with aesthetic judgments" (207, emphasis in original). However, Johnson argues on the contrary, that "those folk theories that are based on Enlightenment Faculty Psychology, its distinction among types of judgment, and its correlative distinction among realms of experience (i.e., the theoretical, moral, and aesthetic) are, for the most part, shown to be wrong by cognitive science" (208). This is one of the major implications of second generation cognitive science, and underlines the significance of the subtitle of Johnson's study. Johnson observes "this folk theory of Faculty Psychology is shared by virtually everyone in Western culture" (15), and it operates for the most part unconsciously. Johnson begins his study by provocatively asserting in contrast to the widely-accepted Aristotelian claim that man is a rational animal: "My central thesis is that human beings are fundamentally *imaginative* moral animals" (1, emphasis in the original). As Johnson concludes in his more recent book, *The Meaning of the Body: Aesthetics of Human Understanding*, "*we need a philosophy that sees aesthetics not as just about art, beauty, and taste, but rather as about how human beings experience and make meaning. Aesthetics concerns all of the things that go into meaning—form, expression, communication, qualities, emotion, feeling, value, purpose, and more....* Insofar as aesthetics concerns the very conditions of meaningful experience and thought, philosophy must be grounded in aesthetics" (212–213, emphasis in original).

As we noted at the outset of this chapter, Johnson, working with George Lakoff, in *Philosophy in the Flesh: The Embodied Mind and Its Challenge to Western Thought*, argues that "there is no ethical system that is not metaphorical" (325). Such moral metaphors, they argue, "are inextricably tied to our embodied experience of well-being: health, strength, wealth, purity, control, nurturance, empathy, and so forth" (331). Lakoff and Johnson argue that these moral "metaphors are grounded in the nature of our bodies and social interactions, and they are thus anything but arbitrary and unconstrained" (290). Cognitive science has shown that the sensorimotor system turns out to be the source domain for moral metaphors. We are embodied beings that walk upright on our own two feet and must literally keep our balance, since, generally speaking, falling down does not contribute to our well being, while staying upright does. Hence we metaphorically speak of taking a balanced approach, or of being an upright citizen, meaning someone of good moral standing. It is easier for us to locate things in the sunlight than in darkness, so we speak, again metaphorically, of bringing things to light, or casting new light on something. We also associate light with good or well-being and darkness with evil and harm. Similarly, we speak about seeing the point of an argument or grasping a difficult concept. We do not *literally* see a logical implication or *physically* grasp with our hands an abstract concept. The source domains for these conceptual metaphors are, of course, literal seeing and physical grasping. This is why such metaphors are said to be derived from and dependent upon the sensorimotor system. Norman Holland, in his book *Literature and the Brain*, is particularly impressed with the results of recent breakthroughs in brain imaging technologies such as positron emission tomography (PET scans) and functional magnetic resonance imaging (fMRIs). He is excited that Lakoff and Johnson have found that "when we use a metaphor (like 'grasping' an idea) that involves doing something with our physical bodies ... the same neurons light up as if we were in fact performing that act" (Holland 98). However Douglas Hofstadter and Emmanuel Sander in their popular book *Surfaces and Essences: Analogy as the Fuel and Fire of Thinking*, argue that "until there are incredibly sophisticated real-time brain-scanning mechanisms, and until we understand the brain infinitely better" we must rely on more indirect evidence for the prevalence of analogy and metaphor in our thinking, such as our use and misuse of language (264). As an example of what they call "lexical blending" they offer the following sentence: "My dad really hit the stack when I got home so late" (265). They go on to explain that "what the speaker meant was that her father grew very angry very fast, which is to say he both *hit the ceiling* and *blew his stack*" (265 emphasis in original). This is an example of multiple influences because each of the previous phrases "contains roughly half of the final blend" (265). But they also point out another common expression which sounds very like the malapropism uttered, "namely, 'hit the sack' ... even though the meaning of 'hit the sack'—'go to bed'—is utterly unrelated to sudden bursts of anger" (265). They suggest "that the 'phonetic pull' or 'sonic attraction' of that standard phrase played ... [a] role in this blend. It was like a huge planet gravitationally pulling the speaker toward it" (265). They call this "phonetic proximity" or "phonetic analogy" as opposed to "conceptual proximity," which the first two phrases of the blend, *hit the ceiling* and *blew his stack* represent. We see Mary Thomas Crane in her cognitive analysis of *The Tempest* as drawing on phonetic analogy when she seizes on Shakespeare's use of a set of terms that are linked chiefly by sound rather than by logical sense: *pinch, pitch, pity, pen*, and *pine* (and its cognate *pain*). We should note in passing that all of these terms evoke embodiment, our confinement to and dependence on a physical body. Hofstadter and Sander, like Crane, build on and in a sense confirm the work of Lakoff and Johnson: "Linguist George Lakoff and philosopher Mark Johnson have shown that there are certain systematic tendencies that guide the construction of a number of metaphors in everyday language. Their studies ... demonstrate that metaphors, far from being just an elegant rhetorical flourish exploited solely by poets and orators, are the coin of the realm in much of ordinary discourse. For example ... life is often spoken of in terms of motion or a trip (the *path* of her success; a *sinuous* career; the *dead end* in which they're trapped), with everyday events as places one passes through (I'm *going* to see them tomorrow; I'll *come back* to that point), and happiness and unhappiness are often represented by the concepts of high and low (*raising* someone's morale; to be in *seventh heaven*; to *plunge* into despair; to be very *down*)" (63, emphasis in original). Note that the "life is a journey" metaphor-schema and the very similar "relationships are a journey" appear right at the beginning of Shakespeare's *The Tempest*. Prospero's relationship with his brother Antonio could certainly be said to be on the rocks since Antonio has usurped Prospero's position as Duke of Milan and abandoned Prospero and Miranda to the mercy of the seas. The beginning of the play literalizes this metaphor in a rather Whedonesque fashion, by having Antonio and his shipmates dashed upon the shores of Prospero's island. At the end of the play, when Prospero has forgiven his brother and regained his Dukedom, when Miranda is betrothed to Ferdinand, Prince of Naples, and they are preparing to leave the island behind, there is the expectation of smooth sailing from here on out. As the actor playing Prospero says to the audience in the Epilogue, "Gentle breath of yours my sails / Must fill" (11–12).

The Whedonverse also makes use of the life as a journey metaphor-schema and at one point actually acknowledges it as a metaphor. In the *Buffy the Vampire Slayer* episode "No Place Like Home" (5.5), Buffy is seen trying to rescue a monk who is being pursued by a monster, and as they run across a vacant lot, he stumbles, falls, and gasping says, "My journey's done, I think." Buffy responds, trying to be encouraging, "Don't get metaphory on me. We're going." Lakoff and Johnson, in *Philosophy in the Flesh*, note that in the "life as a journey" metaphor-schema, there are various sub-mappings, including "Achieving a Purpose Is Reaching a Destination." They give the following examples: "*We've reached the end. We are seeing the light at the end of the tunnel. We only have a short way to go. We're where we wanted to go. The goal is a long way off*" (190, emphasis in original). We learn that the monk that Buffy has attempted to rescue has achieved his purpose. He informs her with his dying breath that he has delivered into her protection a mystical Key, now magically put into human form, a brand new 14-year-old sister called Dawn (Buffy has gone through four seasons as an only child!). The old Guardians of the Key "knew the Slayer would protect" it with her life, and magically altered everyone's memories and even family photographs to retrospectively accommodate the new sister. Rhonda Wilcox, in *Why* Buffy *Matters*, following Roz Kaveney, calls such narrative manipulation "retcon" (retroactive continuity), "giving information that explains an earlier event, especially seeming plot contradictions or lacunae" (9). It suddenly dawned on us that the Key is certainly retcon writ large. The monk's metaphor, "My journey's done, I think," functions at a number of levels. Since he is in the process of dying, his life as a journey is ending. He has obviously traveled to Sunnydale, and thus achieved his destination. He has also achieved his purpose in delivering the mystical Key into the safekeeping of the Slayer. This is not the only instance in this episode in which the audience's attention is drawn to the metaphorical character of the dialogue. Giles, Buffy's now unofficial Watcher, has just purchased a shop called The Magic Box, and is trying to reassure himself of its financial viability: "Still, not to worry. No, I've got feelings about this place. Magic's a small niche market but ... well, think about it. Sunnydale. Monsters. Supply and demand. They'll be lining up around the block in no time." To which Buffy responds, "Yeah. You'll be making money hand over fist." Immediately upon uttering this common metaphor, Buffy seems suddenly puzzled and moves her open hand slowly back and forth above her clenched fist as though trying to plumb the depths of the metaphor. Whedon and his writers are very good at literalizing metaphor, often to humorous effect.

The Hofstatder and Sander book, *Surfaces and Essences*, provides overwhelming evidence for the analogical and metaphorical nature of abstract thought as exhibited in language. Indeed, it contains 530 pages of examples and explanations. To mention only a few, "To be up to one's ears in work, to go in one ear and out the other, to roll out the red carpet, to roll one's sleeves up, to be dressed to the nines, to be in seventh heaven, to be dead as a doornail, to wait until the cows come home, to burn the candle at both ends, to swallow one's pride, to eat humble pie, to take it for granted, to kick the bucket, to let the floodgates open, to drop the ball, to catch the drift, to be caught off guard, to get away with murder, to read between the lines, to read the handwriting on the wall, to lick someone's boots, to have the time of one's life, to drop something like a hot potato, to throw someone for a loop, to throw someone into a tizzy, to get a kick out of something, to play it by ear, to bend over backwards, to fly in the face of evidence, to tie the knot, to get hitched, to open a can of worms, to scrape the bottom of the barrel, to drop a bombshell, to be caught between a rock and a hard place, to paint oneself into a corner, to eat one's words, to let the cat out of the bag, to spill the beans" (95). They note that such analogies can be anything from a single word such as "it's all *Greek* to me," "he *swallowed* her story," "a *blanket* excuse" (63, emphasis in original), "The *leg* of a table, "a *head* of lettuce," a *skeleton* key (62, emphasis in original), to the phrases listed above, and even to proverbs like "*Once bitten, twice shy*" (105, emphasis in original), as well as to entire fables such as Aesop's Fable about the fox and the grapes. To shorten the story considerably, the fox wants to eat the high-hanging grapes but finds he cannot reach them, so gives up, saying, "They look so green that it's simply not worth the trouble" (112). This is, of course, the origin of the *sour-grapes* analogy. Hofstatder and Sander are so thorough that they even distinguish between sour-grapes and silver-linings: "In contrast to *sour-grapes* situations, which involve the expedient distortion of one or more beliefs, *seeing-the-silver-lining* situations are ones in which the protagonist, though upset, does not distort any beliefs but instead is *selective* in terms of which beliefs to focus on" (117, emphasis in original).

In some metaphors, the underlying neural architecture is more apparent than in others. Lakoff notes that we use temperature to describe affection because "temperature is publicly discernible while affection is not" (Lakoff 1993, 84). As children, we experience affection and warmth, often at the same time, "feeling warm while being held affectionately" (Lakoff and Johnson 1999, 50). Lakoff and Johnson point out that this is the origin of the "Affection Is Warmth" conceptual metaphor. Lakoff notes that this is how the metaphorical mapping is written in English. "The mapping it names is neural in character" (Lakoff 1993, 83). As Lakoff puts it: "Neurons that fire together wire together" (83). It should be noted that this neural mapping is in effect a one-way street. The temperature synapses are stronger than those associated with affection, because we experience warmth through the sensorimotor system and thus those synapses fire more often. "As a result, activation will flow from temperature to affection and not in the opposite direction" (Lakoff 1993, 84). Heating food does not make it more affectionate, but a person can be said to be becoming more affectionate when they warm up to another. The "Affection Is Warmth" conceptual metaphor is used on occasion by Shakespeare himself. Take Sonnet 154, for example. We have highlighted the relevant metaphors in italics:

> The little Love-god, lying once asleep,
> Laid by his side his *heart-inflaming* brand,
> Whilst many nymphs that vow'd chaste life to keep
> Came tripping by, but in her maiden hand
> The fairest votary took up that *fire*,
> Which many legions of *true hearts had warm'd*
> And so the general of *hot desire*
> Was sleeping by a virgin hand disarm'd.
> This brand she *quenched in a cool well* by,
> Which from *Love's fire took heat perpetual*,
> Growing a bath and healthful remedy
> For men diseas'd, but I, my mistress' thrall,
> Came there for cure, and this by that I prove:
> *Love's fire heats water, water cools not love.*

Shakespeare's great dramas are also complex metaphors dealing with moral questions and ethical quandaries such as what one ought to do, who one wants to be, and how to achieve such goals. For example, as we have seen above, in

The Tempest Prospero must choose between punishing his brother Antonio for usurping his Dukedom, that is following his vengeful dark side represented metaphorically by Caliban, or forgiving Antonio out of love for family, following his nobler side, represented by Miranda and Ariel. Had he followed his Caliban, *The Tempest* might very well have become a tragedy. Such extended narratives allow us to consider and examine the concrete particularities of moral experience, which is something that abstract reason and general moral principles do not. Philosopher of cognitive science Mark Johnson has noted that "Martha Nussbaum has mounted an extended and quite eloquent argument for the central role of literature in our moral development" (1993, 196). He cites Nussbaum's *The Fragility of Goodness* in support: "A whole tragic drama, unlike a schematic philosophical example making use of a similar story, is capable of tracing the history of a complex pattern of deliberation, showing its roots in a way of life and looking forward to its consequences in that life. As it does all of this, it lays open to view the complexity, the indeterminacy, the sheer difficulty of actual human deliberation.... A tragedy does not display the dilemmas of its characters as pre-articulated [i.e., it does not spell out everything that needs to be noticed]; it shows them searching for the morally salient; and it forces us, as interpreters, to be similarly active" (196–197; see Nussbaum 14). Nussbaum is a leading member of a group of contemporary moral philosophers who have been called "premodern" because they find inspiration in the ancient Greek philosophers (Cahoone 87). According to Nussbaum herself, these include "Bernard Williams, Alastair MacIntyre, Iris Murdoch, John McDowell ... Philippa Foot, Annette Baier, and Cora Diamond," among others (xxiv). They are all, in varying degrees, suspicious of the Enlightenment use of the faculty of reason to dominate the passions and emotions, what Mark Johnson called the "Enlightenment folk theory of Faculty Psychology," as we explained above. This does not, of course, entail a complete rejection of Enlightenment ideals. Nussbaum clarifies her own position in the Preface to the revised edition of her book *The Fragility of Goodness*: "I wish to distance myself from appeals to the Greeks that urge the rejection of systematic theorizing in ethics and of the Enlightenment goal of a social life grounded in reason.... [M]y position ... aims not to reject Enlightenment ideas but to appropriate the Greeks as allies of an expanded version of Enlightenment liberalism" (xvi). Our position is a little more radical than that of Nussbaum. We do, however, agree that you can't really defend a narrative ethics without also discussing ethical theory, what Nussbaum calls "systematic theorizing in ethics." See our Chapter Eight "Reason and Rules in Ethics: The Parfit Pathology." Nor do we totally reject Enlightenment reason. Who can reject enlightenment, casting light on a subject, pushing back the dark ages? The metaphors are, well, enlightening. Certainly advances in science from the

Enlightenment on have led to the discoveries in second-generation cognitive science that we are using here to defend narrative in ethics. Still, when this sense of reason is applied in ethical argument, using what Johnson calls the "Enlightenment folk theory of Faculty Psychology," it seems to diminish ethical thought. The enlightenment that follows, the light that is cast, is more like the "lite" of a lite beer. It doesn't give you much of a buzz and there is less nourishment in it. We have chosen to compare the dramatic works of Shakespeare and Whedon in part because Whedon is postmodern and Shakespeare is early modern. Shakespeare, after all, is writing before the modernity of the Enlightenment has fully taken hold of and suppressed the moral imagination. Comparing the paragraph-long case studies that some contemporary ethicists offer as philosophical examples to something like a full Shakespearian tragedy, Nussbaum argues, "interpreting a tragedy is a messier, less determinate, more mysterious matter than assessing a philosophical example; and even when the work has once been interpreted, it remains unexhausted, subject to a reassessment, in a way the example does not. To invite such material into the center of an ethical inquiry concerning these problems of practical reason is, then, to add to its content a picture of reason's procedures and problems that could not readily be conveyed in some other form" (14). We would add, following Johnson, that it also emphasizes the role of imagination over that of reason.

Johnson's thesis in *The Moral Imagination* is that ethical thinking requires, not moral laws, but imaginative narrative: "If a good many of our basic moral concepts (such as person, rights, harm, justice, love) and many of the concepts that define kinds of action (e.g., murder, lie, educate, natural, sex) have internal prototype structure, then Moral Law theories must be rejected" (189). Hofstatder and Sander provide a useful metaphor, which we think helps to explain what Johnson means here by prototype structure. "Psychological studies have shown that a mental category, rather than having well-defined and context-independent boundaries, is more like a vast cosmopolitan area such as Paris, which first sees the light of day as a tiny, almost solid, central core ... which ... will eventually be baptized the 'old town.'... At every moment in the life of a major metropolis or a 'mature' category, there is a crucial central zone that includes, surrounds, and dominates over the original core.... Further out, one finds an urban ring that is not as dense or as historically important, and then there comes a vast suburban ring, which extends far out from the center while growing gradually less and less densely populated, and which has no precise outermost boundary ... fields filled with wheat and cattle are evidently no longer part of a city" (62). Cognitive science has shown that moral principles really apply only to prototypes, to the "old town" which is often clearly delineated by its ancient walls. Johnson explains, "they 'work' for the prototypical cases—the nonproblematic ones—about which there is widespread agreement within moral traditions. What moral laws we have are precisely those that are formulated to fit the prototypical cases, the central members of a category" (190). To deal with more problematic cases in ethical thinking we do not need more moral rules and principles; rather, we require imaginative narrative, the ability to tell and contemplate stories. Johnson has learned from cognitive science "that narrative characterizes the synthetic character of our very experience.... The stories we tell emerge from, and can then refigure, the narrative structure of our experience.... [B]ecause we are imaginative narrative creatures, we can also configure our lives in novel ways" (163). Through a discussion of both Shakespeare's and Whedon's dramatic texts, the following chapters examine in some detail how various characters "configure [their] lives in novel ways." In the next chapter we explore the more direct impact of Lakoff and Johnson's discussions of cognitive science on the Whedonverses.

THREE

Joss Whedon's "Big Brain": The Espenson Authorship Controversy

Joss Whedon describes Jane Espenson as his Big Brain. What he actually said is "Steve DeKnight and Jane Espenson, two of my biggest brains…" ("Making *Dollhouse*"). DeKnight and Espenson are two of the most prolific writers on Whedon's team, both having contributed to *Buffy the Vampire Slayer*, *Angel*, and *Dollhouse*. Jane Espenson has also contributed to *Firefly*. It is Espenson we are concentrating on in this chapter, since we maintain that she is directly responsible for the influence of cognitive science in the Whedonverse. In our previous chapter, we noted that as early as 2003 Gregory Stevenson used Lakoff and Johnson's work on metaphor and cognitive science to justify discussing metaphor in a TV series like *Buffy the Vampire Slayer*. In 2007 we extended Stevenson's work by noting that in Lakoff and Johnson's *Philosophy in the Flesh* it is argued that all abstract thinking, including moral decision making, is primarily metaphorical in nature (Richardson and Rabb 151). We also drew upon Lakoff and Johnson's argument that morality begins as family morality. We argued that the Scooby gang in *Buffy the Vampire Slayer* as well as, to some extent, the crew of Serenity (in *Firefly/Serenity*), exhibit what Lakoff and Johnson call the nurturant parent metaphor for morality as opposed to the Strict Father Family Morality (159–160). At that time (2007) we took this as further confirmation of Lakoff and Johnson's thesis that abstract and ethical thinking are primarily metaphorical since metaphors abound in the Whedonverse. In 2008 we published "Reavers and Redskins: Creating the Frontier Savage," in *Investigating* Firefly *and* Serenity, edited by Rhonda Wilcox and Tanya Cochrane. During the editorial process, they suggested we look more closely at Jane Espenson since we had criticized her discussion of the Reavers and had discussed the "Pangs" episode of *Buffy the Vampire Slayer* which she had written.

Their suggestion led to what we described as a "most startling discovery" which we subsequently published in the journal *Slayage* under the title "Myth, Metaphor, Morality and Monsters: The Espenson Factor and Cognitive Science in Joss Whedon's Narrative Love Ethic" (Rabb and Richardson 2009).

It is important to consider exactly what we said in that article, since it led to an even more startling discovery. Paragraph 29 of "Myth, Metaphor, Morality and Monsters" reads as follows:

> It turns out Espenson did undergraduate work and graduate research in cognitive science at Berkeley with Lakoff, who singles her out as the graduate student whose own research has contributed to the theory of metaphor. In discussing what he calls location-object duality in our use of metaphors, Lakoff praises Espenson's work in the field: "Duality is a newly-discovered phenomenon. The person who first discovered it in the event structure system was Jane Espenson, a graduate student at Berkeley who stumbled upon it in the course of her research on causation metaphors. Since Espenson's discovery, other extensive dualities have been found in the English metaphor system" (1993, 227). For an example of object-location [location-object] duality think of the sentence "The end of this paper looms up before us." Here the end is an object, like a bus, bearing down on us. Compare "We are coming to the end of this paper." Here the end is a fixed location in the "life is a journey" metaphor system and it is we who are in motion toward it. Such metaphors are pervasive. Consider, for example, "She clawed her way to the top" (location), as opposed to "Throughout her career, promotions were just handed to her" (object). And to think Jane Espenson of the Whedonverse is responsible for this discovery. Mark Johnson, in his book *Moral Imagination: Implications of Cognitive Science for Ethics*, also acknowledges Espenson: "Jane Espenson ... at the Institute for Cognitive Studies, University of California at Berkeley helped me work out some of the metaphorical analyses included in chapter 2" (Johnson xiv). Jane Espenson, as Executive Story Editor, Producer, and Co-Executive Producer as well as writer or co-writer of more than twenty episodes of *Buffy* and episodes of *Angel* and *Firefly*, has had a direct influence on the Whedonverse. Whedon's narratives certainly challenge patriarchal prototypes even before Espenson joined the team. We find that Espenson's training in cognitive science confirms Whedon's more intuitive practice in confronting prototypes. Hence the complexity of moral perspective required by the metaphoric work in "Pangs" (4008), *Firefly*'s Reavers, and so much more of the Whedonverse.

So Jane Espenson has worked with George Lakoff and Mark Johnson and in doing so has both contributed to second generation cognitive science and provided insights from cognitive science to the writing of the Whedonverse. Since it was generally believed that she did not join the Whedon team until season three of *Buffy the Vampire Slayer*, we referred to "Whedon's more intuitive practice" when he was involved in writing seasons one and two. Though Whedon's intuitive use of metaphor in the first two seasons seems to confirm Lakoff and Johnson's findings in cognitive science, we have never been fully satisfied with our appeal to Whedon's intuitions on this matter. Years of worrying about this led finally to our even more startling discovery. In this chapter we argue that Espenson surreptitiously joined Team Whedon, or at least worked personally with Whedon himself, beginning in the first season, with "Welcome to the Hellmouth" and "The Harvest" (1.1 and 1.2, 1997). Whedon is listed as *sole* author of these two episodes as well as of "Prophecy Girl" (1.12), "When She Was Bad" (2.1), "Lie to Me" (2.7), "Innocence" (2.14), and "Becoming, Parts One and Two" (2.21 and 2.22) in seasons one and two. We are not going to claim anything so radical as that Joss Whedon did not write *Buffy the Vampire Slayer*. He most certainly did write the 1992 movie *Buffy the Vampire Slayer*. The TV series is, however, another matter. There is an innocuous sense in which this is true. As we noted in the previous chapter, many of the episodes are the result of a fast-working team of writers. This, as we said, is typical of many weekly TV dramas, even ones that become associated with a single creative individual (e.g., Rod Serling and *The Twilight Zone,* and Gene Roddenberry and *Star Trek*), and is the approach to the Whedonverse taken by David Kociemba in his paper "Understanding the Espensode." In the section of his paper entitled "Alternative Authorship," he argues that "the creative process can be marked by more than just a dynamic of control and ownership; it can include influence and sharing too" (24). In support he cites Rhonda Wilcox's cathedral-builder metaphor: "for years now, when I have thought of the art of a television series, I have thought of the master builder of a cathedral and his workers: a cathedral is a creation which is certainly accepted as art, but which was worked on by many different people over many years ... *Buffy* itself ... has taught me to envision the interaction in a much livelier and less one-way, top-down fashion" [Kociemba 24, see Wilcox 2005, 5–6). Wilcox here is more concerned about justifying such collaborations as works of art. She is not concerned with the niceties of authorship. Kociemba, on the other hand, wants to argue that it is "best to think of creators like Joss Whedon as catalysts to other artists' creations as well as creators in their own right. They are both a muse and an artist" (24). He goes on to discuss "places where Espenson carves out some artistic autonomy and influences others in the creative process" (24). In fact, he gives a 14-point analysis, which he describes as the "Anatomy of the Espensode" (27).

Point (1)—is what he calls "off-the-nose dialogue" (27), or imprecise modes of speech usually found "when a character is REALIZING something" (28) and signaled by hesitancy, trailing off, and awkward and embarrassed overstatement or understatement. One example is of Xander getting tongue-tied while trying to impress Buffy, the new girl at school. He had had a brief encounter with her earlier in which he was helping her pick up the spilled contents of her bag. There he had blurted out: "Can I have you?" Then, after a puzzled look from Buffy, he corrected himself by saying, "Can I help you?" (1.1). His second meeting with Buffy, later that day, occurs when he and his friend Jesse approach Willow and Buffy sitting in front of the school. The following dialogue ensues:

> WILLOW: Buffy, this is Jesse and that's Xander.
> XANDER: Oh, me and Buffy go waaay back, old friends, very close. Then there's that period of estrangement where I think we were both growing as people, but now here we are, like old times, I'm quite moved.
> JESSE: Is it me, or are you turning into a bibbling idiot?
> XANDER: No, it's, uh, it's not you [1.1].

Xander is coming to realize that he is a bibbling idiot when he is around attractive girls and we the audience are also gaining an insight into his character.

Point (2)—is closely related to off-the-nose dialogue. It is "the blurt" (28), which occurs when characters become temporarily inarticulate while attempting to utter a truth that either makes them vulnerable or is potentially painful to their listener. As they struggle mightily to get through the utterance, they often just blurt out the truth. As Espenson herself puts it: "Truth implies tongue-tied. Tongue-tied implies truth. Only the liar is glib" (*Jane in Progress*, October 3, 2006). We have already seen an example above, when Xander blurts out, "Can I have you?" when he meant to say, "Can I help you?" Of course he does want to "have" her, though that is just not said, especially on a first meeting. We know from subsequent episodes that he is very attracted to her and does attempt to date her.

Point (3)—acing the written—is a sort of reversal of point (1) in that it generally involves over-precision in speech. This is a fairly capacious category with room enough for punning and other forms of wordplay, as well as for speech that is far too precise to be spoken naturally by anyone. Espenson explains: "In general, in dialogue writing, you want to avoid language that sounds 'written.' Have people say 'thing' a lot, and speak imprecisely, and search for the word. Unless ... you're going for a joke that plays off the fact that someone is saying something that sounds written" (*Jane in Progress*, May 9, 2006). The character Anya—once an 1100-year-old vengeance demon, now a teenage girl—characteristically speaks in a noticeably non-naturalistic manner. Espenson continues: "But I think the best, subtlest use of this kind of dialogue is when it's suggested that a character is using it on purpose to be self-deprecating. This works because we use it in real life this way sometimes. Here is a nervous Buffy, having brought a date home with her. She hesitates outside her dorm room: "BUFFY: This is it. My door. It's wood. I think. Maybe some kind of wood veneer" ("The Harsh Light of Day" 4.3). How many of us casually use 'veneer' on a date? The word calls attention to Buffy's nervousness.

Which is exactly what the character wanted it to do, since Buffy is subtly laughing at her own nerves in this moment" (*Jane in Progress*, May 9, 2006). Espenson's recommendation that writers, in attempting to portray more natural speech, should have their characters use the word "thing" a lot can be seen in the following dialogue. Xander is trying to get rid of Willow so that he can ask Buffy for a date. He says: "Willow, don't you have a thing?" She responds: "A thing? The thing! That I have! Which is ... a thing that I have to go to. See ya later." Xander turns to Buffy and says hesitantly: "So, uh, Buffy, I wanted to, um.... There was this thing I wanted to ask you, to talk to you about." Xander asks Buffy for the date and she says no because she does not want to spoil the close friendship that they have. Xander replies: "Well, I don't want to spoil it either. But that's not the point, is it? You either feel a thing or you don't" (1.12). This is, of course, an example of natural teenage speech. It contrasts nicely with the stilted speech patterns of this season's Big Bad, the übervamp called The Master. His speech not only sounds like "written" but often seems to be a take-off or reversal of biblical rhetoric: "My blood is your blood. My soul is your soul.... On this ... most hallowed night ... we are as one. Luke is the Vessel! ... Every soul he takes will feed me. And their souls will grant me the strength to free myself. Tonight I shall walk the Earth, and the stars themselves will hide!" (1.2). This is not only quasi-biblical; it also has echoes of Shakespeare. When Macbeth is plotting to murder King Duncan, he invokes the darkness needed to cloak his evil in the following terms: "Stars, hide your fires, / Let not light see my black and deep desires" (1.4.50–51).

Point (4)—analogy: Given Espenson's work on metaphor with George Lakoff, it is little wonder that she "uses analogies as a basic tool in her comedy arsenal" (Kociemba 29). Kociemba cites Espenson herself: "Comparisons, like pictures, are worth a thousand words. They're part of how we understand the world, by conceptualizing things in terms of other things" (29). Such metaphors or comparisons need not be comic; for example, when Xander tells Willow that he has been rejected by Buffy, he uses an election analogy: "The deal's done. The polls are in, and it's time for my concession speech" (1.12). In another example, with a Shakespearean heritage no less, a demon Buffy is fighting draws attention to her mortality, telling her: "You're the one who's barely here. Set on this earth like a bubble. You won't even disturb the air when you go" (6.3). This is derived from Banquo's account, in *Macbeth*, of the vanishing of the witches on the blasted heath: "The earth hath bubbles, as the water has, / And these are of them. Whither are they vanish'd?" (1.3.79–80).

Point (5)—repetition: Once again Kociemba cites Espenson's *Jane in Progress* blog in describing this particular technique. "Tell a joke once, it's funny. Twice, it's not funny. Eight times ... it gets funny again" (Kociemba 31). Such repetitions, which draw upon an earlier joke, are referred to as "callbacks."

A series of such callbacks sometimes across episodes and even across different seasons are called "runners" (29). The runners need not be jokes, though they tend to be funny, sometimes strangely funny. In Season One for example, we have the horrible übervamp called The Master ending a long Biblical sounding speech with the words "Here endeth the lesson" ("Never Kill a Boy on the First Date" 1.5). The same words are repeated by Spike, another, not quite so evil, vampire, in Season Five ("Fool for Love" 5.7). Finally, in Season Seven Buffy herself, in attempting to take charge of a growing army of potential Slayers ends her rant at them with the words "Here endeth the lesson" ("Showtime" 7.11). She is here acting more like a general giving orders to an army, rather than a mentor to her sister Slayers. Her change in behavior is implicitly criticized when she inadvertently repeats the words of the evil übervamp. It draws attention to the fact that she has momentarily moved from a nurturant parent family morality to the worst sort of patriarchal strict father family morality: that represented by the Master.

Point (6)—the two percent solution—is really "a specialized type of callback" (Kociemba 31). It is called "a two-percenter" by Espenson. Again citing the *Jane in Progress* blog, Kociemba explains the two-percenter as "a joke that the writers estimate will be understood and enjoyed by two percent of the audience ... it means you are dealing with a fairly obscure reference" (Kociemba 31). The "runner" we described above with Buffy unknowingly repeating the Master's words, "Here endeth the lesson," is a good example of Espenson's two-percenter. She explains: "As an audience member, when you're part of the two percent that gets it, there's nothing better ... because it feels like the writer is reaching into your own personal brain. In a good way" (quoted in Kociemba 31). The entire seven seasons of *Buffy the Vampire Slayer* actually ends with a two-percenter. After Buffy and the army of newly-empowered slayers have defeated the First Evil, while they stand looking at the huge crater that used to be Sunnydale, Dawn asks, "Yeah, Buffy. What are we gonna do now?" ("Chosen" 7.22). *Buffy* fans will remember that at the end of the first season we have virtually the same question being asked by Jenny Calendar, after this season's Big Bad, the Master, has been defeated: "Well, what do we do now?" Here the question is given an answer. Buffy responds: "We saved the world. I say we party!" ("Prophecy Girl" 1.12). No answer is forthcoming at the end of the series; instead, the camera focuses on Buffy's face and we see just the beginnings of a smile. They have restored hope to the world.

Point (7)—clichés—Espenson likes to use clichés but keeps them fresh by either "reversing the intent" or taking "the common idiom and making it literal" (Kociemba 32). Well of course the whole of *Buffy the Vampire Slayer* is based on a reverse cliché: the horror movie cliché in which the victim is a cute helpless-looking blonde girl with a fluffy name like Buffy, which clearly shouts, "*Victim*, I'm going to walk down this dark deserted ally and get myself killed by a vampire or some such monster." Of course in this case Buffy *is* the Vampire *Slayer*, the "one girl in all the world ... with the strength and skill to hunt the vampires, to stop the spread of ... evil..." (1.1). As for the literalization of clichés: in the previous chapter discussing the use of metaphor in the Whedonverse we noted Buffy using the cliché "making money hand over fist" and then waving her open hand slowly back and forth above her clenched fist, obviously pondering the meaning of this cliché (5.5). This sort of humor based on taking a cliché literally is not uncommon in the Whedonverse. At one point Xander uses a variation on the cliché "sticking out like a sore thumb" which gets Willow to thinking: "Sore thumbs. Do they stick out? I mean, have you ever seen a thumb and gone, 'Wow! That baby is sore!'" (2.7). In this same episode someone uses a line from the song "Five to One" by Jim Morrison and the Doors, a version of which incidentally became the title of the first book-length biography of Morrison: "*No One Here Gets Out Alive.*" Since that time it has become a cliché. In *Buffy* it is used both literally and metaphorically. Buffy has been lured into a large underground bomb shelter/nightclub by an old classmate who, along with a gang of teenagers, wants the immortality promised by being turned into the undead by vampires. They are waiting for nightfall and the arrival of vampires who have promised to turn them if they give them the Slayer. Since the impenetrable door of the shelter can only be opened from the outside it is literally the case that no one is getting out of the shelter until the vampires come to kill them. Since they are all going to be leaving this life, the metaphor is also apt. It is really a variation of the life is a journey metaphor, which we discussed earlier in relation to the work of George Lakoff. It is more a "Life is a prison" metaphor, which is paradoxical because it implies that there is nothing outside this particular prison. There is nothing from which you are barred. The song from which the line is taken also indicates that the "ballroom days" have ended. The bomb shelter confining Buffy and the vampire wannabes is really functioning as a kind of underground Goth ballroom. It even has a mirror faceted disco ball hanging from the high ceiling. This makes the line about getting out alive like a two-percenter, since not everyone watching the show will be familiar with Jim Morrison and the Doors. Neither they nor their song, "Five to One," are mentioned by name in the episode. Only the cliché about not getting out alive is used, and of course the disco ball as part of the set.

Point (8)—throw-away lines. Throw-away lines have the dialogue continuing beyond the funniest word in the joke, the punchline, leaving no time for audience laughter. It is really throwing away the joke, sometimes extending it in a different direction. For example, Willow on her first day at college is really overwhelmed by the difference between high school and university.

Upon entering the massive library of UC Sunnydale, she exclaims: "in high school, knowledge was pretty much frowned upon. You really had to work to learn anything. But here, the energy, the collective intelligence, it's like this force, this penetrating force, and I can just feel my mind opening up—you know?—and letting this place thrust into and spurt knowledge into.... That sentence ended up in a different place than it started out in" (4.1). Then there is the famous Buffy cookie dough analogy, in which Buffy explains to Angel: "OK, I'm cookie dough. I'm not done baking. I'm not finished becoming who-ever the hell it is I'm gonna turn out to be. I make it through this, and the next thing, and the next thing, and maybe one day I turn around and realize I'm ready. I'm cookies. And then, you know, if I want someone to eat ... or enjoy warm, delicious cookie me, then ... that's fine. That'll be then. When I'm done" (7.22).

Point (9)—crickets—are usually a moment of stunned silence, in which there is no dialogue. It is quiet enough to hear the sound of crickets; hence the name of this technique. These jokes do not depend solely upon dialogue. As Espenson herself says, "Like the analogy jokes that we talked about earlier, I think these jokes work because they come directly out of character" (*Jane in Progress*, May 2, 2006). For example, when Buffy is explaining that she has to enter the Master's lair in order to rescue a friend, she asks Angel, who is still such a stranger that she has just learned his name, "Do you know what it's like to have a friend?" This is followed by a long silence during which the camera is focused on Angel's blank face. In this case, Buffy breaks the silence by saying "That wasn't supposed to be a stumper" (1.2). One of the longest crickets ever used in a television series begins at the end of the fourth season episode entitled "Hush." The fact that it appears here accentuates the theme of the entire episode, as "fairy tale monsters" have stolen the voices of everyone in Sunny-dale. Hence there is very little dialogue in the entire episode. Once things have been restored to normal, it is apparent that both Buffy's secret identity and that of her boyfriend Riley have been compromised. Neither had thought the other was involved in fighting monsters, or even the paranormal. The episode ends in Buffy's college dorm room with the two of them sitting across from one another. Riley says: "Well, I guess we have to talk." And Buffy replies: "I guess we do" (4.10). The stare at each other in silence for several beats, and finally the closing credits roll. The airdate for this episode was December 14, 1999. The first episode of the new year, entitled ominously "Doomed," which aired on January 18, 2000 begins with Buffy and Riley sitting in silence across from each other in her college dorm room, just where we left them. Buffy breaks the long silence: "Somebody should speak before one of us graduates" (4.11).

Point (10)—Put-downs. Kociemba, citing *Jane in Progress*, notes that "rather than just revealing something about the butt of the put-down, Espenson argues, 'almost all of them are flashlights trained on the character that says them,' ... Espenson tries to use put-downs to foster understanding, not gall or hate" (33). Almost anything that comes out of Cordelia Chase's mouth in the first three seasons could serve as examples of put-downs. We learn most about her character from her put-downs of other people. She is certainly not self-deprecating. Commenting on Willow's wardrobe, she says, "Willow! Nice dress! Good to know you've seen the softer side of Sears.... No wonder you're such a guy magnet" (1.1). The fashion-conscious Cordelia is suggesting that Willow gets her fashion sense from a store that also sells appliances and hardware. This really tells us as much about Cordelia as it does about Willow. Cordelia, like her counterpart in Shakespeare's *King Lear*, is willing to speak what she sees as the unvarnished truth regardless of other people's feelings. As Clinton P.E. Atchley notes of the Shakespeare play: "Cordelia [is] blunt and honest but tactless in [her] handling of Lear" ("*King Lear, Buffy*, and Apocalyptic Revisionism" 83). Both Cordelias are blunt and tactless. This is confirmed by Gregory J. Thompson and Sally Emmons-Featherston in their article "What Shall Cordelia Say?": "Likewise, *Buffy the Vampire Slayer*'s Cordelia is far more concerned with her own integrity, however skewed that integrity may be, than she is in protecting the feelings of those around her. Tact is not a common denominator of either Cordelia's personality" (161). Cordelia's sense of entitlement is also evident when she is incensed at Willow's interrupting her gossiping about Buffy with her in-group, the Cordettes, while they are working on an assignment in the computer lab: "Excuse me? Who gave you permission to exist? Do I horn in on your private discussions? No. Why? Because you're boring" (1.2). Willow, a first-rate hacker, is shortly able to get revenge with an implicit put-down of Cordelia's computer skills. When the assignment is done Cordelia asks, of no one in particular, "Okay, so how do we save it?" and Willow, quietly and unobtrusively, says, "Deliver." Cordelia searches for the "deliver" key and finding the one labeled "del" presses it and looks on in stunned horror as the whole program they had been working on vanishes, is deleted not delivered.

Point (11)—Trait-based humor. Jane Espenson argues that "a joke that pokes fun at a person is sharpest, funniest, when it finds that perfect detail, the most subtle observation of what sets that person apart. Someone's race or gender is unlikely to be the most subtle thing about them, and certainly it's not the most specific" (*Jane in Progress* January 19, 2006). Given that Buffy Summers' calling is to be the warrior who protects humanity from vampires and all sorts of other large and scary monsters, one might very well expect such a hero to be a man who is physically imposing and even threatening. In actual fact, the Slayer is always a girl, and this particular Slayer, Buffy, has the bodily appearance of a petite blonde cheerleader. So the series naturally has a number of scenes in which characters presupposing the warrior stereotype express some surprise that Buffy is not only a girl, but a smallish one at that. In Buffy's first encounter with Angel, she knocks him down. Angel, knowing she is the Slayer, remarks, "Truth is, I thought you'd be taller, or bigger muscles and all that. You're pretty spry, though" (1.1). Jenny Calendar also has preconceptions or unwarranted assumptions about the physical qualifications of a Slayer. Upon first learning that Buffy is the Slayer, Jenny remarks: "The part that gets me, though, is where Buffy is the Vampire Slayer. She's so little" (1.12). A most prominent trait of Buffy's watcher, Giles, is an almost compulsive ostentatious removal and cleaning of his glasses. When the new watcher, Wesley Wyndham-Pryce, arrives and first meets the new Slayer, Faith, who seems to have no time for him, he and Giles simultaneously remove their glasses and start to clean them. Giles notices what Wesley is doing and, embarrassed, immediately puts his own glasses back on before Wesley has a chance to see him (3.14).

Point (12)—Food. Kociemba begins his discussion of this point by noting that "Espenson uses food and the rituals that build up around meals to reveal character, which should come as no surprise from a writer who ends every entry of her blog with a description of what she had for lunch" (34). He mentions the episode "Pangs" in which Buffy is attempting to put together a traditional Thanksgiving dinner while dealing with the threat of the vengeance spirit Hus and Willow's concern about the unfair treatment of Native Americans. In discussing "Pangs," Espenson claims that "the core of it was something that Joss had wanted to do for a long time, which is have a dead Indian at Thanksgiving—a very poetic illustration ... that we do kind of live in this country by virtue of some very ugly conquest" (Kaveny 111–112). He discusses a number of other episodes written by Espenson, including, later on, "Doublemeat Palace" (6.12), in which the suspicion arises that the burgers in the fast food joint where Buffy is forced to take a menial job are made of human flesh. They turn out to be veggie burgers, not even containing the beef and chicken that give the "doublemeat" franchise its name. Kociemba says that this is "Espenson's most extensive use of food-based horror-comedy to date" (35). In our book, *The Existential Joss Whedon*, we argued "that the 'Doublemeat Palace' episode (6.12) is central to understanding the existential import of the entire Whedonverse. It is also important ... for emphasizing the implied link between the metaphorical nature of morality and its grounding in our physical being, our corporeal consciousness.... The unwholesomeness of everything represented by the 'Doublemeat experience' ... is manifested in the all-but-indelible odor it leaves on the body" (158). Even vampires are offended by it. One even refuses to fight Buffy upon learning that her offensive odor comes from working at the Doublemeat Palace: "You know what? Let's just call it a night. If it's all the same to you, and you've been eating that stuff, I'm not so sure I want to bite you" (6.15). The Doublemeat odor is a metaphor for Buffy's moral failings at this point. However, with Riley's help, Buffy does recognize that things don't have to stay this way. She says that the odor "goes away with many bathings" and Riley assures her, "Wheel never stops turning, Buffy. You're up, you're down ... it doesn't change what you are. And you are a hell of a woman" (6.15). The Doublemeat experience marks the nadir in terms of the food symbolism in *Buffy*. From this point on, Buffy begins to accept the role of nurturant parent to her little sister, Dawn, providing her with the "sustenance she needs both for her body and her moral development, both physically and metaphorically" (Richardson and Rabb 159). As Buffy herself confesses to Dawn: "I got it so wrong. I don't want to protect you from the world. I want to show it to you" (6.22).

What Kociemba misses by concentrating on food episodes written by Espenson is the bigger picture comparing food references made by vampires with those of the humans. Right from the first episode, the vampires refer to the humans as food and the activity of sucking their blood as feeding. In "Welcome to the Hellmouth" a member of the Master's vampire family says, "I've sent your servants to bring you some food" (1.1), meaning by that that he has sent them out to hunt humans and to bring them back alive. In the next episode, one of the "offerings" was brought to the Master already bitten, arousing the Master's ire: "You've tasted it.... I'm your ... faithful dog. You bring me scraps" (1.2). There is, of course, a pecking order among vampires. The vampires decide to use this offering to lure the Slayer to their lair since he is Xander's friend Jesse and Buffy is sure to come to the rescue. Jesse is told, "I thought you nothing more than a meal, boy. Congratulations. You've just been upgraded. To bait" (1.2). Vampires treat humans as animals to be hunted for food. Spike even refers to them as "billions of people walking around like Happy Meals with legs" (2.22). Buffy is only too well aware of how vampires treat people and warns the teenagers in the Goth bomb shelter ballroom waiting to become immortal that when evening comes "Spike and all of his friends are going to be pigging out at the all-you-can-eat moron bar" (2.7). In order to be turned into a vampire, the vampire needs to suck your blood and you need to suck its blood; as Buffy says, "It's like a whole big sucking thing" (1.1). This is how vampires perpetuate their kind. With vampires procreation and feeding are closely related; with humans they are separate activities. When we discussed food in the Whedonverse, we noted that "hunger for food and hunger for sex are fundamental, powerful bodily and social imperatives. The 'normal' hunger for food serves at least three primary functions: (1) giving sustenance, nutrition, maintaining the life of oneself or of others ... 2) giving sensual pleasure via the tastes, aromas, and textures of food; and (3) cementing social relations, establishing community, making connections, etc.... Similarly, the 'normal' hunger for sex serves at least three primary functions: (1) sustenance of the life of the species via procreation, creating new life; (2) sensual pleasure; and (3) cementing or establishing deep connections with another individual (at least in a monogamous system)" (Richardson and Rabb 153).

Point (13)—Loss of dignity is hilarious. Espenson explains in her blog, *Jane in Progress*, "If you've got a scene that you want to leaven with comedy without having the characters crack jokes, this is a really good way to go about it. Give them something undignified to do, or an undignified place to be. Let them have that heart-to-heart on a carnival ride, or while sitting in very small chairs in an elementary school, or while dangling from a cliff-face in groin-pinching harnesses, pathetically awaiting rescue" (December 29, 2006). She goes on to explain, "The kind of humor I've been talking about is just a few degrees skewed from poignancy, a point well understood by anyone who's ever had the misfortune to get very angry while wearing a chipmunk costume. It's funny if you're not the chipmunk, it's terrible if you are." Think of Anya in her huge, furry, and very funny bunny costume. She was asked to pick out a *scary* costume for a Halloween party. In one of her previous lives, she had an unfortunate experience raising rabbits and really does suffer from leporiphobia. When Xander looks at her and says, "That's your scary costume?" Anya, looking offended, replies, "Bunnies frighten me" (4.4).

Point (14)—Jane's progress. This section does not add a new writing technique to the above list. It is an implicit acknowledgement of Espenson's blog *Jane in Progress* and does give a number of further examples of Espenson's techniques such as off-the-nose dialogue, blurts, loss of dignity, and so forth. Kociemba illustrates how Espenson's comic writing techniques have been developed into more serious, even tragic, writing techniques. He notes that "Doublemeat Palace" (6.12) "was her first successful foray into horror" (36). "I Was Made to Love You" (5.15) was "her first successful tragic climax" (36). Kociemba claims that "Espenson adapts her comic writing techniques to writing a fully tragic episode for the first time" in "After Life" (6.3).

Kociemba concludes with a useful list of writing techniques particular to an episode written by Jane Espenson: "An Espensode is marked by the use of inventive word play, a preference for observational comedy over the situational, imprecise and overly precise dialogue, reflexive references, empathic humor and a keen interest in secondary characters—and food is more likely than not to serve an important narrative function" (37–38). Kociemba stresses the fact that these writing techniques appear in Espenson's scripts "independent of the series for which she writes" (27). He gives examples from a number of TV series outside the Whedonverse, such as *Tru Calling, Gilmore Girls,*

Battlestar Gallactica, and *Andy Barker, PI*. He argues that "if the Espensode is strictly a feature of Jane Espenson's work with Whedon, then she is simply an adept craftswoman" (27). He shows that this is not the case and argues that when she is working with Whedon we should see her "as an auteur working within another auteur's series" (38). We want to go further and argue that Jane Espenson is an auteur in her own right, that her contributions to the Whedonverse are much greater than have generally been recognized. This claim is more radical than it may seem at first, and we would ask readers to keep an open mind until we have presented all of the evidence and worked through a fairly complex argument in support of our thesis.

Our argument will take us into the next chapter dealing with Shakespeare in popular culture. There, among other things, we discuss at some length the movie *Anonymous*, which in all seriousness urges the controversial claim that Edward de Vere (1550–1604), the seventeenth Earl of Oxford, is the true author of Shakespeare's works. Yes, we are arguing that Jane Espenson is playing Edward de Vere to Joss Whedon's William Shakespeare. Spoiler alert! The case for Espenson's Whedon is much stronger than that for de Vere's Shakespeare, though the logic of the arguments are somewhat similar. Again we ask readers to reserve judgment until we have presented the entire case. Kociemba's 14-point analysis of the Espensode is but a very small part of this argument. Observant *Buffy* fans (i.e., all *Buffy* fans) will have already noticed that we, unlike Kociemba, have illustrated Espenson's writing techniques with examples coming primarily from seasons one and two, ostensibly *before* Espenson joined Team Whedon. In fact, we concentrated particularly on those episodes in which Joss Whedon is credited as the sole author. Even if all thirteen Espenson writing techniques can be found in Whedon's first and second season scripts, this in itself doesn't really prove very much. But, as we said, this is only a very small part of a much larger argument, and we ask readers to keep an open mind. As we said, in the next chapter we will examine in some detail the de Vere case, which is often called the Oxford position because he was the Earl of Oxford. We will show how the Oxfordian arguments interact with the Espenson authorship controversy. We conclude this chapter by examining piece by piece the growing evidence for the Espenson authorship position.

In our last chapter, we discussed the literalization of the Lakoff "life is a journey" primary metaphor: "In the *Buffy the Vampire Slayer* episode 'No Place Like Home' (5.5), Buffy is seen trying to rescue a monk who is being pursued by a monster, and as they run across a vacant lot, he stumbles, falls, and gasping says, 'My journey's done, I think.' Buffy responds, trying to be encouraging, 'Don't get metaphory on me. We're going.'" It is our contention that much of the metaphorical reference in the Whedonverse is due to the Espenson influence. Given Buffy's metatextual imperative "Don't get metaphory on me," we would certainly expect an Espenson quill-wielding hand in this episode. But the episode is written by Doug Petrie and directed by David Solomon, two of the other members of Team Whedon. However, if you watch the credits for the show, you will see that Jane Espenson is listed as a producer. Many of the episodes where she is not listed as author or co-author have still felt her influence. As she tells us herself: "Writing on the actual staff of a television show is more about talking than it is about actual writing. After all, you only get to write somewhere between one and, at the outside, four episodes a year on any given show. What you do between those writing weeks (and often during them, too), is work as a group breaking and re-breaking the episodes that others will write. That means talking. Pretty much nothing but" (*Jane in Progress* April 15, 2007). Although she ostensibly wrote only one episode of the TV series *Firefly*, in the special feature "Here's How It Was: The Making of *Firefly*," Joss Whedon is labeled as creator and executive producer, while Jane Espenson is called "writer, 'Shindig.'" We accept Whedon as creator of all of the shows that make up the Whedonverse, and, of course, no one would claim that he wrote all of the episodes for all of these shows. In comparing the Espenson case with the de Vere case, we are really claiming that Espenson's role in the Whedonverse is much greater than has hitherto been acknowledged, particularly in the first two seasons of *Buffy the Vampire Slayer*. It is in these seasons that the metaphorical nature of the story is firmly established. For example, not only is the Master a symbol of evil, he is also a metaphor for patriarchy. As Rhonda Wilcox notes in *Why Buffy Matters*, "There could hardly be a nastier incarnation of the patriarchy than the ancient, ugly vampire Master" (27). The Hellmouth itself is a metaphor whose source domain is our physical bodies as are the mouths of rivers, volcanoes, tunnels, bottles, and so forth. If this is at first a little difficult to swallow, remember that things are both disgorged from the Hellmouth and swallowed by it, which is why Buffy and the Scoobies are constantly trying to close it or to prevent it from opening. Such metaphors are synonymous with Jane Espenson, who, in relation to *Firefly/Serenity*, admits: "Sci-fi tends to work through metaphor. Some Other-World is intended to represent our own world through some sort of mapping. The details of the correspondences are not stated explicitly; that work is left to the viewers…. [I]t … fosters debate: points of view, passionately contested. In other words, metaphor leads to books of essays. Go metaphor!" (2007a, 3). Not only did Espenson do graduate work on the theory of metaphor under the direction of George Lakoff, as we explained above, she also worked with him as a research assistant developing the Cognitive Linguistics Group's *Master Metaphor List*, first edition compiled by George Lakoff, Jane Espenson, and Adele Goldberg (August 1989), second edition compiled by George Lakoff, Jane Espenson, and Alan Schwartz (October 1991).

As we explained in the last chapter, Lakoff rejects what he and Mark Johnson call "the Enlightenment folk theory of faculty psychology" on the very good grounds that it conflicts with the findings of contemporary cognitive science. Lakoff, in applying cognitive science to contemporary moral and political issues, speaks of a New Enlightenment: "In a New Enlightenment, cultural narratives will not be gone, replaced by cold, hard reason. Cultural narratives are part of the permanent furniture of our brains. But in the New Enlightenment we will at least be self-aware. We will recognize that we are all living out narratives. It will be normal to discuss what they might be, to raise the question of what influence they have, and whether we can or should put them aside" (2008, 36). He explains "cultural narratives" in terms of certain cognitive structures which he calls frames: "complex narratives—the kind we find in anyone's life story as well as in fairy tales, novels, and dramas—are made up of smaller narratives with very simple structures.... Those structures are called 'frames' or 'scripts'" (22). These simple structures or frames become part of a specific culture when they use that culture's prototypes, icons, themes, and images: "in Russian fairy tales, there is the Baba Jaga, a powerful and villainous old hag ... in Indian mythology and folklore there are Rama (the Perfect Man), Sita (the Perfect Wife), Hanuman (Rama's helper ... able to appear in the form of a talking monkey), and Arjuna (the archer). In America, there are the comic-book figures: Superman, Batman, Spider-Man, and other superheroes. Then there are the movie and TV heroes: Rambo, Rocky, Rick in *Casablanca*, the Lone Ranger, Captain Kirk in *Star Trek*, Luke Skywalker in *Star Wars*" (24). Beneath all of these cultural specifics there is what Lakoff calls a "deep narrative," a general case in which they all participate. He gives as an example a "general Rescue narrative" which reminds us of a number of episodes of *Buffy*: "the Hero is inherently good; the Villain is inherently bad. The main actions form a scenario, usually in this order: the Villainy, committed by the Villain against the Victim; the Difficulties undergone by the Hero; the Battle of the Hero against the Villain; the Victory of Hero over Villain; the Rescue of the Victim by the Hero; the Punishment of the Villain; the Reward of the Hero. The Villainy upsets the moral balance. The Victory, Rescue, Punishment, and Reward restore the moral balance" (24). In Whedon's narratives, the Hero is seldom rewarded, though is occasionally thanked—doing the right thing seems to be its own reward. Still, these stories seem to follow this deep narrative structure, but with more ethical ambiguity such as vampires with souls, for example. This is why we find Whedon's stories so useful when discussing narrative ethics. Narrative ethics, as Lakoff keeps reminding us, has the support of contemporary cognitive science. He is most anxious that it should be used more broadly in ethical and political thought today: "We can never go back to the naiveté of the eighteenth-century philosophers. But nor can we escape from having human brains and thinking with real human minds. What we can do is become as self-aware as possible, using what the science of the mind has to teach us" (36). Whedon has been quoted as saying, "If I made *Buffy the Lesbian Separatist*, a series of lectures on PBS on why there should be feminism, no one would be coming to the party, and it would be boring. The idea of changing culture is important to me, and it can only be done in a popular medium" (cited in Nussbaum 2011, 65).

Whedon has become noted for creating "stories that are not merely true to life but are metaphors for a deeper level of human experience" (Nussbaum 2011, 65). With the Whedonverses, Lakoff and Espenson have such complex metaphoric structures and ramifications that the deep narratives have attracted world-wide academic discussion. There have in fact been, and continue to be, academic conferences on the Whedonverses in Australia, Canada, Turkey, the United Kingdom, and the United States. The famous *Slayage* conference, now sponsored by the Whedon Studies Association (WSA), has been meeting every two years since 2004. *Slate*, the online magazine, posed to itself the question "Which pop culture property do academics study the most?" *Slate* came up with the following result: "*Buffy the Vampire Slayer* by a mile. More than twice as many papers, essays, and books have been devoted to the vampire drama than any of our other choices—so many that we stopped counting when we hit 200. Buffy even has its own journal: *Slayage*, a publication of the Whedon Studies Association (named for the show's creator, Joss Whedon), which features titles like 'Real Vampires Don't Wear Shorts: The Aesthetics of Fashion in *Buffy the Vampire Slayer*' and 'Killing us Softly? A Feminist Search for the 'Real' Buffy'" (2012). This number gets considerably larger if we go on to include works attributed to Joss Whedon since *Buffy the Vampire Slayer*. We count at least 40 scholarly books on *Buffy the Vampire Slayer*, *Angel*, *Firefly/Serenity*, and *Dollhouse* alone. If Lakoff and Espenson were attempting to influence the deep structure of these narratives to appeal to the intellects of the viewers, to make them active probers of the stories rather than passive consumers, then they were spectacularly successful. We must admit that we have no evidence that Lakoff was involved in this purported cognitive studies experiment, other than the fact that Espenson has served as his research assistant on numerous occasions.

We do know and have shown above that Espenson has been exerting some influence on the Whedonverse since season three of *Buffy the Vampire Slayer*. But can we substantiate our further claim that Espenson influenced Whedon's writing in the first two seasons of *Buffy the Vampire Slayer*? The evidence we have is purely textual. It might be possible to hack into Whedon and Espenson's emails and phone conversations, but that sort of thing is just not done in a free, democratic society, which values individual privacy and human freedom.

We could, of course, just ask Whedon, but whether or not he is involved, he is more likely than not to answer with a Whedonesque quip such as "Well, yes, of course I'm Jane Espenson." We must rest content then with the textual argument. The kind and depth of metaphor we find in the episodes attributed to Whedon in the first two seasons are quite different from those found in his movie, *Buffy the Vampire Slayer* (1992). There is, we admit, one metatextual reference to metaphor in the film script. Buffy is just discovering that she has Slayer skills and speed. She is sitting in a restaurant with some girlfriends when a couple of drunken teenage guys, Pike and Benny, come in and have only enough money to order one hot dog. In a typically vulgar teenage attempt to impress the girls, Benny takes the hot dog out of the bun and holds it dangling from his crotch, saying, "Hey, Buffy, you hungry? I got something for you.... " Buffy takes the knife at her place and slices a large piece off the hot dog so quickly that all we see is her hand closing on the knife back on the table. This is a wonderful metaphor for emasculation and is underlined by Pike who smiles and says, "Bummer metaphor" (16). In discussing food metaphors in seasons one and two, we noted that the vampires described humans as "offerings." There is one such reference to an "offering" in the film script, though it is more of a religious metaphor. Lothos, the vampire King who has already killed five Slayers, in speaking to Merrick, Buffy's watcher, says, "I know who you are. She's out here, as well, isn't she? Another Slayer. Who is it this time? What *offering* have you brought me?" (53, emphasis added).

Nothing Lothos says approaches the biblical-sounding rhetoric of both the Master and Luke in "Welcome to the Hellmouth" and "The Harvest" (1.1 and 1.2), which we have cited above. The closest the film gets is a Whedonesque critique of capitalism by having Lothos, a vampire, a metaphor for evil, praising it: "I've seen this culture, the wealth, the greed, the waste ... it's truly heartwarming. The perfect place to spread my empire. Honestly, Eastern Europe was so dead, the Communists just drained the blood out of the place. It's livened up a bit in the past few years, but it's nothing compared to this ... this Mecca of consumption. The city of Angels. What are we? We are man, perfected. We exist to consume" (26–27). This is rather clever in that it is a take-off, or rather reversal of, Karl Marx's famous comparison of capitalists to vampires, "capital is dead labor which vampire-like, lives the more, the more labor it sucks" (cited by James South). Philosopher James South in "'All Torment, Trouble, Wonder, and Amazement Inhabits Here': The Vicissitudes of Technology in *Buffy the Vampire Slayer*," actually uses the quotation from Marx as he posits vampires as symbols of the evils of technology and exploitation (96). South is discussing "The Wish," episode 3.9 of *Buffy the Vampire Slayer*, which depicts an alternate reality where Buffy never went to Sunnydale and the vampires were victorious. It's a loose take-off on the 1946 movie *It's a Wonderful Life*, starring Jimmy Stewart. In "The Wish," the vampires build an assembly line "blood extractor machine" (South 98). The humans are strapped onto a conveyor belt. Several prongs are mechanically lowered and inserted into their bodies and their blood is pumped through a series of tubes to a spigot where it can be elegantly dispensed into wine glasses. The übervamp Master who has not been killed in this reality presides over this machine, praising the technology he has appropriated from the humans: "Vampires, come! Behold the technical wonder, which is about to alter the very fabric of our society. Some have argued that such an advancement goes against our nature. They claim that death is our art. I say to them ... Well, I don't say anything to them because I kill them. Undeniably we are the world's superior race. Yet we have always been too parochial, too bound by the mindless routine of the predator. Hunt and kill, hunt and kill. Titillating? Yes. Practical? Hardly. Meanwhile, the humans, with their plebeian minds, have brought us a truly demonic concept: mass production!" (3.9). South argues that "there is present in *Buffy the Vampire Slayer* a real worry about the uses of technology and the ways in which it can dehumanize humans" (98). He goes on to conclude that "it is significant that the show recognizes that technology cannot fight technology, since we would merely end up being subjugated by yet another technology" (99). The depth of metaphor in this episode, which supports South's moral examination of technology, is just not present in the movie. In fact, we found it most difficult to isolate examples of Kociemba's 13-point taxonomy of the Espensode in the movie. As we show above, we have no difficulty in finding such examples in the "Whedon-authored" episodes of the TV series, including those in the first two seasons. We have illustrated Kociemba's point 3, "acing the written" in Lothos' "we are man, perfected" speech above, but that is about as close as the movie comes. Our claim here is falsifiable and we invite readers to go through the film script attempting to find examples of Kociemba's 13-point taxonomy. The URL for the movie script can be found in our Works Cited. We are under no illusions (some readers might say "delusional" is the appropriate word) that this argument by itself proves anything conclusively. It could of course be argued that all it suggests is that Whedon's writing matured and developed with experience. One could even advance Emily Nussbaum's claim that Whedon, "in a classic Hollywood tale of disillusionment, ... lost control of his screenplay—only to see his vision of 'populist feminism' turned into a schlocky comedy. He recalls sitting in the theater, crying. 'I really thought I'd never work again,' he recalls of the experience. 'It was that devastating.' But in a second chance few get, Whedon was able to resurrect 'Buffy' on television, restoring the show's powerful central metaphor: adolescence is hell, and any girl who makes it through is a superhero" (66). This is why we used the original script of the film in our search for Kociemba's 13-point anatomy of the Espensode. We remind readers that this is only part of our argument and to keep an open mind until we have presented the entire body of evidence supporting our claim that "Jane Espenson is playing Edward de Vere to Joss Whedon's William Shakespeare."

The final two parts of our argument in this chapter consist of a discussion of the Espenson-authored *Buffy* episode "Pangs" (4.8), and an analysis of the way in which the Whedonverse deals with stereotypes, which turns out to be compatible with the way Lakoff and Johnson use cognitive science to handle stereotypes as prototypes. We are fortunate to have an article by Rhonda Wilcox entitled "'Let It Simmer': Tone in 'Pangs'" which includes a discussion based on two of Espenson's early drafts of this episode. She says, "I will also draw on Jane Espenson's draft versions of the episode, to enhance understanding of the final version by comparing some of the choices available to the writers" (par. 2). It was Wilcox's willingness to use the plural, "writers," when discussing this single-authored episode attributed to Jane Espenson that inspired us to consider that the episodes attributed to Whedon might in fact have been coauthored by Espenson as well. Wilcox presented a version of her paper, "Let it Simmer," as a keynote address at the fourth biennial *Slayage* conference on the Whedonverses at Flagler College in St. Augustine, Florida, in 2010. At that time, we drew her attention to the fact that Espenson reports that Whedon had done extensive rewrites on this episode and that "much of Acts Three and Four are pure Joss, not me" (Rabb and Richardson 2008a, 131). In the published version of her paper Wilcox thanks us for drawing her attention to this fact, and though she quotes Espenson's claim that Joss had done extensive rewrites, we can't see that it has made any difference to Wilcox's main thesis. We would like to argue that Espenson is constantly attributing revisions to Whedon, especially those that markedly improve the script or the concept behind it, in order to maintain the Joss-as-genius illusion, and to mask the breadth of her own contributions: "I've commented before that if anyone ever compliments a line from an episode, it's a Joss line" (Espenson 2002). She goes on to say that in one episode of *Buffy* in which Whedon was said to have made numerous changes as the script developed, the first draft of one of her scenes was kept exactly as she wrote it: "I was very fortunate that it stayed how I wrote it. I surprised myself a little with that" (Espenson 2002). It seems that even single-authored episodes get revised and polished by Team Whedon. Espenson's happiness that a first draft of her scene "stayed how I wrote it," as she puts it, is the exception that proves the rule.

Wilcox's paper on the Espenson-authored episode "Pangs" concludes that it is "a problem play, not a solution play" because "the problem of the U.S. past with Native Americans is certainly not sorted out in this 48-minute television show" (par. 27). She quotes Whedon's own comment on the episode: "'Pangs' is 'to me, among the most radical and potentially offensive and necessary messages we ever played. American History has fictionalized itself, and in an attempt to deconstruct it, we find ourselves repeating it'" (par. 3). As we noted above, Espenson indicates "the core of it was something that Joss had wanted to do for a long time, which is have a dead Indian at Thanksgiving—a very poetic illustration ... that we do kind of live in this country by virtue of some very ugly conquest" (Kaveny 111–112). Though it deals with very serious and controversial issues, centered on a series of tragic events concerning Native Americans, it also contains comedic scenes in which Buffy attempts to prepare a traditional Thanksgiving dinner. Hence the ambiguous title of Wilcox's paper, "Let it Simmer": while the dinner is simmering on the stove, the anger of the Chumash vengeance spirit, Hus, also simmers and reaches the boiling point. In this highly controversial episode, pangs of guilt are intermingled with, and some critics say superseded by, pangs of hunger. Wilcox explains: "At the height of the debate on how to deal with Hus, Buffy talks with Willow while simultaneously giving Anya cooking directions.... Willow says Hus ... 'is an oppressed warrior guy who's just trying to—' and when she pauses, Buffy fills in with 'Kill a lot of people?' 'I didn't say he was right,' concedes Willow; and Buffy launches into her speech: 'Will, you know how bad I feel about this. It's eating me up—[to Anya:] (a quarter cup of brandy and let it simmer)—but even though it's hard, we have to end this. Yes, he's been wronged. And I personally would be willing to apologize—' 'Oh, someone put a stake in me,' Spike injects. This passage is perhaps richest in implication of any in the episode" (par. 18). Wilcox is also intrigued by Anya, a thousand-year-old vengeance demon, who defines Thanksgiving as "a ritual sacrifice, with pie" (par. 8). Wilcox continues: "This bald description is not only humorous but accurate; her objective tone might make us laugh, but it might also make us look at ourselves from a slightly different, thousand-year-long perspective" (par. 8). The pangs of guilt are re-emerging, which is why she calls this a "problem play."

Though Wilcox may not have intended it, her notion of a problem play calls to mind debates about how to define and interpret Shakespeare's so-called problem plays, which are neither comedies, nor tragedies, but may even be both. The designation of a few of Shakespeare's plays as "Problem Plays" can be traced to F.S. Boas' 1896 book *Shakespere and his Predecessors*, in which Boas, when discussing *All's Well That Ends Well*, *Measure for Measure*, *Troilus and Cressida*, and *Hamlet*, observes that "throughout these plays we move along dim untrodden paths, and at the close our feeling is neither of simple joy nor pain; we are excited, fascinated, perplexed, for the issues raised preclude a completely satisfactory outcome, even when, as in *All's Well* and *Measure for Measure*, the complications are outwardly adjusted in the fifth act. In *Troilus and Cressida* and *Hamlet* no such partial settlement of difficulties takes place, and we are left to interpret their enigmas as best we may. Dramas so singular in theme and temper cannot be strictly called comedies or tragedies" (345). Shakespeare scholar Arthur F. Kinney notes that Richard Hillman's *William Shakespeare: The Problem Plays* redefines "the genre of 'problem play' ... seeing the genre as itself radically unstable in its attempts to fuse the content of traditional romance with a realistic style, comedic overlays with the mechanics of power" (vii). Espenson's "Pangs" deals with the conservative power of colonialism overlaid with the comedic attempt to have a traditional Thanksgiving dinner. E.L. Risden, in *Shakespeare and the Problem Play: Complex Forms, Crossed Genres and Moral Quandaries* describes Shakespeare in terms that virtually evoke Joss Whedon as well, especially with the liberalization of conservative ideals: "from studying the problems of Shakespeare's problem plays we do learn something about Shakespeare as a thinker ... he turns out to be what in our time we'd have to call a social conservative: his plays tend to affirm old ideas of degree, of the importance of fidelity and duty.... But artistically and in terms of how he treats the human individual we must term him liberal: he takes the traditional, conservative stories, genres, and ideas and radically revises them for powerful and troubling effects: he never lets his audience off with easy resolutions or judgments or simple answers. He prepares us according to common expectations, and then he transgresses, breaking boundaries of form and technique and theme to push what drama can do and what the heart can feel. His ... explosion of old limitations of thought with new language make him one of the greatest poets; his sometimes painfully elastic metaphors and lively yet deeply troubling characters create a literary genius that we continue to admire above all others" (12–13).

Whedon, with his horror comedies and space westerns, certainly takes traditional "stories, genres, and ideas and radically revises them for powerful and troubling effects." As Wilcox is at pains to point out, "Pangs" is not only a horror comedy; with its stereotypes of Native Americans, it is also "unquestionably one of the most controversial episodes of *Buffy*" (par. 1). She notes that Dominic Alessio in "'Things Are Different Now?': A Post-Colonial Analysis of *Buffy the Vampire Slayer*" and Sally Emmons-Featherston in "Is That Stereotype Dead? Working with and Against 'Western' Stereotypes in *Buffy*" both condemn "Pangs" as being "essentially colonialist" (par. 3). Emmons-Featherston is of "Choctaw and Cherokee descent." Jes Battis, in his book *Blood Relations: Chosen Families in* Buffy the Vampire Slayer *and* Angel, and Matthew Pateman in *The Aesthetics of Culture in* Buffy the Vampire Slayer are both offended on behalf of Native Americans. This is not exactly how Wilcox puts it. She says that "Battis calls the episode 'infamous' ... and ... 'a highly misguided and patronizing attempt to discuss cultural relativism within

Buffy'" (par. 3). She notes that Pateman claims that the infamous "comment that 'the only good Indian is a dead Indian' is disturbingly mirrored in [the resolution of] 'Pangs'" (par. 3), where Hus and his spirit warriors are killed by Buffy and others defending "Fort Giles." On a more positive note, she says that "Gregory Stevenson, in his book *Televised Morality* ... argues for 'Pangs,' saying that while both the colonizers and the indigenous people used violence, Buffy, in his declared Christian view, represents moving on to forgiveness, because of the fact that she and the Scoobies take in both the ex-demon Anya and the vampire Spike—and vampires and demons can represent oppressed, demonized peoples" (par. 3).

We are more critical of Stevenson's position than Wilcox allows. Commenting on our book, *The Existential Joss Whedon*, she says, "J. Michael Richardson and J. Douglas Rabb acknowledge Stevenson and further emphasize the fact that *Buffy*, as a television series, will have done a great deal to bring to light the atrocities inflicted on Native Americans by the colonizers— much more than the books that Willow unearths, and that Giles seems to think sufficient to have spread the truth" (par. 3). Though we do acknowledge that Stevenson attempts to deal with cultural guilt, we are critical of his method of dealing with it though Christian forgiveness and the taking in strangers (Spike and Anya) for a contemporary Thanksgiving dinner. As we said in our book: "because Stevenson concentrates on the contemporary concept of Thanksgiving, rather than on its historical origins, what is missing from his argument is any understanding of the reasons for cultural guilt or the necessity of learning anything from first contact with the Indians. Near the beginning of the episode, Willow reminds us of what every American has learned in school about the original Thanksgiving: 'they make animated specials about the part where, with the maize and the big, big belt buckles. They don't show you the next scene, where all the bison die and Squanto takes a musket ball in the stomach'" (165).

We use the "Pangs" episode to illustrate how narrative ethics can deal with controversial issues. "Pangs," we argue, "illustrates in a positive way how moral decisions are made and how ethical judgments are justified" (161). Most commentators, including Wilcox herself in "Let It Simmer," seem to ignore Willow's comments about the death of the bison and the treatment of Squanto. Hus, the Chumash vengeance spirit, represents Native Americans from the Pacific coast. Squanto and the bison extend the representation right across the prairies "where the buffalo roam[ed]" to the east coast, where Squanto, representing the Wampanoag, despite having suffered mistreatment at the hands of the colonizers, nonetheless chose to "help the helpless" by, for example, teaching the settlers how to fertilize their fields using fish and helped them to celebrate the first Thanksgiving in 1621. "This Thanksgiving episode of *Buffy* is not just about the Chumash or the Wampanoag. It is about learning from those our forefathers oppressed, the Indigenous peoples of North America. Squanto and the Chumash represent these peoples and what they still have to teach us" (Richardson and Rabb 166).

Hus is a vengeance spirit, and in a sense a stereotype of his people. His death can be seen as the death of a savage stereotype whose savagery was at least in part a result of confrontation with invading colonists. Wilcox's examination of earlier drafts of this episode, where "Espenson ... gave Hus a much more human voice and, in fact, a name" (par. 11) confirms our claim that in the broadcast version, his destruction is the destruction of a stereotype or symbol and does not represent the continued oppression and massacre of his people by Buffy and her friends. Though Giles' house is called, humorously, "Fort Giles," it is not in fact a fort. The cavalry do ride back to bring reinforcements to the battle at the "fort," but this cavalry, humorously, consists of Xander, Anya, and Willow on "borrowed" bicycles, though the diegetic music is appropriate to the cavalry of the wild west. As Wilcox indicates, in the earlier drafts, "Huluyanawchet and Buffy have an actual conversation, and among other things he says, 'Our people were slaughtered! Imprisoned in your Missions [sic], forced into labor. Cut down by the thousands by your diseases. Our lands taken. Our women raped. Our children starved. The men driven to theft. And when we fought back, we tried to take back what was ours ... we ended up like the priest here. Like this seller of lies' (First Draft 24–25).... In the broadcast version, the information about atrocities is presented mainly by Willow rather than Hus.... Hus seems to be less of a person and more of a symbol—as the story specifies, a spirit rather than a living being" (pars. 11–12).

We should acknowledge that our reading of "Pangs" has been criticized by Sally Emmons-Featherston. However, her critique is based on a misreading of our account. Emmons-Featherston writes, "In the *The Existential Joss Whedon*, J. Michael Richardson and J. Douglas Rabb praise this episode for depicting Hus cutting off Dr. Gerhardt's ear, writing that 'many more people now know about this kind of atrocity' (163). What is missing in Richardson and Rabb's logic is that most viewers will be totally unaware that early settlers were paid by government officials for killing native people and that these settlers proved how many victims they had killed by showing their collection of scalps, skins, and sometimes ears. Instead, what viewers will see is Hus behaving like a bloodthirsty savage" (57–58). Contrary to Emmons-Featherston, we do not praise Whedon for perpetuating the bloodthirsty savage stereotype. Nor do we say that he does. What we do say is, "Hus materializes in the old anthropology department and takes a Chumash knife from their artifact display case. He then slits the throat of Dr. Gerhardt, the head of the anthropology department, and cuts off her ear, because, we learn, that's what was done to his people by early settlers. Many more people now know about this kind of atrocity thanks to the popularity of *Buffy the Vampire Slayer*. The episode is partially about cultural guilt after all" (163). We go on to argue, as Wilcox acknowledges, that "a popular television program like *Buffy the Vampire Slayer* has been much more successful at drawing the public's attention to these issues than the numerous history books that nobody but intellectuals like Willow reads.... These history books are usually written by the winners and do not tell the whole story. As Cherokee historian Jace Weaver ... points out ... 'The native people in a colony are not allowed a valid interpretation of their history, because the conquered do not write their own history. They must endure a history that shames them, destroys their confidence, and causes them to reject their heritage.... A fact of imperialism is that it systematically denies native people a dignified history.' ... As Whedon himself puts it, through his character Mal in *Serenity*, 'Half of writing history is hiding the truth'" (167). Contrary to Emmons-Featherston, we do *not* read Whedon as attempting to perpetuate a stereotype of Native Americans.

It is our contention that under the influence of Jane Espenson the Whedonverses deal with negative stereotypes in a unique "New Enlightenment" way, compatible with, indeed required by, recent findings of second generation cognitive science. Stereotypes are a particular kind of prototype, and cognitive science has shown that our thinking necessarily uses prototypes to make sense of the world, to make sense of experience in general, including moral experience. In our previous chapter we cited Hofstatder and Sander's metaphorical description of prototype structure from their book *Surfaces and Essences: Analogy as the Fuel and Fire of Thinking*: "Psychological studies have shown that a mental category, rather than having well-defined and context-independent boundaries, is more like a vast cosmopolitan area such as Paris, which first sees the light of day as a tiny, almost solid, central core ... which ... will eventually be baptized the 'old town' ... At every moment in the life of a major metropolis or a 'mature' category, there is a crucial central zone that includes, surrounds, and dominates over the original core.... Further out, one finds an urban ring that is not as dense or as historically important, and then there comes a vast suburban ring, which extends far out from the center while growing gradually less and less densely populated, and which has no precise outermost boundary ... fields filled with wheat and cattle are evidently no longer part of a city" (62). They cite the seminal work of psychologist Eleanor Rosch to show just how our thinking relies on prototypes (55, 345, 435–6). We discussed Rosch's work in some detail in our *Slayage* paper on the Espenson factor in the Whedonverse, noting that her experiments with the category of birds are cited so often that they have almost become the prototype of experiments on prototypes (par. 22). In her experiments she showed subjects photographs of birds and other creatures, and asked them to hit a button as soon as they saw a bird. She measures the time it takes from the appearance of the photograph to the hitting of the button. It turns out that birds like robins and sparrows are the prototypes (prototypical of birds), at least in the West, since they are identified much more quickly than, say, kiwis, ostriches, and penguins. In variations on this experiment she required subjects to identify as true or false sentences like "chickens are birds." Again, the identification is much quicker with robins and sparrows than it is with seemingly obvious birds like chickens or ducks. She also discovered an "asymmetry" in the treatment of members of such categories. Subjects who were told that robins had succumbed to a particular disease also indicated that they believed that ducks in the area would also be at risk, whereas, if they were told that the ducks had the disease they did not believe that the robins were in any danger of contracting it (Rosch 1973, 1977, 1978). These and many similar experiments demonstrate that we tend to think in terms of prototypes and do not treat all members of these radial categories in the same way. The term "radial category," which is also used by Lakoff and Johnson and their followers, has been explained in terms of a solar system metaphor. The central members of the category, the prototypical members, like robins and sparrows in some of Rosch's experiments, are located at the center of the system, and radiating out from there are less and less typical members of this fuzzy category, like ostriches and penguins in Rosch's work. There is today, for example, a debate about whether or not dinosaurs should be included in the "bird" category. Physician and cognitive scientist, Gary H. Wright, who did his Ph.D. in Philosophy and Cognitive Science under the direction of Mark Johnson, further explains the solar system analogy for radial categories by noting that metaphors function as the glue or gravitational pull holding radial categories together: "Analogies and metaphors act cognitively like forces (such as gravity) or links in that the easily identified clear cut central members present a cognitive pull on the marginal examples drawing them into association" (56). We think it is significant that in Whedon's *Firefly/Serenity* we get a literalization of this metaphor for radial categories with the most centralized and civilized planets in this 'verse forming the "core" planets, and radiating out from them are less and less civilized worlds, under only nominal control of the Alliance government. The more marginal members are sometime referred to as "rim" worlds beyond which we get the Reavers about whom there is some question as to whether or not they are even human. As we noted in the previous chapter, the Reavers have been metaphorically regarded as stereotypes for Native Americans.

Since cognitive science has shown that the brain naturally uses prototypes and radial categories, it must deal with ways to avoid stereotyping, racial profiling and other such morally questionable but perfectly natural practices.

Philosopher of cognitive science Mark Johnson suggests becoming what he calls transperspectival, by allowing one prototype (or stereotype) to confront another, thus enlarging the overall perspective: "Here is a vision of a realistic human objectivity. It involves understanding, and being able to criticize, the way in which you and others have constructed their worlds, and it involves ... a limited freedom to imagine other values and points of view and to change one's world in light of possibilities revealed by those alternative viewpoints" (Johnson 1993, 241). Commentators on Whedon who object to the portrayal of negative stereotypes, such as Hus and the Reavers, seem to be looking for a way of abolishing stereotypes, thinking without the use of prototypes at all. This kind of impossible ideal, outmoded as it is, still appears in university textbooks today. For example, in *Social Research Methods: Quantitative and Qualitative Approaches* by Lawrence Neuman, we find the claim that "science is value free, unbiased, and objective ... free of prejudice.... With complete value freedom and objectivity, science reveals the one and only, unified, unambiguous truth" (116–117). The prototypes, which cognitive science has shown that our brains automatically use, are often regarded as prejudices. They certainly are prejudices when they become negative stereotypes. Cognitive science has taught us that it is not possible to think without such prejudices, at least in the form of prejudgments, since it is through these prototypes that we make sense of the world. As Mark Johnson argues, drawing on the German philosopher Hans Georg Gadamer, "Our prejudgments are conditions for our being able to make sense of things. Without them, we could understand nothing.... Rather than overthrowing all our prejudgments, we need to open them up to possible transformation through our encounters with others, whose prejudgments may confront our own" (1993, 231–232). We make sense of our world in terms of our expectations (pre-understandings), which are either confirmed or modified by further experience (see McPherson and Rabb, 2003, 136–142). We think it is significant, in this context, that Johnson's notion of the transperspectival, what is sometimes called polycentrism or the polycentric perspective, also turns out to be a traditional Native American value closely related to noninterference and respect for difference (McPherson and Rabb 2001). This polycentrism is illustrated in an account of the traditional "sharing circle" by Cree scholar Michael A. Hart. He suggests since everyone is sitting in a circle "they will each have a different perspective of the topic" which is metaphorically located in the centre of the circle. "Everyone expresses their views so that a full picture of the topic is developed. Individual views are blended until consensus on the topic is reached. A community view is developed and knowledge is shared for the benefit of all members" (Hart 65).

Patrick R. LeBeau, in his co-authored article, "Reading and Composing Indians: Invented Indian Identity through Visual Literacy," which appeared in a recent issue of *The Journal of Popular Culture*, presents an account of dealing with stereotypes which is compatible with the findings of cognitive science on the necessary use of prototypes in thought. LeBeau is himself Native American, being "a descendent of the Turtle Mountain Chippewa Tribe of North Dakota" on his mother's side and "an enrolled member of the Cheyenne River Sioux Tribe of South Dakota" on his father's side (77). He is drawing on an ancient Native tradition that has not directly suffered through the 17th and 18th-century European Enlightenment, and is therefore, we contend, closer in spirit to what Lakoff calls the "New Enlightenment." Rather than trying to develop a picture of Native Americans completely devoid of stereotypes, such stereotypes, even well-worn negative ones of Native Americans "can be recognized as base knowledge—as an established set of cultural and visual literacies—upon which more dynamic, accurate, contemporary understandings of Native Americans and Native cultures can be formulated" (DeVoss and LeBeau 55). For the past twenty years or more LeBeau has been giving lectures and presentations to audiences "that range from elementary schoolchildren to college age adults" on Native American studies in general, and on the history of "Michigan Indians, yesterday and today" more specifically (DeVoss and LeBeau 2010, 55). At each presentation, whether he is "introducing a film, giving a lecture, teaching a class, presenting at an elementary school assembly, or conducting a teacher training workshop," LeBeau asks his audience right at the beginning of the session "to draw what they think the [presentation] is about" (68). They know the presentation will be about Native Americans, and they have a contemporary Native American standing right in front of them, providing "a physiognomic prompt" (68). They nonetheless inevitably draw pictures which are "predictable, stereotypical and frozen in the past" (68), most of which could be "reduced to teepees and warriors, with war weapons and feathered headdresses" (68–69). LeBeau raises the question: "Why are the same pictures drawn over and over again by all age groups regardless of gender, age, or educational background? Clearly, the participants came equipped with knowledge of Indians, albeit oversimplified, standardized, and ahistorical" (69). These stereotypes obviously come from "old westerns, dime novels, movies, and myriad other cultural artifacts [that] reflect the Indian as either a war-weary yet majestic chief or a blood-thirsty, untrustworthy brute.... These two representations have watered down to a generic Indian icon prevalent today in a multitude of visual sources, including food wrappers, billboards, and sport utility vehicles" (DeVoss and LeBeau 2010, 49). These are the materials educators have to work with. LeBeau and his co-author argue, "The challenge teachers face is not to avoid these ... or to use them without thought.... [T]here must be room for that ... understanding to change and grow as students and teachers develop new knowledge" (65). We cannot simply dismiss or ignore stereotypes: "Ignoring the rich practices and understandings of students—or dismissing them—erases the potential moments and spaces within which we can make change; ignoring students' preconceived notions negates the fissures within which we can move our understandings of Native Americans into more robust, more appropriate representative spaces" (67).

It should now be obvious why Whedon and company felt it necessary to depict negative stereotypes in their controversial narratives dealing with the treatment of Native Americans. We are arguing that Jane Espenson's influence on Team Whedon imported the insights of cognitive science concerning stereotypes, prototypes, and radial categories into their stories. We should note in passing that the "problem plays" in Shakespeare as well as the problem episode "Pangs" show that the generic categories of horror, comedy, tragedy, etc. are inadequate containers for the creations these writers actually give us. In actual fact, genres turn out to be radial categories with necessarily fuzzy boundaries.

This completes our purely textual argument for the thesis that Jane Espenson is playing Edward de Vere to Joss Whedon's William Shakespeare. We hope readers will keep an open mind until they read our discussion of the de Vere case in the movie *Anonymous*, in the following chapter on Shakespeare and popular culture.

FOUR

Shakespeare and Popular Culture: Uses and Echos of the Bard in the Whedonverses and Ours as Well

The allusions to Shakespeare in Joss Whedon's television and film narratives are just the tip of the iceberg, so far as Shakespeare and popular culture is concerned. Although Shakespeare has long been a staple in the film industry, as seen for example, in the Shakespearean film adaptations of Orson Welles (*Othello*, *Chimes at Midnight*, and *Macbeth*) and Lawrence Olivier (*Hamlet*, *Richard III*, *Henry V*), up through Zeffirelli's *Romeo and Juliet* and later *Hamlet*, Burton and Taylor's *Taming of the Shrew*, and Polanski's *Macbeth*, none of these prepared us for the sustained attention that Shakespeare has received from Hollywood since the 1990s. Certainly, Kenneth Branagh charted the course: his *Henry V* was a critical, and more importantly for Hollywood, a financial success. Shakespeare became a hit in the art houses and film societies with Al Pacino's *Looking for Richard*. Shakespeare became a hit with the teens, in *Ten Things I Hate About You*, *Deliver Us from Eva* (both adaptations of *The Taming of the Shrew*), *Never Been Kissed* (an *As You Like It*), *O* (*Othello*), *A Midsummer Night's Rave*, *Get Over It* (*A Midsummer Night's Dream*), *Gnomeo and Juliet*, and *She's the Man* (*Twelfth Night*). Shakespeare even became a hit with the Academy of Motion Pictures; witness *Shakespeare in Love*. Since Branagh's *Henry V* got the ball rolling in 1989, we have had, in addition to the movies mentioned above, major films of *Twelfth Night*, *Much Ado About Nothing*, *A Midsummer Night's Dream*, *Romeo and Juliet*, *Hamlet* (many times, including, of course, *The Lion King*), *Othello*, *Titus Andronicus*, *The Merchant of Venice*, *Richard III*, *Loves Labour's Lost*, *As You Like It*, *Macbeth*, *Coriolanus*, and *The Tempest*.

Though the 2011 film *Anonymous* is not an adaptation of Shakespeare, it does capitalize on the current Shakespeare industry in its badly misguided attempt to bolster the case for Edward de Vere's authorship of the Shakespeare canon. As we note in Chapter Three, de Vere (1550–1604), was the seventeenth Earl of Oxford. Those supporting the claim that he wrote the Shakespeare plays are called Oxfordians. The movie takes this claim very seriously, even though de Vere died before many of the plays were written, requiring the Oxfordians to re-date some of the canon and to exaggerate the uncertainties surrounding some of the dating. There do remain some awkward problems for the Oxfordians, such as the allusions to Bishop Garnett and the Gunpowder Plot in *Macbeth*, since this event occurred in November 1605, while de Vere died in April 1604. Moreover, as Alan H. Nelson demonstrates in his article "The life and theatrical interests of Edward de Vere, Seventeenth Earl of Oxford," although we have evidence that de Vere did write comedies, the absence of playtexts "from Oxford's pen" makes it impossible to compare them with plays in the Shakespeare canon. "Chronology, however, presents a fatal stumbling-block to the Oxfordian hypothesis" (43). Nelson also points out that the evidence for dating *The Tempest* to around 1611, many years after Oxford's death, is compelling. For example, this play is "clearly based on reports of a shipwreck which occurred off the island of Bermuda in late 1609. The earliest documented performance of the play was at court during the winter of 1611-12" (43). We discussed the origins of *The Tempest* in Chapter Two, citing Charles H. Frey's "*The Tempest* and the New World." The play's metrics indicate a late date of composition and its "elaborate stage-directions are consistent with indoor performance at the Blackfriars Theatre, which opened in 1609" (43). After citing this and further evidence, Nelson asks pointedly: "So how could *The Tempest* have been written by Oxford?" (43). He points out that the first Oxfordian, J.T. Looney, "dealt with this obstacle by the simple expedient of ejecting the play from the Shakespeare canon" (43), a conclusion that later Oxfordians balk at and instead generally resort to three basic strategies: "(1) they invent an Oxford-friendly chronology by pushing every play and every poem back to before April 1604, the month of Oxford's death; (2) they fantasize that Oxford left drafts which were released after his death, perhaps touched up by a reviser; and (3) they ... imagine that Oxford faked his death and continued to write from some place of hiding" (Nelson 44). The movie *Anonymous*, however, while devising a fantastical history, does not utilize the faked death scenario. Nelson points out that "equally fatal to the Oxfordian cause is the fact that Oxford was a patron of his own theatrical company" from 1580 to 1602 and that "it is impossible to imagine that he would have given his plays to the Lord Chamberlain's Men, a rival company" (44). Nelson even quotes a 1602 letter of incorporation in which de Vere is transferring his company,

Oxford's Men, to the Earl of Worcester. They were thereafter known as Worcester's Men. The movie *Anonymous* suppresses any reference to Oxford's having his own theatre company. Indeed, its Edward de Vere is initially very disdainful of the theatre, linking it exclusively to the sort of low life's who enjoy bear-baiting. When he is induced to actually enter a theatre to see one of "his" plays in performance, he asks suspiciously, "there won't be puppets, will there?" something that someone with his own theatre company would never ask. As he watches, allegedly for the first time, a play being performed, he discovers how easy it is to whip a theatre audience into a frenzy. He later capitalizes on this revelation when he decides to stage *Richard III* to work its audience into the rage required to march against the Queen in support of the Earl of Essex's rebellion. Apart from the fact that, historically, *Richard II* was the play staged on the eve of the Essex Rebellion (a play which does not allow for the cheap shot at Robert Cecil's hunchback), it would make no sense at all to have Oxford use a rival playhouse for his own political purposes when he already has his own company and his own actors to do it for him. And, of course, patronizing a company of players would be totally inconsistent with the film's Oxford's disdain of acting. It is, of course, never made clear in the film why a man who distrusts the theatre and despises actors would even decide that it was a good idea to become a playwright. As an aristocrat, Oxford, if he had had any elevated literary ambitions, had many more obviously serious genres to choose from; for instance, epic verse such as that favored by Edmund Spenser in his *The Faerie Queen*, or pastoral romance like Sir Philip Sidney's *The Countess of Pembroke's Arcadia*. Aristocrats with literary ambitions need not engage with and usually disdained from dabbling in theater, the popular culture of their time.

Another line of argument followed by the Oxfordians, and emphasized by *Anonymous*, is based on the questionable assumption "that all literary composition is quintessentially autobiographical" (46). So they comb the plays for anything they can tie to events in Oxford's life and comb the biography for anything they can tie to the poems and plays. Nelson points out that such "[p]arallels between Oxford's life and aspects of the Shakespeare canon are both superficial ... and inexact" (44). In short, there is no reason whatsoever to think that Oxford had anything at all to do with the works we know as Shakespeare's. The book in which Nelson's article appears, *Shakespeare Beyond Doubt: Evidence, Argument, Controversy*, presents an impressive series of articles that not only deal with the standard, and non-standard, alternative authors, but also with all the relevant issues such as the contemporary documentary evidence, the nature and extent of theatrical collaboration in the period, how Shakespeare's probable schooling informs the plays, etc. Needless to say, despite its thoroughness and clarity of argument, this book will, alas, do little to persuade diehard conspiracy theorists. The original Oxfordian conspirator, J.T.

Looney, in his 1920 book, *'Shakespeare' Identified in Edward de Vere the Seventeenth Earl of Oxford*, "drew up a list of propositions declaring what Shakespeare must have been like given the particular characteristics of his surviving poems and plays" (Nelson 39). The movie *Anonymous* uses this kind of ploy, especially the assumption that "because the plays often portray aristocrats, the author himself must have been an aristocrat" (39), as, of course, the Earl of Oxford was. Likewise, many of the plays are set in Italy, and Oxford was known to have spent some time in Italy. Douglas Lanier, in his appropriately entitled article, "'There won't be puppets, will there?': 'Heroic' authorship and the cultural politics of *Anonymous*," indicates how the film shows Oxford devising plays that "allegorize elements of his life. The biographical foundations upon which Oxford supposedly draws as an author—his training as a soldier and statesman, his classical education, his years on the continent—are sketched in, and the film focuses on how Oxford's vexed relationship with the venal Cecil family and failed romance with the young Queen Elizabeth shape his character and thus his writing" (217).

We had Looney's list of "Shakespearean" characteristics in mind when we were discussing in Chapter Three Kociemba's fourteen-point "anatomy of the Espensode" as part of our argument that Jane Espenson plays Edward de Vere to Joss Whedon's William Shakespeare. We have asked the reader to keep an open mind until we completed the argument with our discussion of de Vere. There is a sense in which we still stand by our statement that Jane Espenson plays Edward de Vere to Joss Whedon's William Shakespeare. However, given our anti–Oxfordian stance, it should be clear that de Vere is *not* Shakespeare, and thus equally clear that Espenson is *not* Whedon. Our discussion of what we called "the Espenson authorship controversy" is, in actual fact, part of our unique argument against the Oxfordian position. The absurdity of the claim that Jane Espenson is really Whedon serves to emphasize the absurdity of the claim that Edward de Vere is really Shakespeare. In fact, Espenson contributed a good deal more to the Whedonverses than de Vere did to the Shakespeare canon. Whedon has always acknowledged that he has had the best writers in the world to draw on. Still, as we would all agree, Joss Whedon is the genius that brings them all together and is the one that shapes the narrative goals and trajectories of all the stories in all the Whedonverses. In fact Whedon has edited some of his writers' episodes so heavily that he says at one point, "There are entire episodes of *Buffy* that I have written every word of that my name is not on" (Lavery and Burkhead 97). Since we are claiming that Whedon is the Shakespeare of our time, we thought it only appropriate, and indeed a somewhat backhanded compliment to Whedon, to raise authorship issues, since it seems that the true authorship of Shakespeare is a question that refuses to die, no matter how many times it is staked.

The movie *Anonymous* does inadvertently raise some useful authorship issues, questions dealing with the very concept of authorship itself. Douglas Lanier, for example, argues that the film runs contrary to current scholarly conceptions of how Elizabethan play production works: "Whereas recent scholarship has stressed the collaborative nature of Elizabethan stage production, the interplay between writers, actors, anticipated audiences, *Anonymous* prefers to conceive of Oxford working entirely in isolation, writing plays independently of any intention of their being performed, his shelves filling up with unproduced manuscripts" (216). Moreover, he notes that "this conception of authorship, the model of the lone, transcendent poet whose work stands apart from the vulgar marketplace and resists authoritarian powers-that-be, has deep roots in Romantic myths of literary genius.... The author, a heroic figure near-tragic in his isolation, writes out of his personal experience" (217). Lanier gives as an example the "ballroom scene between Romeo and Juliet [which] echoes a ballroom scene between the young Oxford and Elizabeth that we see in flashback, 'confirming' that the play originated in Oxford's personal experience rather than, as scholars have long known, in Arthur Brooke's *Tragical History of Romeus and Juliet*" (218). The movie *Shakespeare in Love* takes the much lighter approach of showing Shakespeare breaking various story ideas such as *Romeo and Ethel, the Pirate King's Daughter* before eventually settling on *Romeo and Juliet*, but telling his lead actor, Ned Alleyn, misleadingly, that the title of the play is *Mercutio* (the character that the egotistic actor is to play). Lanier goes on to contrast *Shakespeare in Love* and *Anonymous* by pointing out that *Shakespeare in Love* is a "playful, postmodern biographical fantasy" while *Anonymous* ploddingly presents itself "as earnestly historical" (221). *Anonymous* gives us a radical disjunction between writing, an intellectual activity or process, and acting, a bodily activity or process. In the film, Ben Jonson claims, "Writers do not have time to act! One can either write or act—not both." According to Donovan Sherman's 2013 article "Stages of Revision: Textuality, Performance, and History in *Anonymous*," the film attempts to "show a model of authorship so absolute that the human body is almost entirely removed from the process" (130). *Anonymous* insistently links the bodily with the mud of urban London, so that the body is seen as muck, filth, that which cannot be readily contained, an ever-present threat of contamination. The film often shows Oxford and Shakespeare in scenes in which they are walking—Oxford walks on wooden planks above the urban mud while Shakespeare "trudges obliviously through the muck" (130). As Lanier points out, "The muddy streets of London owe to *Shakespeare in Love* and especially to the sloppy battlefields of Agincourt in Branagh's *Henry V*" (215). *Anonymous* attempts to look historical by borrowing from other contemporary popular culture representations of Shakespeare.

Class of course enters the picture in a strong way: Oxford the aristocrat is linked to the intellect and the text, while the plebeian lout Shakespeare is linked to the body and performance—i.e., the mud and muck that Oxford stands above. Writing is seen as elevated and performing in the theatre as reveling in the muck. Sherman's reading is compelling and fits nicely with Lanier's image of a cynical author manipulating the malleable mucky commoners, a feature of the film that rather stains the image of the rebellious Byronic author-hero in some peoples' eyes (221). *Anonymous* even attempts to separate the writing from de Vere's own body. De Vere tells his wife Ann that he "channels," to use Lanier's term (217) mysterious voices: "The voices, Anne. The voices. I can't stop them. They come to me when I sleep, when I wake, when I sup. I walk down the hall, I hear the sweet longings of a maiden, the searching ambition of a courtier, the foul designs of a murderer, the wretched pleas of his victim. Only when I put their words, their voices, to parchment are they cast loose, freed. Only then is my mind quieted, at peace. I would go mad if I did not write down the voices" (quoted by Lanier, 217–218). This passage is in fact quoted by both Lanier and Sherman. It is troublesome for the ways in which the film depicts the notion of the author and authorship as transcending the body. It also depicts actors, who must use their bodies, as nothing better than slaves. Indeed, it assumes an Aristotelian separation of mind and body. "Wherever there is the same wide discrepancy between two sets of human beings as there is between mind and body or between man and beast, then the inferior of the two sets, those whose condition is such that their function is the use of their bodies and nothing better can be expected of them, those I say, are slaves by nature" (Aristotle 33–34). *Anonymous* depicts William Shakespeare as not only an actor, but a semi-literate one at that, who can read but who cannot write. He even has trouble signing his name. He exemplifies the slave-like actor who uses only his body and "nothing better can be expected of [him]." Oxford, the aristocratic author, is associated with mind, not with body. The voices he hears represent how far above the body the writer is said to be. It is almost as if the script comes from the voices, not from Oxford. If this were the case, then the authorship of Shakespeare, even if it were Oxford, really would be anonymous.

As we noted above, Kenneth Branagh has directed a number of movie versions of Shakespeare, for example, *Henry V, Much Ado About Nothing, Hamlet, Love's Labour's Lost*, and *As You Like It*. Less well known perhaps is that he directed a movie version of Stan Lee's Marvel comic superhero, Thor. Stan Lee, incidentally, is probably more widely known beyond comic book circles since his brief appearance on the TV series *The Big Bang Theory*. At any rate, we find it intriguing that both Branagh and Whedon have directed movie versions of *Much Ado About Nothing* and Marvel superhero blockbusters. Whedon too, we suspect, finds this amusing. At least he includes a Shakespeare reference in *Marvel's The Avengers* which obviously has Branagh in mind. When the superhero Iron Man (Robert Downey, Jr.) starts to fight the Norse god Thor (Chris Hemsworth) in a clearing (not a cabin) in the woods, Thor threateningly says to Iron Man, "You have no idea what you're dealing with." Iron Man, looking around, replies somewhat dismissively, "Uhh ... Shakespeare in the park?" The camera angle changes so that the back of Thor's large red cloak is in the foreground, and Thor and the camera look down on Iron Man. Iron Man demands, in a take off on the declamatory style of speech and gesture typical of old-fashioned Shakespearean acting, "Doth mother know you weareth her drapes?" This is the only Shakespearean reference we have found in *Marvel's The Avengers*. It is not, however, the only nod to Shakespeare in the Whedonverses.

In actual fact, one of us was originally turned on to *Buffy the Vampire Slayer* when, surfing through the channels one night, he landed upon a show in which a vampire asked some of his minions "Now, what news on the Rialto?" (3.9 "The Wish"). This is a question which appears twice in *The Merchant of Venice*: it is first asked by Shylock in 1.3.39 and later by Solanio in 3.1.1. It is this second version of the question that is used in *Buffy the Vampire Slayer*, "Now what news on the Rialto?" Shylock's question does not use the word "now." The Rialto has long been the major commercial and financial district of Venice, and in Shakespeare's time housed merchants both for wholesale and retail, banks, insurance agencies, tax offices, and, even the city's abbatoir. So, the line essentially means "how's business" or "let's get back to business." This allusion is especially apt for this particular *Buffy* episode, since "The Wish" concerns the alternate history created when Cordelia wishes that Buffy had never come to town. In this alternate reality, the vampires have, in effect, assumed complete control over Sunnydale and consumed so many of its citizens that the school is half empty, there are few cars in its parking lot, and no one stays out after sundown. The ancient übervamp known as the Master, whom Buffy killed at the end of Season One, is not only still there, he is also in charge. When he asks, "Now, what news on the Rialto?" it signals that he wants to return to the business at hand—the grand opening of his industrial innovation, a production line for mechanically and efficiently draining victims of their blood, without the inconvenience and messiness of biting them: "the humans, with their plebeian minds, have brought us a truly demonic concept: mass production!" (3.9). We have discussed this episode in Chapter Three. Since this mass production of vampire food involves efficient blood extraction for profit, it links up nicely with the abbatoir in the Rialto banking district of Venice in Shakespeare's time. The subtextual linkage of abbatoirs, banks, and bloodsucking is especially prescient given the banking crisis and mortgage foreclosures in the United States. This brings to mind *Buffy* episode 6.4 ("Flooded") in which Buffy, while applying for a loan, fights off a demon that has attacked the bank and injured some of its patrons. Nevertheless, Buffy is denied a loan on the grounds that, as Carl Savitsky, the loan officer, patiently explains, "the problem is, you have no income. No job." Or as Willow later puts it, "they're like, 'Oh, we're not gonna give you money unless you prove you don't need it.' I mean, what kind of system is that?" Loan Officer Savitsky's intransigence parallels Shylock's when Bassanio offers to repay Antonio's debt (with Portia's "buckets of ducats"), but Shylock refuses, still vengefully demanding his pound of flesh (*The Merchant of Venice* 4.1).

"The Wish" episode is not the only time that *Buffy* refers directly to *The Merchant of Venice*. In the aptly entitled episode "Out of Mind, Out of Sight" (1.11), we see *The Merchant of Venice* being taught in a Sunnydale High classroom, by the English teacher, Ms. Miller. The classroom scene occurs before the opening credits, and not unlike the complex relationships between subplots and main plots in Shakespeare, serves as a parallel to the main plot and themes of the episode. More importantly, though Shakespeare is not mentioned again in the episode, "Out of Mind, Out of Sight" also parallels primarily the characters and thematics of the Shylock subplot in Shakespeare's play, *The Merchant of Venice*. The viewers are left to draw these parallels for themselves, a typical Whedon technique. In this episode, a shy Sunnydale student, Marcie Ross, is treated by most of the students and teachers as invisible. She often has her hand up in the classroom when questions are asked, but is never called upon. We see a scene in which she finally puts her hand down in resignation and watches as it becomes translucent and then disappears. In another scene, she attempts to join a conversation between Cordelia and her friends and is rudely rebuffed, and then ignored, though the point she was trying to make is taken up by Cordelia, and her friends laugh with approval. Having been for so long treated as invisible, she literally becomes invisible and starts to spy on her fellow students, eventually seeking out the most popular girl, Cordelia, on whom she intends to exact revenge. The parallel with Shylock, who fashions his identity in large part from how he is treated by others, is striking:

> He [Antonio] hath disgrac'd me, and hinder'd me half a million; laugh'd at my losses, mock'd at my gains, scorn'd my nation, thwarted my bargains, cool'd my friends, heated mine enemies; and what's his reason? I am a Jew. Hath not a Jew eyes? Hath not a Jew hands, organs, dimensions, senses, affections, passions; fed with the same food, hurt with the same weapons, subject to the same diseases, heal'd by the same means, warm'd and cool'd by the same winter and summer, as a Christian is? If you prick us, do we not bleed? If you tickle us, do we not laugh? If you poison us, do we not die? And if you wrong us, shall we not revenge? If we are like you in the rest, we will resemble you in that. If a Jew wrong a Christian, what is his humil-

ity? Revenge. If a Christian wrong a Jew, what should his sufferance be by Christian example? Why, revenge. The villainy you teach me, I will execute, and it shall go hard but I will better the instruction [3.1.54–73].

Though Shylock does not become invisible, like Marcie he does want to exact revenge, but under the guise of open justice. He forces Antonio, the merchant of Venice, to guarantee his loan with a pound of his own flesh if his merchant ships do not arrive on time: "Go with me to a notary, seal me there / Your single bond; and in a merry sport / If you repay me not on such a day, / In such a place, such sum or sums as are / Express'd in the condition, let the forfeit / Be nominated for an equal pound / Of your fair flesh, to be cut off and taken / In what part of your body pleaseth me" (1.3.144–151). Marcie likewise wants to exact her revenge upon the body of her enemy by cutting and disfiguring Cordelia's face. This is especially disturbing since Cordelia has just been elected May Queen in a beauty contest: "You should be grateful. I mean, people who pass you in the street are gonna remember you for the rest of their lives.... Children are gonna dream about you. And every one of your, your friends who comes to the coronation tonight will take the sight of the May Queen to their graves ... we really have to get started. The local anesthetic's gonna wear off soon, and I don't want you to faint. It's less fun if you're not awake.... Let me see. I think we should start with your smile. I think it should be wider" (1.11). Buffy, of course, saves the day though she has some difficulty fighting an invisible opponent. Marcie is eventually taken away by dark-suited government agents and is forced to join a special government spy agency made up of invisible people like herself. The episode ends with a shot of Marcie in a classroom of invisible students. We see a textbook on her desk being opened to a chapter eleven entitled "Assassination and Infiltration." The final word of the episode is Marcie exclaiming under her breath: "Cool!" She has finally found a place where she belongs and is needed, at least by the government. The implication seems to be that being invisible and criminally insane is an asset when working for some departments of the government, a typically Whedonesque denouement.

Julia L. Grant's contribution to *Buffy in the Classroom: Essays on Teaching with the Vampire Slayer*, entitled "Slaying Shakespeare in High School: Buffy Battles *The Merchant of Venice* and *Othello*," draws attention to the fact that in Shakespeare's time Jews were still "officially banished from England" (204). She notes that "though Jews were banished from England does not mean that there were no Jewish people living in England, but that they lived quiet secretive lives. Fearing arrest, persecution and exile, they made themselves as invisible as possible" (204). Grant suggests that *The Merchant of Venice* and "Out of Mind, Out of Sight" can be used together in the classroom to discuss bullying in general and not just that motivated by religious and racial hostility. She also points out that the connections between the play and the *Buffy* episode are numerous and quite complex. For example, not only is Marcie similar to Shylock as the principal alienated Other, but Cordelia is similar in some respects to both Antonio and Portia, and Buffy herself is similar to Antonio, Bassanio and Portia (204–207). Grant recommends playing at least the opening teaser for "Out of Mind, Out of Sight" in the classroom when teaching *The Merchant of Venice*. It can serve "as the real world students' introduction to *The Merchant of Venice*:

> Ms Miller: "If you prick us, do we not bleed? If you tickle us do we not laugh? If you poison us, do we not die? And if you wrong us, shall we not revenge?" OK, so talk to me people. How does what Shylock says here, about being a Jew, relate to our discussion—about the anger of the outcast in society? ... Cordelia, what's Shylock saying?
>
> Cordelia: How about, "color me totally self-involved."
>
> Ms. Miller: Care to elaborate?
>
> Cordelia: With Shylock it's whine, whine, whine, like the whole world is about him! He acts like it's justice, him getting a pound of Antonio's flesh. It's not justice, it's yicky [203].

Cordelia's answer certainly draws attention to her own self-centeredness and is consistent with the Cordy we know and love. Her massive insensitivity, especially towards Marcie as well as Shylock, rivals that of Antonio in *The Merchant of Venice*. As we noted above, Shylock complains about Antonio's disgracing, mocking, and scorning him. When Antonio asks Shylock for a loan, Shylock's response is to say: "you spet on me on Wednesday last, / You spurn'd me such a day, another time / You called me dog; and for these courtesies / I'll lend you thus much moneys?" (1.3.126–129). Antonio's reply confirms everything that Shylock has complained about: "I am as like to call thee so again, / To spet on thee again, to spurn thee too. / If thou wilt lend this money, lend it not / As to thy friends ... / But lend it rather to thine enemy, / Who if he break, thou mayst with better face / Exact the penalty" (1.3.130–137). This treatment of Jews may be familiar to Shakespeare's audience. As Grant points out, children of the time were taught by their parents that Jews were "monsters or bogeymen who would come to get you if you did not behave" (204). It is little wonder, then, that Jews living in Britain during Shakespeare's lifetime and beyond, "made themselves as invisible as possible" (204).

Grant also compares characters in *Buffy* to characters in *Othello*. She argues that "Faith plays Iago to Buffy's Othello throughout Season Three" (208). In "Earshot" we get another classroom scene in which Shakespeare is being taught. This time the topic is *Othello*. The English teacher, Ms Murray, notes that "jealousy is clearly the tool that Iago uses to undo Othello" (3.18).

Later in the discussion, commenting on Othello's readiness to believe that Desdemona, his new bride, has been unfaithful, she notes that "we all have our little internal Iago's that tell us our husbands or girlfriends or whatever don't really love us. You can never really see what's in someone's heart" (3.18). As Grant rightly notes, "The *Othello* classroom scene's pertinence is not limited to the episode which contains it but speaks to the Buffy-Faith dynamic at work throughout Season Three. If, as Buffy states, Iago is 'the dark side of Othello' (3.18), Faith could be construed to represent the dark side of Buffy" (209). In the preceding episode, "Enemies" (3.17), Faith confesses her jealousy of Buffy, whom everyone seems to regard as the actual Slayer: "You know, I come to Sunnydale. I'm the Slayer. I do my job kicking ass better than anyone. What do I hear about everywhere I go? Buffy. So I slay, I behave, I do the good little girl routine. And who's everybody thank? Buffy" (3.17 "Enemies"). Faith's jealousy and resentment of Buffy here echoes Iago's jealousy and resentment of Cassio and Othello, which was the subject of the classroom lesson on *Othello*. Iago, who has had much military experience with Othello, has been anticipating a promotion to Othello's lieutenant, but is passed over in favor of Cassio, whom Iago regards as an inferior soldier to himself. Moreover, there are rumors that Othello has slept with Iago's wife Emilia. Iago is thus angry with both Othello and Cassio, and decides to destroy them both. He does this in part by creating in Othello a strong sexual jealousy of Cassio, by various insinuations that Othello's wife Desdemona has been sleeping with Cassio. "Enemies" picks up on this motif when Faith tries to make Buffy think that her vampire boyfriend Angel has been similarly unfaithful with Faith and thus become the evil soulless vampire Angelus again. Angel is playing along well enough to convince Faith that he has become Angelus (through a magic spell, not sex) and to make Buffy somewhat unsure of the stability of her own relationship with Angel. Both Othello and Buffy are susceptible to such manipulation because of a few vulnerabilities of their own (their little internal Iagos, as Ms Murray would say). Othello is not only a Moor and thus subject to racial taunts and stereotyping that create vulnerabilities, he is also considerably older than Desdemona, and hence may have doubts about his sexual performance. Buffy, despite her professed trust in Angel's fidelity, has had that faith shaken when she witnessed Faith kissing Angel. This scene, in which Buffy sees the kiss but does not hear Angel and Faith speaking and thus does not know that Angel has rebuffed Faith's advances, resembles Act 3, Scene 3 in *Othello* in which Othello can see that Desdemona has been speaking with Cassio, and Iago then cleverly guides Othello into misconstruing what is happening as signs of Desdemona's alleged infidelity. In Act 4, Scene 1, Iago continues to cleverly and maliciously lead Othello to misunderstand what is happening around him. He has brought Othello to a place where he can overhear a conversation between Cassio and Iago. They are talking about a woman named Bianca with whom Cassio has been having an affair, but Othello assumes they are talking about Desdemona and works himself into the homicidal fury in which he says he will "chop her into messes" (4.1.197).

As Othello has doubts related to his age, Buffy has doubts related to her age compared to Angel's—namely, that he, being a 250-year-old vampire, will remain young and attractive while the teenaged Buffy will age as people do, and there is no possibility of children or anything else that would suggest that a "normal" life is possible for them. In subsequent episodes, the evil Mayor of Sunnydale raises this issue directly to Buffy, while Buffy's mother, Joyce, has a very similar conversation with Angel. By the end of the season, not only has their relationship ceased to be as amorous, but Angel has left Sunnydale for good. So, Faith is playing Iago to Buffy's Othello, which makes Angel's role parallel to that of Desdemona, except, of course, for the fact that Othello eventually murders his new wife.

Before discussing Faith's story arc in more detail, which involves references to *Macbeth* even more than to *Othello*, we should note in passing that "Earshot" is not the only episode that alludes to *Othello*. In the very first episode featuring the vampire Spike, we find him promising his insane vampire girlfriend Drusilla that he will kill Buffy the Vampire Slayer for her: "I'll chop her into messes" ("School Hard" 2.3). These are the exact words used by Othello when Iago has stirred him up to jealous madness and rage at the thought that Desdemona has betrayed him: "I'll chop her into messes. Cuckold me!" (*Othello* 4.1.200). Many seasons later in *Buffy*, when Spike has fallen in love with Buffy and offers to kill Drusilla for her as proof of this love, Buffy finds the thought of having such feeling for Spike revolting, and tells Spike that he cannot love because "you can't love without a soul." Drusilla rightly counters that "we can, you know. We can love quite well. If not wisely" ("Crush" 5.14). This line echoes Othello's final assessment of his love for Desdemona. At the end of the play, he is confessing to killing her and indicating how he wishes his tragic story to be told, from his military service to Venice to his life story's unfortunate conclusion. He says, in part, "Then must you speak / Of one that lov'd not wisely but too well" (*Othello* 5.2.343–344).

Faith's story arc, as we have said, invokes both *Othello* and *Macbeth*. From her first arrival in Sunnydale, she obviously wants to be the center of attention. When Faith first appears in the episode "Faith, Hope, and Trick" (3.3), Buffy becomes jealous of her as Faith immediately slays a vampire with considerable flash and panache, even grabbing a stake from the very startled Buffy to complete the job. She then rhetorically diminishes Buffy by handing back the stake and saying, "Thanks, B. Couldn't have done it without you" (3.3). Faith then just walks away, leaving Buffy staring speechlessly after her as we break for a commercial. With the Scooby Gang's rapt attention to Faith's stories of naked slaying and wrestling alligators, and her revelation that slaying makes her "hungry and horny" (3.3), it is Buffy who is made to feel invisible. When she goes off to take a couple of high school tests, Willow invites Faith to hang with them, and Xander excitedly asks her to be sure to bring her stories. After the tests, Buffy says, "I'm two for two for makeup tests," which echoes Faith's favorite phrase indicating well-being, "I'm five by five" (3.3). Buffy continues to feel displaced by the presence of Faith as is illustrated by the dinner conversation with her mother Joyce while Faith is eating, quite ravenously, at their place. Joyce thinks that having Faith around can make Buffy's life as Slayer easier, that Buffy has much to learn from Faith, and that Faith could even take over for her. Joyce tells Buffy how much she likes Faith, and Buffy replies: "She's very personable. She gets along with my friends, my Watcher, my mom." Buffy then looks back into the dining room where Faith is devouring everything in sight, and says, "Look, now she's getting along with my fries" (3.3). Giles is also, at first, similarly taken in by Faith and her account of what she is doing in Sunnydale, a response that further confirms Buffy's sense that she is being "single-white-femaled" here. After a fight in which Faith got carried away with the violence and simply whaled away on a vampire, beating him to a pulp while Buffy remained in great danger, Giles explains it away as the enthusiastic actions of a plucky fighter focused entirely on the slaying. Giles points out to Buffy that Faith is so focused because unlike Buffy she does not have another life here in Sunnydale, to which Buffy responds revealingly: "She doesn't need a life. She has mine" (3.3). We later discover that Faith's uncontrolled violence here is a form of compensation for her own fears, frustrations, and sense of inadequacy, as she was unable to prevent the brutal killing of her Watcher by the ancient cloven-hoofed vampire Kakistos, whose name means the worst of the worst. In fact, Faith's arrival is due to the fact she is running in terror from Kakistos who is hunting her. Upon learning that she has been pursued to Sunnydale, she prepares to flee again, but with Buffy's help is persuaded to stay and fight, and eventually stakes Kakistos, using a gigantic stake, the only kind effective against such a monster.

Faith's propensity for flight is seen again when she accidentally kills a human being, mistaking him for a vampire. Though she says she is "five by five," she finds she cannot really accept what she has done. Buffy finds her in her motel room obsessively washing her bloodstained shirt. The scene visually reminds us of Lady Macbeth, who says right after her husband has murdered the sleeping king, "A little water clears us of this deed" (*Macbeth* 2.2.64). Later in the play, Lady Macbeth's steely composure and nerve give way to overwhelming and crippling guilt, as she is seen frantically but fruitlessly attempting to wash away the blood that she imagines as permanently and indelibly staining her hands. This guilt eventually drives her to suicide. Though Faith also attempts to commit suicide, she initially claims that the homicide has not affected her. While Faith is scrubbing her shirt, Buffy tells her that "being a Slayer is not the same as being a killer.... Faith, you can shut off all the emotions that you want. But eventually, they're gonna find a body" (3.14 "Bad Girls"). Faith rebuts this argument: "Okay, this is the last time we're gonna have this conversation, and we're not even having it now, you understand me? There is no body. I took it, weighted it, and dumped it. The body doesn't exist" (3.14). Buffy's response is: "Getting rid of the evidence doesn't make the problem go away.... Faith, you don't get it. You killed a man" (3.14). Faith then says, "No, you don't get it. I don't care!" (3.14). But it turns out that on some level Faith does care.

She seems to be driven to a life of crime, working for the season's big, bad, Mayor Richard Wilkins III, significantly suggesting Richard III, one of Shakespeare's most wicked kings. Richard, like Macbeth, finds it necessary to kill children in order to secure his ascendency to the throne he craves. The Mayor's plans for his ascendency to a pure demon involve eating students at Sunnydale High during their graduation ceremony. While Faith is working for the Mayor, as his hit man in effect, she encounters a demon who has the important "Books of Ascension" that the Mayor needs for his transformation ("Enemies" 3.17). Rather than haggle with the demon over the asking price, Faith simply stabs him to death and takes the books. At that moment she looks at her bloody hands, then heads to Angel's mansion with her hands still bloody. She is using her bloody hands almost as a stage prop in her scheme to seduce Angel and turn him back into Angelus on the orders of her boss, the Mayor. She accosts him in his mansion claiming that she is becoming afraid of what she is turning into and begging him for help: "I got nowhere else to go. Look, I hate asking for help, but I'm asking, cause, uh, I'm in trouble. I'm in trouble. The real bad kind.... I'm scaring myself.... That's why I came to you. I don't want to get all twelve steppy, but remember when you told me that killing people would make me feel like some kind of god?" (3.17). Showing Angel her bloodstained hands, she continues: "I think I just came down to earth. It's not human if that's what you're thinking. Not that that makes me feel any better or this guy any less dead.... For real now, I'm scared. Scared of what I am, what I'm turning into. Cold-blooded straight up killer" (3.17). Though this is in part a ruse to seduce Angel and turn him back into Angelus, it foreshadows *Angel* 1.18, "Five by Five," in which Angel does attempt to help Faith, who by this time sincerely regrets her career of crime. Her guilt has become so overwhelming that she seeks out Angel in hopes that he will kill her: "I'm evil! I'm bad! I'm evil! Do you hear me? I'm bad! Angel, I'm bad! I'm ba-ad. Do you hear me? I'm bad! I'm bad! I'm bad. Please. Angel, please just do it. Angel please, just do it. Just do it. Just kill me. Just kill me" (*Angel* 1.18). In our book, *The Existential Joss Whedon*, where we discuss Faith's story arc in much greater detail, we liken this scene to the phenomenon of suicide by cop (26–47). Unlike Lady Macbeth, Faith does not succeed in committing suicide. "Eventually, Faith, with Angel's help, freely chooses to turn herself in to the police and serve time in prison for the crimes she has committed" (Richardson and Rabb 46), which is why her story is not a tragedy, unlike the stories of Macbeth and Othello.

Othello is not the only Shakespearean play dealing with deceit and sexual jealousy that has captured the imagination of Joss Whedon. As Shakespeare scholar Stephen Greenblatt notes, *Much Ado About Nothing* is based in part on an Italian story by Matteo Bandello (2013, 50). However, Shakespeare averts the tragedy of the slandered lady plotline partly by emphasizing the subplot of two "minor companions of the heroine and hero" out of which he creates Beatrice and Benedick (Greenblatt 2013, 50). Whedon picks up on this emphasis and extends it in his film version by opening with a wordless bedroom scene in which we see that Benedick and Beatrice have a sexual history, but one in which things did not work out well. They have had a falling out since this night together, at the end of which Benedick almost furtively leaves the room as Beatrice pretends to be sleeping, so that neither is forced to speak to the other. Ever since that moment of romantic failure and subsequent loneliness, Beatrice and Benedick hurl verbal barbs at each another incessantly, neither being able to refrain from talking obsessively about the other. As Rhonda Wilcox aptly notes in her keynote address to the 2013 *Joss in June* conference, "consider Whedon's brilliance here: in choosing to add a scene which is not in the play, Whedon makes it a *wordless* scene. And that very wordlessness communicates with excruciating clarity the difficulty of becoming genuinely intimate. With beautiful irony and psychological appropriateness, the famously loquacious Beatrice and Benedick *do not speak* in the first scene" (15, emphasis in the original). Beatrice's uncle, Leonato, remarks of his niece that "there is a kind of merry war between Signior Benedick and her; they never meet but there's a skirmish of wit between them" (1.1.61–64). As Wilcox observes, "Beatrice and Benedick are two of the most famously verbal characters in the history of literature. Even people who have never read or seen *Much Ado* are familiar with the names of the witty Beatrice and Benedick" (2013, 15). Greenblatt in his *New York Review of Books* article notes that Beatrice and Benedick "dominate the film, as they seem … to have dominated the play" (2013, 50). Leonato and his houseguest Don Pedro conspire to bring Beatrice and Benedick back together by arranging for each to overhear staged conversations (little plays within the play) designed to make Beatrice think that Benedick is in love with her and to make Benedick think Beatrice is in love with him. This lighthearted form of deception and manipulation parallels the darker deceit in which Don Pedro's bastard brother Don John creates a fictive scene of infidelity designed to undermine the marriage plans of Beatrice's cousin Hero and her fiancé Claudio. It is interesting to note that the dark deceit is largely visual while the deception of Beatrice and Benedick was done verbally. It is especially and ironically appropriate that Benedick and Beatrice, the masters of quick-witted words, are taken in by the very medium in which they excel. The younger, more naïve, Claudio is taken in by Hero's maid Margaret wearing one of her mistress's dresses and leaning out of Hero's bedroom window, wishing one of Don John's men, Borachio, goodnight, "a thousand times goodnight" (3.3.147–148). This malevolent deception leads Claudio to spurn Hero at the altar where he publicly denounces her alleged infidelity. Hero is so traumatized by this humiliation that she collapses in a faint, whereupon Claudio leaves, along with the other male accusers who have contributed to the vilification of Hero. Benedick however, does not leave and out of genuine concern immediately asks, "How doth the lady?" (4.1.113). Beatrice is afraid that Hero might be dead, but Hero's enraged father Leonato joins the crew of accusers and says that if she does not quickly die he will kill her himself. Benedick urges Leonato to be patient and says that he himself is puzzled by the events he has just witnessed. At this point, the Friar who was conducting the wedding ceremony intervenes, and points out that he has been carefully "noting of the lady" (4.1.158) and has concluded that "there is some strange misprision in the princes" (Claudio, Don Pedro, and Don John, 4.1.185). Benedick suggests that Claudio and Don Pedro have been somehow misled by the bastard Don John "whose spirits toil in frame of villainies" (4.1.189). The Friar proposes that since the princes left Hero for dead, her family should "publish it that she is dead indeed" (4.1.204) since that deception might at least stir some remorse in Claudio and give the family some time to work out the truth. In the end, this ruse produces better results in *Much Ado About Nothing* than the similar scheme of the famous Friar Lawrence in *Romeo and Juliet* to fake Juliet's death as part of a grand plan to reunite her with Romeo. Benedick shows genuine concern for Hero's wellbeing. As Wilcox notes, "it is the pain of Hero's public rejection by Claudio that brings Beatrice and Benedick, in their shared sympathy for Hero, to confess their feelings for each other" (2013, 4). In response to Benedick's offer to do anything for her, Beatrice whispers (at least in Whedon's version) "Kill Claudio" (4.1.289). Benedick ultimately agrees to challenge Claudio to a duel, upon hearing Beatrice curse the limitations placed on her as a woman, and with Lady Macbeth–like ferocity impugn Benedick's masculinity: "O that I were a man.... O God, that I were a man! I would eat his heart in the market-place.... O that I were a man ... or had any friend would be a man for my sake! But manhood is melted into cur'sies, valor into compliment, and men are only turn'd into tongue" (4.1.303–320). Somewhat cowed by Beatrice's rage, Benedick finally says, "Enough, I am engag'd, I will challenge him" (4.1.331–332). The potential tragedy of the duel is averted by the bumbling night watchman, Dogberry, and his associates, when they finally reveal their discovery that Claudio had been duped. We discussed Dogberry's multiple malapropisms in Chapter Two, a "linguistic ineptitude" which Wilcox rightly contrasts with the linguistic mastery of Beatrice and Benedick (2013, 4). The deceptions do not stop with the revelations of Dogberry. Claudio, in recompense, agrees to marry Hero's look-alike cousin, still believing that Hero has died as a result of his ill-considered and vehement accusations. In a modernized film version of *Much Ado*, like Whedon's, the presence of such an arranged marriage could well cause what Wilcox calls cognitive dissonance in the viewer. As she puts it, "Most of us know that there are societies which still engage in arranged marriages, but they presumably do not populate Southern California. Even if Claudio is making the marriage to atone for Hero's death, what about the anonymous young woman he is supposed to be marrying? She just hops to it because Uncle Leo says so? Not even Tony Soprano would expect such obedience" (2013, 11). This, and Beatrice's need to have Benedick challenge Claudio to a duel, runs against contemporary feminist sensibilities. Wilcox confesses, "part of my mind is horrified that Beatrice would not just briefly wish for Claudio's death, but also follow up on the progress of the challenge later; and part of my mind is troubled that she would not try to act on some kind of vengeance herself" (2013, 12). Following the musical metaphor, "cognitive dissonance," she introduces the term "cognitive counterpoint" to describe this phenomenon when watching a modernized rendition of a Shakespearean play: "I connect to the emotions of the Elizabethan/modern characters, and at the same time I am mercifully conscious of the difference in the gender rules of their world and ours" (2013, 12–13). We believe that the concept of cognitive counterpoint is a useful addition to the theory of narrative ethics. Whedon's modernized *Much Ado* shows us that some moral progress has been made since Elizabethan times, while still suggesting that we all have a long way to go.

We suggest that *Much Ado*'s Beatrice might well be the Shakespearean forerunner of Whedon's Buffy. Both are fiercely independent and quick with verbal putdowns. To the suggestion that *Much Ado*'s Beatrice is a Whedonesque heroine, Whedon himself has replied, "I like her pretty well, I'm not going to lie. Knowing that, it still astonished me, when I went back to the text, how that one scene, "Oh, that I were a man"—how bald it is, how unapologetic it is. It's one of the most important things Shakespeare ever wrote, particularly in this play in which libertines treat women not just appallingly, but publicly" (Orr 2013). We are going even further and suggesting that there is much of

Beatrice in Buffy. At least she uses a Beatrice-like wit to verbally spar with her attackers, cutting them down with her wit before staking or otherwise dispatching them—cutting and dusting so to speak. As Karen Overbey and Lahney Preston-Mattau note in "Staking in Tongues: Speech Act as Weapon in *Buffy*," "Joking at the moment of combat places Buffy in a long tradition of sardonic heroes: from Hamlet to Sherlock Holmes, from James Bond to Jackie Chan. Not only does it 'throw vampires off' and make them 'frightened,' the joke disarms, making the foe witless. And in this witlessness, they are vulnerable" (76). In episode 12 of the first season, just before their first battle, the big bad of that season, the ancient übervamp called The Master, actually comments on Buffy's proclivity for witty prose. This episode, written and directed by Whedon, is in actual fact his directorial debut, and we should not be surprised that it contains such postmodern self-metadramatic comments, as well as, incidentally a sophisticated allusion to Shakespeare. As Buffy enters the Master's dark, damp underground lair we hear the Master's voice seemingly echo off all the walls of this cavernous space, "Welcome" (1.12 "Prophecy Girl"). Buffy, wearing the prom dress her mother has just bought her, with a short leather jacket over it, and carrying a crossbow, responds: "Thanks for having me.... Y'know, you really oughtta talk to your contractor. Looks like you got some water damage." It is here that the Master comments on the sort of witty repartee audiences have come to expect of the Slayer by the end of the first season. He says, "Oh, good. The feeble banter portion of the fight. Why don't we just cut to the..." (1.12). At this point he is interrupted by Buffy turning quickly and firing her crossbow at him. He catches the arrow in mid flight right in front of his heart, calmly responding with an evil smile: "Nice shot." This is the famous episode in which it has been prophesied that the Slayer will fight the Master and die. Giles, her Watcher has read it in one of his ancient tomes, *The Codex*, as opposed to all the other bound books. As he explains to Angel, "There is nothing in it [*The Codex*] that does not come to pass ... it's very plain! Tomorrow night Buffy will face the Master, and she will die" (1.12). And kill her he does. Having overcome her with his vampire hypnotic powers, just before drinking her blood he tells her in a demonic whisper, "You tried. It was noble of you. You heard the prophecy that I was about to break free and you came to stop me. But prophecies are tricky creatures. They don't tell you everything. You're the one that sets me free! If you hadn't come, I couldn't go. Think about that!" He doesn't drain her blood, he needs only enough Slayer blood to gain the strength to break free and open the Hellmouth, which we learn in this episode is directly below the library in Sunnydale high school. Having acquired the strength he needs, the Master lets Buffy fall face down in one of the many pools of water on the floor of his lair. As Buffy has quipped, "Looks like you got some water damage." Angel and Xander arrive in the nick of time. Angel is unable to find her pulse and declares her dead. She is revived with CPR, performed by Xander, since the vampire Angel does not breathe. Buffy goes off to fight the Master again who has by now ascended to the roof of Sunnydale High School to survey his kingdom. While Buffy, Angel, and Xander march into battle, we hear the series' opening theme music, played by the band Nerf Herder. This is the only time in the show's seven seasons that this theme is played as part of the action of an episode. It is during this second confrontation with the Master that Shakespeare's words enter the narrative. The Master seems to like quoting Shakespeare. As we have seen above, it is he who uses the line from *The Merchant of Venice* "Now, what news on the Rialto." Here he echoes a line from the famous gravedigger scene in *Hamlet* where Hamlet is holding Yorick's skull in his hand and addresses it, saying, "Where be your gibes now, your gambols" (5.1.189). The Master has seized Buffy by the throat in such a way that it looks like he is holding her skull in the palm of his hand. He addresses Buffy, saying, "Where are your gibes now?" Buffy has already used a number of Beatrice-like witty gibes in this scene, the most famous of which is her response to the Master as he, quite taken aback upon seeing her after he has bitten and drowned her, says in stunned amazement: "You're dead.... You were destined to die! It was written!" (1.12). Buffy responds: "What can I say? I flunked the written" (1.12).

It is not just that Beatrice lies behind Buffy, but allowing for cognitive counterpoint, all of Shakespeare's leading women can be seen as forming the foundation for the feminism of today. *As You Like It*'s Rosalind, *Twelfth Night*'s Viola, and *The Comedy of Errors*' Adriana, like Beatrice, are intellectually, emotionally, and ethically superior to the men they find themselves married to. Shakespeare's leading women are either strong, if sometimes somewhat villainous like Lady Macbeth, Goneril and Regan, or equally strong but victims as in some stage portrayals of Desdemona and Emilia in *Othello*. If they are portrayed as victims, the play makes it very clear that this is disapproved of. It is usually a tragedy. The influence of literature on societal values and individual behavior we believe is best understood through a discussion of the transformative nature of narrative, which is the topic of the next chapter.

FIVE

Persons, Personation and Character Development: The Transformative Nature of Narrative

One of the principal themes in both Shakespeare and Whedon is the transformation of self through stories and narrative. Shakespeare often handles these motifs of transformation via mentoring (as in *Titus Andronicus*) or disguise scenarios (as in *Twelfth Night*), while Whedon frequently deals with them via assumed identities (as in *Dollhouse*) or fragmented identities and other crises in *Buffy the Vampire Slayer*.

Dollhouse turns out to be quite a troubling narrative in that it raises controversial issues about prostitution and the violation of individual autonomy, the selling of the self! Though we find these issues troubling as well, they are not what *really* troubled us about the show. Certainly at the beginning of this narrative, the Dollhouse, a division of the Rossum Corporation, signs five-year contracts with individual men and women who were made aware that they would have their identities, memories, their very persons, wiped from their minds (brains) and would be from time to time imprinted with other identities and skills needed by clients, very rich clients, of the Rossum Co. We are shown the imprinting technology on which the wiping and imprinting occurs. According to the contract, after five years the original person is restored with no memory of the intervening five years. Indeed after each assignment their minds are wiped again. The programming information is stored on "wedges," external portable hard drives. This includes the original information, which is what facilitates the restoration of the original personalities after the five-year contract. The contract includes a very high financial incentive and a guarantee to be set up in a new life, with unpleasant memories removed if that is what motivated them to run to this five-year escape. Though the contract seems to be entered into freely, it does raise ethical questions about prostitution, though here the prostitutes are not pretending, they have actually been programmed to be in love with the paying client. Further it is not all about sex. Some of these dolls, as they are called, are programmed with the skills and background necessary to negotiate with kidnapers, for example.

On our first viewing of *Dollhouse*, the violation of individual autonomy, the prostitution and so forth, did not really worry us because we felt we knew Whedon's work and were confident that the morality of the situation would eventually be challenged in this narrative. As we explained in previous chapters, when Whedon uses narratives in order to explode certain stereotypes, he first has his audience confront and live with them for a while. We could see that in *Dollhouse* Whedon was probably doing something similar and were more than willing to allow the narrative to develop, even though the terms "doll" and "dollhouse" conjured toys to be played with, an obvious objectification of the person.

However the technology portrayed for wiping and imprinting the Dolls was too much for us. We literally screamed at the television set (in a metaphory kind of way), "No! Noooooo! That is outmoded first generation cognitive science! Whedon can't be using *that*!" We had recently discovered that Jane Espenson, with her background from the Institute for Cognitive Studies, University of California, Berkeley, had been working with Whedon and his team for some time. She would not let him get away with this sort of nonsense. Was she not involved in the *Dollhouse* project? It turns out that she was, being consulting producer of eight episodes and writer and co-writer of two episodes. But we did not know that when we viewed the first few episodes. We were upset. We were confused. We were disappointed. Let us explain why, using the work of cognitive scientist George Lakoff and philosopher of cognitive science Mark Johnson, two scholars Espenson has worked with closely.

In their book *Philosophy in the Flesh: The Embodied Mind and Its Challenge to Western Thought,* Lakoff and Johnson explain: "First-generation cognitive science evolved in the 1950s and 1960s, centering on ideas about symbolic computation.... [I]t seemed natural to assume that the mind could be studied in terms of cognitive functions, ignoring any ways in which those functions arise from the body and brain. The mind from this 'functionalist' perspective, was seen metaphorically as a kind of abstract computer program that could be run on any appropriate hardware. A consequence of the metaphor was that the hardware—or rather 'wetware' was seen as determining nothing at all about the nature of the programs. That is the peculiarities of the body and brain contribute nothing.... This was philosophy without flesh. There was no body in this conception of mind" (75–76). This outmoded computational, artificial intelligence (AI) approach to cognitive science, *seemed* to be assumed as a working hypothesis in *Dollhouse.*

As Bronwen Calvert observes in her *Slayage* article "Mind, Body, Imprint: Cyberpunk Echoes in the Dollhouse": "The language of computing plays an important role in *Dollhouse's* narrative, and helps to reveal the way in which, as in cyberpunk narratives, the mind or brain is often privileged over the organic body. Those controlling the Dollhouse and its processes use the language of computing to refer to the dolls, describing them as 'glitching' or needing to be 'wiped' or 'scrubbed' like computer hard drives. This is underlined when Topher and his Washington counterpart Bennett are referred to as 'the programmers.' The mind/brain is privileged and clear connections made between the way the dolls are viewed and aspects of computing or cybernetic technology" (par. 10). Calvert goes on to point out that in the episode "Needs" Topher, the principal programmer, describes what he does to the dolls saying simply, "I put them in a chair and I program them." Topher goes on to explain that "our brains are natural motherboards.... I just hack the system" (par. 10). The assumption that they can download a person, memory, identity and all, on to a hard drive, and then program that neurally-wiped brain with the identity and skill sets of various other persons (which have also been stored on hard drives) is an assumption that presupposes the truth of first-generation cognitive science. The brain or computer on which the program is run contributes nothing; the program is everything. But these assumptions are just false.

First-generation cognitive science is not true, though a few "holders-on" still think that its fundamental tenets are strong and that with some modest revisions it can still be made to work (see Dennett 1991, 1993, 1996 and 2013). But as Lakoff and Johnson argue: "By the mid-to-late 1970s, a body of empirical research began to emerge that called into question ... these fundamental tenets of Anglo-American 'cognitivism' [as first-generation cognitive science came to be called]" (1999, 77). They go on to point out that two kinds of evidence led to the gradual rejection of first-generation cognitive science and to the development of "a competing view of cognitive science." These two kinds of evidence were first, "a strong dependence of concepts and reason upon the body" and second, "the centrality to conceptualization and reason of imaginative processes, especially metaphor, imagery, metonymy, prototypes, frames, mental spaces and radial categories" (75).

We discussed prototypes and radial categories in Chapter Three in the context of the research of psychologist Eleanor Rosch. This research led her to coauthor an important foundational book with biologist/philosopher Francisco Varela and philosopher Evan Thompson entitled *The Embodied Mind: Cognitive Science and Human Experience,* which is cited with approval by

Lakoff and Johnson (78). The notion of an embodied mind is what is important here, as the main title of the book suggests. We noted in Chapter Two that the source domain for most of our moral metaphors, such as, for example Whedon's preoccupation with restoring the *balance* between good and evil, can be traced back to our sensorimotor systems. As we explained: We are embodied beings that walk upright on our own two feet and must literally keep our balance, since, generally speaking, falling down does not contribute to our well being, while staying upright does. Hence we metaphorically speak of taking a balanced approach, or of being an upright citizen, meaning someone of good moral standing. As Lakoff and Johnson argue, "our very idea of what morality is comes from those systems of metaphors that are grounded in and constrained by our experience of physical well-being and functioning" (331).

In fact, Lakoff and Johnson are so committed to the notion of an embodied self that they insist that the distinction between first-generation and second-generation cognitive science "could just as well be called 'disembodied' versus 'embodied'" cognitive science (78). They are dealing with cutting-edge research in cognitive science here. Besides the Varela, Thompson and Rosch book, *The Embodied Mind: Cognitive Science and Human Experience,* we would recommend Evan Thompson's more recent studies, *Mind in Life: Biology, Phenomenology, and the Sciences of Mind* (2010), and *Waking, Dreaming, Being: New Light on the Self and Consciousness from Neuroscience, Meditation, and Philosophy* (2014). There he expands upon Francisco Varela's important notion of "neurophenomenology," using self-consciousness and consciousness of self to guide experiments in cognitive science. This goes far, far beyond the computer model of cognitive science. It recognizes, for example, that the kind of sensorimotor systems we have will influence our *interactions* with, and understandings of the world around us, around our bodies. This is called an "enactive" approach to cognitive science, yet another term for second-generation cognitive science, one that emphasizes both the interaction of the (human) body with its environment, and how such activity rewires the brain and thus enacts meaning. The source of this metaphor, incidentally, is a government enacting, creating, legislation, (passing laws).

What has all this to do with Joss Whedon's *Dollhouse*? Are we simply criticizing him for using a naive computer model of cognitive science, first-generation cognitive science, in this science fiction narrative? Not at all, though as we said, we were concerned, indeed, deeply disturbed by the first few episodes. As the story developed, interesting and exciting things started happening. Some of the Dolls, or "Actives" as they are also called, started not only remembering but also integrating and acting on supposedly wiped "programs," developing a sense of self through bodily interaction with the world both in and out of the Dollhouse. The technology wasn't working as expected, much to Topher's dismay. Now *he* appeared concerned and disturbed, *deeply* disturbed. We on the other hand were getting excited, very excited. Bodily experience seemed to be trumping so-called neural programming in this fascinating science fiction narrative.

Could *Dollhouse* possibly be exposing the shortcomings of first-generation cognitive science by imagining an attempted technological application of this outmoded cognitive theory, and then showing the disastrous results by depicting the importance of the body in determining the sense of self and understanding of the world, not to mention survival in it? We are convinced that this particular thought experiment is exactly what is happening in the *Dollhouse* narrative. We were pleased to see that a number of academic articles on *Dollhouse* discuss the importance and significance of the body, though these articles themselves make no direct reference to cognitive science (see, for example, *Slayage* 8.2 & 3 [30 & 31], 2010, special issue on *Dollhouse*; and Espenson, 2010). We take this as independent corroborating evidence for our reading of the narrative. The most important of these articles from our point of view, "The Mind Doesn't Matter, It's the Body We Want," by Kate Rennebohm actually does have a sort of indirect link with cognitive science through Jane Espenson. It is published in the anthology, *Inside Joss' Dollhouse: From Alpha to Rossum,* edited by Jane Espenson. But that is not all. The essays that make up this anthology "were submitted as entries in a contest open to anyone who wanted to give it a shot" (Espenson 2010, 2). Rennebohm's "The Mind Doesn't Matter, It's the Body We Want" was the Grand Prize Winner and Jane Espenson was the judge. As Espenson puts it: "My job was to select a winner and three other finalists, and ultimately to choose the eighteen entries that comprise this book" (2). Given Espenson's grounding in second-generation cognitive science through George Lakoff and others, we find it most interesting that she chose Rennebohm's entry as the Grand Prize Winner. Of course it is a well-written, well-argued piece, and certainly deserves the prize. But we suspect that it also spoke to Espenson with her background in cognitive science as, indeed, it spoke to us for the same reason.

Rennebohm's article begins by noting that in much of Whedon's work such as *Buffy the Vampire Slayer, Angel,* and *Firefly* the protagonists seem to develop their identity through their actions: "good people make themselves ... through their actions" (Rennebohm 5). This brings to mind Varela and Thompson's "enactive" approach to cognitive theory, discussed above. *Dollhouse,* however, is seen at first as departing from this notion of making and developing one's self through action because, as we explained above, the "Dolls" in the Dollhouse "have thoughts and beliefs planted in their brains, so [asks Rennebohm] how can they 'make themselves' through their actions? How can they think and act for themselves if there is no real 'self' there?" (6). It turns out that the answer to these important questions lies in the way our identity is linked to our conception of the human body. As Rennebohm puts it, "By addressing the body in ways that have been largely untouched in Whedon's previous shows, *Dollhouse* alters and expands the conception of identity found in the Whedonverse" (6). Topher and the other "programmers" at the Rossum Corporation seemed to assume "that the electrical and chemical activity of the brain alone stored the memories, habits, and feelings that constitute a person's identity" and further that these could be programmed to the specifications and requirements of the Dollhouse. (7). They were wrong, of course; they did not take into consideration the role of our physical bodies, as Rennebohm argues in some detail. "As we know, though, things didn't go the way they were supposed to at the Dollhouse.... It would seem that the masterminds at the Dollhouse missed something in their conception of human identity, something that turned out to be very important" (7–8).

The story of Caroline/Echo is used to illustrate. We are shown Caroline being offered the infamous five-year contract we described above. She is told that she will be able to start over with a "clean slate," whereupon she replies, "you ever tried to clean an *actual* slate? You always see what was on it before" ("Ghost" 1.1). This we later learn was a kind of forewarning or portent of things to come. When Caroline becomes the "Doll" called, appropriately enough, "Echo" (see Coker 228), we find that, unlike most of the Dolls, imprinted "programs" or "personas" cannot be completely "wiped" from her brain. Echoes of them remain behind. Flashbacks of previous imprints begin to interfere with current assignments. Echo eventually learns how to live with and integrate these implanted memories, calling on imprinted knowledge and skills as needed. But as she does so she becomes more and more like the Caroline whose body was forced to cope with these imprints. As Rennebohm puts it, "Echo eventually became fully self-aware, and by the middle of the second season she had developed an identity which resisted the wipes and absorbed the imprints.... Caroline's body, wiped of Caroline's set of memories and thoughts, interacted with the world around her; this produced an individual, Echo, who was very similar to Caroline" (9). When Rennebohm says Echo and Caroline turn out to be "very similar" she does not mean that they simply look alike. Rather, Echo seems to act like Caroline and to share a number of values and goals. We learn in season two that the real reason Caroline was being offered a "clean slate" through a five-year contract with the Dollhouse is that she was caught bombing a Rossum research facility, protesting their unethical use of animals. In the process of breaking into the research facility, she discovered that Rossum was experimenting with humans as well. Seeing that humans were held captive in the facility, she went back to deactivate her bomb and save the people. As Rennebohm observes, "Both Caroline and Echo had a desire to help and protect other people; both were capable and driven; both lived to take down the Rossum Corporation"; and Rennebohm adds humorously "both had the skills to cultivate endlessly perfect hair" (9). The important point here is that identity depends upon the body and its interaction with the world. It does, however, get somewhat complicated. Once Echo was imprinted with Caroline's personality on top of all the other imprints, "Echo's identity came from the interactions of all these various personalities with one another, with each other, and with the world, as experienced through Caroline's body" (Rennebohm 10–11). We would add that adopting Caroline's original goal of bringing down Rossum allowed Echo to integrate and use all her accumulated memories and skills to this end, thus facilitating the development of her new identity. They finally become meaningful to her as opposed to something imposed upon her. Her accumulated memories, most of which being imprints, are interpreted in the light of the new goals she has adopted, bringing down the Rossum Corporation.

Rennebohm also discusses what we like to call interpretive memory. The discussion centers around the episode "Briar Rose" (1.11), which is, incidentally, the only episode written solely by Jane Espenson. Echo's assignment is to help a traumatized young girl, Susan, who has had to cope with abuse. Echo is imprinted with a possible version of Susan's future personality, which Susan might in fact become if she gets the right kind of help and learns to deal with past abuse. Rennebohm argues, "This didn't mean that Susan could forget her past and create a new identity from scratch, but it did mean she could think differently about that past ... re-think her memories and feelings ... and ... affect Susan's understanding of the world, which would in turn affect Susan's actions" (14). Rennebohm then quotes Bennett Halverson who like Topher was a "programmer," an imprinter. This is supposedly from a Dollhouse instructional video: "Every action affects our neural topography. We literally become what we do, not what we've done, or what we will do. We're best defined by our actions in the moment" ("Epitaph Two," Rennebohm 15). We like to think of this instructional video as an upgrading video for the programmers, since we see it as covertly introducing something closer to second-generation cognitive science. It is certainly more sophisticated than anything Topher talks about. After all, our actions require our bodies, are done with our bodies, so the body is being introduced as an influence on our "neural topography." At any rate importance of the body is emphasized, and this is the point Rennebohm is making in her article. Her arguments are very carefully constructed. For example Echo's ability to retain imprints and develop her own identity is attributed at least in part to the uniqueness of Caroline's body. Rennebohm is careful to point out that the "view that identity is related to the body was not limited in *Dollhouse* to Echo and her special body.... Rather Echo's specialness only underlined the uniqueness of bodies and the identities they produced" (11).

Rennebohm goes on to discuss the post-apocalyptic "Epitaph" episodes in which remote wiping has been "perfected" and everyone left is afraid to answer the telephone or listen to the radio, TV and so forth. Most "had had their personalities remotely wiped; some had become 'dumbshows'—figures similar to Dolls, who wandered around will-less—and the rest had been imprinted as animalistic killers with orders to destroy anyone who was not a 'burner' like themselves" (16). Those few who had escaped programming, remote or otherwise, were known as Actuals. They "tattooed their names on their bodies—not because it would help them keep their bodies, but because it would trouble any other personality's attempt to claim it as their own.... Actuals feared having their consciousness separated from their body as if it were death" (17). Rennebohm concludes that what is most terrifying about this post-apocalyptic world is that the "events of 'Epitaph One' and 'Epitaph Two' and the behavior of the Actuals prompt the question: If 'I,' this consciousness, woke up one day without my body, would I be the same person? Would my 'self' exist and more ... what would life mean without our bodies?" (17–18). She notes that those heads of the Rossum Corporation who attempted to cheat death by transferring from body to body "were already dead and gone, 'living' in a never-ending state of conscious meaninglessness" (18). Rennebohm suggests that the ultimate lesson of *Dollhouse* is that should "we forget that our bodies constitute our identities—the physical entity which makes it possible for us to decide and act for ourselves—then we really are just a set of 'imprints' insubstantial and entirely dependant on the whims of others" (18).

The episodes "Briar Rose" (1.11) and "Omega" (1.12) are most important for the first/second generation cognitive science subtext we find in *Dollhouse.* In these episodes we meet the rogue Doll, Alpha, "an early recipient of the never-quite-perfected wipes" as Rennebohm astutely observes (13). In "Briar Rose," with seeming reluctance he helps disgraced FBI agent Paul Ballard sneak into the Dollhouse. Ballard is in disgrace, and under suspension, because he is the only FBI agent who believes there is a Dollhouse engaged in programming the minds of innocent victims. No one else at the Bureau thinks such a thing is even remotely plausible. This may be one of the ways the narrative is covertly laughing at itself, since running these kinds of computer-like programs on peoples' brains really is implausible according to second-generation cognitive science, that is, embodied cognitive science. At any rate, despite orders to the contrary, Ballard keeps looking for the Dollhouse, intent on rescuing Caroline, the one victim his diligent research has unearthed. He believes he has also discovered the whereabouts of one Stephen Keple who supposedly helped design the Dollhouse. He hopes to convince or force Keple to help him rescue

Caroline from the Dollhouse. Unfortunately for both Ballard and the Dollhouse, not to mention Stephen Keple, Alpha has murdered Keple and assumed his identity. So, though agent Ballard thinks he is forcing the seeming psychotic Keple to help him break into the Dollhouse and rescue Caroline, actually the truly psychotic rogue Doll, Alpha, is using Ballard as a diversion to sneak into the Dollhouse and kidnap Echo/Caroline. Each seems to see himself as the hero rescuing the damsel in distress. The name of this episode in which all this occurs is important. It is, as we noted above, "Briar Rose." It begins with Echo imprinted as an older and wiser Susan reading the story of Briar Rose, Sleeping Beauty, to the younger traumatized Susan, in order to help her deal with the abuse she has suffered. The young girl seems not impressed, asking why Sleeping Beauty needs a prince to rescue her. Why can't she save herself? This of course has been a recurrent theme in Whedon's narratives since *Buffy the Vampire Slayer.*

In what we are tempted to call a truly brilliant narrative parallel to the Sleeping Beauty story, Alpha awakens Echo from her Doll-like state by imprinting her with a persona he had worked with on an earlier assignment in which both he and this persona believed they were on a Bonnie-and-Clyde–like criminal rampage across the country. Echo thus recognizes Alpha as her boyfriend and is more than willing to go with him as both escape the Dollhouse, leaving Ballard detained as the intruder he is. Alpha takes Echo to his mad scientist "lair" where he imprints her with some thirty-eight personalities from her past assignments. He had stolen the wedges containing them from the Dollhouse while "rescuing" Echo. He also took the wedge containing Echo's original identity, Caroline, and destroyed the only backup. Before imprinting Echo with her past assignments, he had imprinted a woman they had kidnapped on the way to the lair with the Caroline wedge. The confrontation between Caroline and Echo in Caroline's body is most informative. Once they sort things out as best they can, Echo, or Caroline's body through Echo, scolds Caroline embodied in this stranger, raising some interesting and profound questions: "You walked out on me, you left me alone in that place. Why did you do that?" ("Omega" 1.12). As Rennebohm argues, "This odd moment in *Dollhouse,* brought to us by the magic of science fiction, captured a much larger idea: that the unique, specific human body is an integral aspect of identity, not to be forgotten or left behind" (8).

The subtext, arguing that cognitive science needs to pay attention to the body and its interactions, should not distract us from the principal purpose of *Dollhouse,* which we take to be that stories or narratives influence lives and transform identities. The various "downloads" can be taken as metaphors for stories that we hear or tell ourselves. It is how we deal with them that determines how they will influence, or transform us, if at all. Echo was able to integrate all thirty-eight downloads as well as eventually that of Caroline, and as we learn in "Epitaph Two," even that of Ballard who died in the chaos following the remote mass imprinting. He had had his persona stored on a wedge by Alpha. That it was downloaded into Echo is a nice Whedonseque literalization of the metaphor that deceased loved ones can always be with you so long as you remember them and the influence they have had on you.

A variation on this idea appears in the Season 9 graphic narrative continuation of *Buffy the Vampire Slayer*, where Dawn, Buffy's little sister created by magic to hide "the Key," is beginning to fade away due to Buffy's smashing "the Seed" which held magic in the world. As Buffy and friends attempt to restore magic to the world, Xander assures Dawn, "You're **not** going to die." Dawn replies, "But you're all forgetting me..." to which Xander responds, "Listen.... Even if Buffy forgets, even if you vanish from that loft, even if no one remembers you ever existed—there's one place you **can't** disappear from. Here. [as he places his hand over his heart] You're part of me. And as long as you're part of me—I will **never** stop fighting for you" ("The Core, Part Three," 9. 23; emphasis in the original). Dawn's crisis is unique in that everyone was magically given "false" memories of her growing up as Buffy's sister. Even family photographs were magically "photoshopped" to include her before her actual arrival. She has become a "real girl" both to herself and to others because everyone has incorporated these memories into their own stories. In *Dollhouse*, Dolls like Echo become real persons when they incorporate all their downloaded memories toward a specific goal, e.g., bringing down the Rossum Corporation, an original goal of Caroline herself. It is important to note that Echo calls herself a person even before Caroline, the original inhabitant of this body, is downloaded back into it.

We regard the "Tabula Rasa" episode (6.8) of *Buffy the Vampire Slayer* as an early attempt to explore the relationship between memory, identity, and body. Jane Espenson was involved in the production of this episode. She is listed as Supervising Producer, which, as we all know, like "co-producer," means "not-producer." Still, though the memory wipe is produced by magic instead of Dollhouse technology, it does not stretch the bounds of credibility too too far. We suspect that this has something to do with Espenson's input. The episode also depicts Willow's further dependence on magic. She has already used Lethe's Bramble in a spell to erase Tara's memory of a fight they had had. Tara is now aware of this and regards it as a violation of her mind, telling Willow that she (Willow) doesn't get to design their relationship. Willow is very apologetic and offers to go an entire month without resorting to magic. Tara suggests she try going an entire week, which Willow fails to do. Willow had wanted to make things right with Buffy by making Buffy forget that she had been "in heaven" when Willow's resurrection spell dragged her back to Sunnydale, which, it will be remembered, is on a Hellmouth. In spite of promising Tara that she would not violate Buffy in this way, Willow is so addicted to magic that she goes right ahead and performs the spell using Lethe's Bramble again. This a good name for this memory-erasing bramble, since in Greek mythology Lethe is a river in Hades from which the dead must drink in order to obliterate their memories of their earthly life, to give them a clean slate, a *tabula rasa*, so that they can then be reincarnated into new bodies. *Dollhouse* is, in part, just a technological literalization of this mythology. In ancient Greek, the word "Lethe" means "forgetfulness," "oblivion," or "concealment." Hence the Greek word *aletheia*, meaning "truth," "un-forgetfulness," or "un-concealment." In clandestinely performing this spell, Willow is quite literally being false to her friends. We do means friends in the plural, since the spell works too well, affecting not only Buffy and Tara, but also everyone in close proximity to her, namely Giles and those he has gathered in his store, the Magic Box, to announce that he is returning to England (Buffy, Dawn, Anya, Xander, Spike who has burst in seeking sanctuary, and, of course, Tara, and Willow herself). Willow had left a measured amount of the brambles burning in the fireplace. When it was fully consumed, Buffy's memory of "heaven" was supposed to be locked in a crystal in Willow's pocket. Willow would know that it worked if and when the crystal turned black. The incantation of the spell goes as follows and gives the episode its title: "For Buffy and Tara, this I char. Let Lethe's Bramble do its chore. Purge their minds of memories grim, of pains from recent slights and sins. When the fire goes out, when the crystal turns black, the spell will be cast. *Tabula rasa, tabula rasa, tabula rasa*" (6.8). Unfortunately, Willow left a plastic bag full of Lethe's Bramble on the floor in front of the fireplace. We are shown a spark jumping from the fireplace, igniting the entire bag. This presumably explains why the spell works too well, obliterating not only all of Buffy's memories, but also those of her friends, as we noted above.

Having passed out when the spell took effect, they all awaken in the Magic Box with no clue as to who or where they are. Although it is usually said that all their memories have been wiped, as with the Dolls in *Dollhouse*, this isn't quite accurate. Their sensorimotor systems seem to be intact. They can move their limbs, walk, and talk, and indeed speak English. In fact Giles and Spike both "discover" that they are British by hearing, with some surprise, their own accents and vocabularies. Giles seems pleased, while Spike says in disgust, "Bollocks ... I'm English." For a detailed discussion of different kinds of memory, we recommend psychologist Sherry Ginn's *Slayage* article "Memory, Mind, and Mayhem: Neurological Tampering and Manipulation in *Dollhouse*," and her book *Power and Control in the Television Worlds of Joss Whedon*.

How Buffy and friends attempt to (re)build their identities, based on what little memory and documentation is available to them, tells us a great deal about how identity, person, and moral agency are constructed and transformed through story and narrative. Giles, Willow, Tara, and Xander are able to discover their names from documentation in their wallets. Spike is not so fortunate, since he is in disguise, hiding from a loan shark. He reads inside his "borrowed" suit jacket "made with care for Randy." Spike glowers at Giles, whom he suspects, on too little evidence, might be his disaffected father, and shouts at him scornfully, "Randy Giles? Why not just call me 'Horny Giles,' or 'Desperate for a Shag Giles?' I knew there was a reason I hated you!" Giles too is participating in this narrative construct. Anya has noticed and remarked upon the "ruggedly handsome resemblance" between Giles and Spike. Giles seems pleased that Anya regards him as "ruggedly handsome," but then notes that seeing Spike as a possible son or younger brother does, nonetheless, "inspire a, um ... particular feeling of ... familiarity and ... disappointment" (6.8). The sexual attraction between Anya and Giles and the fact that Spike knows the meaning of the terms "randy" and "shag" suggests that a rather bodily (bawdily?) memory is involved here.

Bodily memory also plays a role in the narratives Willow and Tara use to (re)construct their identities. From their student cards, they realize that they both study at UC Sunnydale, and Willow hypothesizes that they may well be "study buddies" (6.8). Looking at her student card, Willow says: "I'm Willow Rosenberg. Heh, Willow. Funny name." And then Tara responds, "I think it's pretty." Tara and Willow as we have seen above are in fact in a relationship, and Tara's response suggests that in spite of the memory wipe the attraction is still there. Willow at this point is in a heteronormative mode. Since she is wearing the jacket that Xander lent her before the memory wipe, they speculate that she must be dating him, or perhaps his brother. When she takes off the jacket and reads the name "Harris" written across the back, Xander says: "That's my last name. Maybe I have a brother and you go out with him. Or maybe you go out with me" (6.8). At which point, Willow adduces another piece of apparently confirming evidence: "Well, we did wake up all snuggly-wuggly" (since they were sitting side-by-side when the memory-wiping spell hit). She understandably but incorrectly concludes that they must be dating. There is still an old bodily attraction between them since they have known each other since they were small children and have dated in the past (a history that proves decisive at the end of the season). Xander is in fact at this point engaged to Anya, though no one in the Magic Box is able to remember this at the moment. The introduction of Xander's brother, though somewhat humorous in itself, since Xander keeps offering it as an alternative possibility, is probably introduced to amuse the most knowledgeable and dedicated fans of the show; it is what Espenson would call a "two-percenter" since only two percent of the audience would pick it up (see Chapter Three above and Kociemba 31). In an episode from the previous season, entitled "The Replacement" (5.3), an episode written and produced by Espenson, Xander is inadvertently split into two separate people by a demon called Toth, who was actually trying to kill the Slayer by separating Buffy Summers from the Slayer Buffy Summers. If he then kills the weaker one, they both die. Fortunately for Buffy, Toth missed her and hit Xander. As Giles explains: "the rod device, it's called a ferula-gemina. It splits one person in half, distilling personality traits into two separate bodies. As near as I can tell, Toth was attempting to split the Slayer into two different entities.... One with all the qualities inherent in Buffy Summers, and the other one with everything that belongs to the Slayer alone ... the, uh, the-the strength, the, uh, speed, the heritage. And when it hit Xander, I think it separated him into his strongest points and his weakest" (5.3). Toth's device is appropriately named, since *ferula* is Latin for rod and *gemina* is Latin for a twin. While the character Xander does not have a brother, Xander in "Tabula Rasa" may vaguely remember his qualities being split into two "different but identical" bodies in the previous season, a trauma for any body. While the character Xander does not have a brother, the actor, Nicholas Brendon (Schultz) does in actual fact have a twin brother, Kelly Donovan (Schultz), who played one of the Xanders in the episode "The Replacement." This is what makes it a "two-percenter," appealing to those fans who are very familiar with the show and its cast. Once the weak Xander and the suave Xander are put back together through Willow's undoing spell, we see a much more confident Xander since he is now aware that he has that within him. He is able to incorporate both narratives. In "Tabula Rasa," however, he has forgotten this integration and we see both a panicky Xander praying and a much braver vampire-fighting Xander. When the loan shark demon shows up with his vampire henchmen, looking for Spike, it is interesting that everyone seems to remember what vampires are, that they are real, and what they look like. No one in the Magic Box is skeptical of or surprised by their existence, though Buffy does say: "Monsters are real. Did we know this?" The rest of Sunnydale has always been ignorant of the supernatural threats lurking around and beneath their town, puzzled by the unusually high murder rate.

The longer Willow and Tara are together fleeing from the vampire threat, the more Willow seems attracted to her until she finally begins to realize, with some surprise: "I think I'm kinda gay" (6.8). It is significant that these are the exact words Willow uses in the much earlier episode "Doppelgängland" (3.16), when she sees her leather-clad vampire double. Willow seems intrigued by this idea, but has not yet incorporated being gay into her narrative of self. She is at this time dating Oz (Daniel Osbourne), a guitarist in a local band. Her gayness must be more than a social construct, since she recognizes it in "Tabula

Rasa" when she is trying to piece together who she really is. Tara too, as we have said above, is attracted to Willow and therefore at some level is recognizing her gayness. More than this, she also displays some consciousness of being a witch, since she notices that they are not only in a magic shop, but in "a-a-a *real* magic shop" (6.8), as opposed to the kind of magic shop that sells only what Giles calls "balderdash and chicanery." It is interesting that in (re)constructing their identities on such limited information, how close they come to their actual identities.

There are humorous exceptions, of course. Anya and Giles come to the conclusion that they are engaged, on the basis of the fact that Anya is wearing an engagement ring (Xander's engagement ring) and documents they find that show that they jointly own the Magic Box. Their conclusion, and the life narrative they try to build on it, is not unreasonable, but it is incorrect. The further narrative elaboration that Giles constructs, that he is leaving Anya, is based on his discovery of a one-way ticket to London in his jacket pocket. He makes this discovery while he and Anya are arguing over how best to deal with the current situation: Buffy and Spike have run outside to distract the demon loan shark and his vampire henchmen, the rest of the gang have gone down into the tunnels to try to find a route to the hospital, and Giles and Anya are upstairs in the Magic Box, trying to help with spells. In accordance with her true self, Anya has declared: "I'm not leaving the shop. I have to protect the cash register, and ... do some spells." Giles weakly agrees: "Oh. Well, magic might help, yes, it's worth a shot" (6.8). Anya's declaration shows her enduring connection to her avaricious true self in wanting to protect the money, and some awareness of a link to the supernatural in wanting to try spells (she was, after all, a vengeance demon in another life). Unfortunately most of her spells go wrong and generate legions of rabbits, and her actual leporiphobia comes hilariously to the surface, as she stands panic-stricken on a table creating more and more rabbits. Giles points out that it is clearly the wrong set of spells. The fact that they are now arguing leads Giles to the conclusion that he has some grounds for leaving her, continuing the false narrative.

Though Giles incorrectly deduces that he is engaged to Anya and is also likely Spike's father, or older brother, Buffy and Dawn, on much less evidence, correctly conclude that they are sisters. This fact suddenly dawns on them when they are bickering. One is saying, "Boy, you're a pain in the..." while the other is complaining, "Boy, you're bossy!" They stop and look at each other, and Dawn says, "Do you think we're—" while Buffy completes her sentence: "sisters?" (6.8). They then hug, while the camera spans to Spike who says to Giles: "You never showed me affection like that! ... I'd wager." There were earlier hints of the filial connection between Buffy and Dawn. The first thing Buffy does upon awakening with a wiped memory is to console Dawn who is cringing fearfully in a corner, telling her not to worry and that she, Buffy, doesn't know anyone there either. It is significant that of all the strangers in the room it is Dawn that Buffy immediately shows concern for. A little bit later on, when they realize they are in a strange magic shop, and people are having trouble sorting out their respective identities, Dawn turns to Buffy and confides, "I don't like this," to which Buffy responds parentally, "It's okay, don't worry. We'll take care of each other" and brushes the hair back from Dawn's face. Buffy is in fact not only Dawn's older sister but since the death of their mother Joyce, her legal guardian. It is of little wonder that she is instinctively acting as a parent in this situation. It must be in some sense a bodily memory. It was Buffy's body that was, after all, sacrificed to save Dawn (and the rest of the world) at the end of Season Five. What nicely complicates matters is that originally Dawn was magically made from the essence of Buffy's body to conceal the Key, and all memories of her are, in a sense, false memories.

Buffy not only parentally protects Dawn, but very quickly begins to take charge of the entire situation. She is after all Buffy the Vampire Slayer, the Chosen One, though no one at the moment remembers this, least of all Buffy herself. Everyone else has found some kind of personal documentation; even Dawn is wearing a necklace which says "Dawn," or "Umad" when read upside down, as Dawn reads it. Buffy declines Dawn's offer to name her and, in the absence of any evidence whatsoever, decides to call herself "Joan," because she feels "like a Joan" (6.8). In taking charge, Buffy/Joan announces, "Well, we need to figure out what's going on. We need to get help." In case we haven't noticed that she is assuming control, we are shown Spike saying somewhat derisively, "Looks like Joan fancies herself the boss." It is at this point that they try to leave for the hospital to get help, but upon opening the front door of the Magic Box, they are confronted by the demon loan shark and his minions. Everyone screams, and it is Spike who, without pause for analysis, identifies the minions as vampires. Spike at this point does not realize that he is himself a vampire and of course Buffy does not remember that she is the Vampire Slayer, but gets a hint of her special powers while fighting the vampire minions and instinctively staking one. Everyone, including Buffy, is amazed at her fighting abilities. Buffy/Joan rightly concludes, "I think I know why Joan's the boss. I'm like a superhero or something!"

Spike doesn't discover he's a vampire until he and Buffy/Joan attempt to lead the vampires away from the Magic Box and fight them in the open. During the fighting, Spike manifests his vampire face, complete with fangs and bulging forehead. It is Buffy who tells him, with some surprise, "You're a vampire! ... Check the lumpies. And the teeth." This revelation brings about a major shift in the narrative selves they are constructing. Buffy has now come to the realization not only that vampires exist, but that there is a Slayer and that it is her, as she reminds Spike "I kill your kind." Spike similarly absorbs the awareness that he is a vampire, but also that he seems to be somehow outside the traditional vampire vs Slayer narrative, that he is transgressing what would seem to be a significant requirement of the usual mythology and its embedded morality. Hence, he attempts to construct an alternative story to account for the information he currently has. He tells Buffy that, as a vampire, "I bite your [kind.]" But then he is faced with cognitive dissonance: "So how come I don't wanna bite you? And why am I fightin' other vampires?" The only explanation he can come up with is a marvelous bit of metafictional commentary as well: "I must be a noble vampire. A good guy. On a mission of redemption. I help the hopeless. I'm a vampire with a soul." Buffy is underwhelmed by this new narrative, and remarks skeptically: "A vampire with a soul? Oh my god, how lame is that?" (6.8). This, of course, is the *Buffy*verse laughing at itself. It can get away with as much fantasy as it does because it never takes itself too seriously. However, it can and does still raise serious issues. In this case, it deals with how stories shape character and develop persons. We adopt stories that others tell us about ourselves, both transforming these stories and allowing these stories to transform us. Willow, for example, was obviously influenced by seeing (and being kidnapped by) her lesbo Doppelgänger. Although the narrative Spike constructs about himself is, at this point, really a humorous parody of Angelus/Angel's narrative arc, Spike himself goes in quest of a soul and ends up joining Angel in Los Angeles in helping the hopeless. In other words, he adopts this narrative, complete with having an affair with Buffy.

Adopting stories and integrating them in our own narratives can lead to a transformation of self, but may also result in violence and tragedy, as William Shakespeare well knew. The clearest example of this in Shakespeare is the catastrophic choice and emulation of only partially digested stories from ancient history, literature, and mythology that lead to escalating violence, bloodshed, and destruction in *Titus Andronicus*. In her excellent introduction to *Titus Andronicus* in *The Norton Shakespeare*, Katharine Eisaman Maus notes that Shakespeare has, in this play, imagined "Rome" as a series of, an anthology of, stories, reflective of Shakespeare's own education via such narratives and texts (373). Everyone in the play is "acutely conscious of the glorious Roman past as it is enshrined in narrative" (Maus 373), but their "dependence on old stories means that their lives have a curiously derivative quality. The characters not only model their behavior on these stories, but they consistently exceed the prototype" (Maus 373–374). Titus himself, for instance—with "his austere patriotism, his intolerance of dissent, his acute sense of personal and private honor, his traditional piety, and his ferocious commitment to patriarchal hierarchy" (Maus 372)—is modeled on a number of ancient Roman precedents, in such a way that he is, in essence, "a recurrent Roman personality type" (Maus

372), what we have been calling a prototype or stereotype. One such model to which Maus draws our attention is Horatius, in the war against Alba Longa from 672 to 642 BCE, who after his victory in the war kills his sister, Horatia, for mourning the death of "her betrothed, a man of the enemy nation whom [Horatius] himself had slain in combat" (Maus 372). Another is Gaius Mucius Scaevola, who "burned off his right hand in the presence of an enemy king to demonstrate the resolution of the Romans" (Maus 372). Titus Andronicus cuts off his hand and presents it to the emperor, thinking thereby that two of his sons who had been unjustly arrested would be spared. The emperor returns Titus's hand along with the heads of the two sons. Yet another ancient Roman model is Titus Manlius Torquatus, a severe general who had his own son executed for jumping the gun in an attack on the enemy (Maus 372). Shakespeare's Titus kills one of his own sons for allegedly violating family and political honor. Still another Roman prototype on which Titus is modelled, and one explicitly alluded to in the play, is Virginius who killed his daughter Virginia because "her sexual honor was compromised" (Maus 372). At one point in Shakespeare's play, Titus's own daughter, Lavinia, is raped and mutilated by the two sons of the new Empress, Tamora. At the climax of the play, ironically during a feast—the typical ending of a comedy—Titus asks the emperor, Saturninus, "Was it well done of rash Virginius / To slay his daughter with his own right hand, / Because she was enforc'd, stain'd and deflower'd?" (5.3.36–38). Saturninus approves of Virginius's action, at least in the abstract, "Because the girl should not survive her shame, / And by her presence still renew his sorrows" (5.3.41–42). Titus takes this as a license to do the same in real life, calling Virginius's actions "A pattern, president [precedent], and lively warrant" (5.3.44) for him to do likewise, and promptly kills Lavinia before all the dinner guests.

Titus, true to his internalized stereotype, orders the sacrifice of the eldest son of Tamora (a Goth) to Roman gods. At this very early point in the play, Tamora is not yet the empress of Rome, but is in fact the captured Queen of the Goths whom Titus had been fighting on behalf of Rome for the past ten years. Titus has lost twenty-one of his twenty-five sons in the wars with the Goths, and explains to Tamora, "Religiously they ask a sacrifice: / To this your son is mark'd, and die he must, / T'appease their groaning shadows that are gone" (1.1.124–126). The brutality of some of the language used by Titus's son Lucius clashes with the alleged religiosity of the sacrifice (e.g., he speaks of hewing (1.1.129) and lopping (1.1.143) the limbs of Tamora's son) thus confirming Tamora's characterization of this act as "cruel, irreligious piety" (1.1. 130). Titus's execution of a prisoner of war is the decision that leads to all the tragic consequences which befall him and make this play a tragedy. When Tamora becomes empress by marrying the new emperor, Saturninus, she uses her elevated position to get her revenge on Titus and his whole family, by encouraging her remaining two sons to rape Titus's daughter Lavinia. These sons obviously know their Ovid, as would Shakespeare's audience since Ovid was a major part of a grammar school education. Tamora's sons pattern their assault after Ovid's version of the myth of Philomele and Progne. They indeed, one-up the Ovidian original. In Ovid, Philomele is raped by her brother-in-law, Tereus, who cuts out her tongue to prevent her telling anyone. Philomele cleverly reveals the crime to her sister Progne by weaving an illustration of it into a tapestry. The two sisters then slaughter Progne's son by Tereus and make the father eat him. Tamora's sons may have read their Ovid, but they have missed the point of the story entirely: the story is designed to discourage rape and mutilation, but Tamora's sons, egged on by Tamora and her advisor / lover Aaron the Moor, treat it is as a handbook for sexual violence. They imagine that they can avert the fate that Tereus experienced by not only cutting out Lavinia's tongue, but also lopping off her hands.

Shakespeare clearly does not want his audience to miss the Ovidian connection. When Titus's brother Marcus comes upon the violated Lavinia, he first asks "what stern ungentle hands / Hath lopp'd and hew'd and made thy body bare / Of her two branches" (2.4.16–18), picking up on the very language Lucius had earlier used to describe the sacrifice of Tamora's eldest son, and thus confirming the essential brutality of that act too. Marcus continues, "But sure some Tereus hath deflower'd thee / And, lest thou shouldst detect [him], cut thy tongue" (2.4.26–27) and later comes to a more complete realization of the extent of the horror, saying, "Fair Philomela, why, she but lost her tongue, / And in a tedious sampler sew'd her mind; / But, lovely niece, that mean is cut from thee. / A craftier Tereus, cousin, hast thou met, / And he hath cut those pretty fingers off, / That could have better sew'd than Philomel" (2.4.38–43). Eventually Lavinia finds a way to communicate to Titus and Marcus what had happened to her, and in revenge, Titus kills the rapists / mutilators and cooks them in a pie for their mother to eat. Titus, as well as Tamora's sons, knows his Ovid. While Tamora's sons one-up Ovid by having two rapists instead of one and by lopping off Lavinia's hands as well as cutting out her tongue, Titus not only one-ups Ovid by having a parent eat two sons instead of one, he also improves on Ovid's story by making it more just despite its being more violent. In Ovid, the son eaten by his father was totally innocent, while in *Titus Andronicus* it is the perpetrators themselves who are killed and eaten. To paraphrase Sir Francis Bacon, revenge is a very wild justice indeed. Just as today we have Shakespeare transformed and adapted in many popular culture genres and forms, so in Shakespeare's own day we have Ovid and Roman history transformed and adapted into what is, in essence, the popular culture of the day.

Titus Andronicus is, as Vernon Guy Dickson cogently argues in his article "'A Pattern, Precedent, and Lively Warrant': Emulation, Rhetoric and Cruel Propriety in *Titus Andronicus*," a probing, and ultimately scathing, critique of emulation, as taught in the grammar schools, as a "character-shaping" practice (377). In this play, "characters are continually presented as modeling themselves on their history and historical fictions, forming their lives and actions in response to what has gone before, seemingly bound to communal precedents too 'mighty, strong, and effectual' to break away from" (377). Dickson shows in detail that "as the characters compete to outdo available texts and each other's imitations of these texts and precedents, they weave throughout *Titus* a destructive pattern of conflicted, partial, and uncritical emulations" (379). The conclusion is almost inescapable that "with its rehearsal of almost all of the forms and patterns of the grammar school ... the play can be read as a kind of schoolboy's revenge on his own education" (380).

Dickson cites a number of problems with this emulative mode of developing character and ethics, but chief among them is the problem of circularity: "Judgment ... is always tied to the very acts and texts it judges, a troubling circularity that *Titus* explores. Judgment and excellence are learned through reading the same texts that are to be evaluated. Excellence is gained by accurately judging and following—and, where appropriate, superseding—the necessarily imperfect texts of others" (387). One suggested way out of this circularity is to have the best teachers and tutors, so that the students can emulate the models chosen and explicated by their teachers. But this "solution" really just defers the problem since the teachers are also products of the same problematic process and its inherent circularity (Dickson 387–388).

A related set of problems with the system is the danger that the texts to be emulated could be misconstrued by the student or teacher, followed simply by rote rather than by careful analysis, and even be the wrong, or inappropriate, texts altogether. We have already noted an instance of this kind of problem when Tamora's sons use Ovid as a handbook for rapists. Dickson generalizes the issue as follows: "Thus, the germ of *Titus*'s tragedy—for both the play and its title character—lies in Titus's rote following of precedent. Equally, the personal failures of the play, tied up in imitative acts, are replicated and intensified in the political failures of Rome, deriving from traditional emulative models of action. These include virtues that have been torn from their roots through rote followings of precedent not all that dissimilar from the play's uncritical and indecorous patternings of Ovidian imitation, which have also been torn from their root moral messages and humanist beliefs" (395). The scenes of education that appear in the play, Titus, his son Lucius, and his brother Marcus, teaching Titus's grandson, Young Lucius, all indicate that that this young boy is being trained into the same kind of bloodthirstiness and hatred that characterize his elders and the models they choose for emulation, despite the fact that these models have produced nothing but disaster and chaos for the Andronici and for Rome itself. These characters repeat ancient models, whose cultural appropriateness has been long susperseded, and which are also decidedly Romano-centric, when what is needed is thoughtful analysis and a search for better models of behavior and action. As Dickson puts it, "After the final banquet, as Marcus and Lucius take over the education of the Boy and, indeed, all the people of Rome (and likely the Goths as well), their lessons of emulation and judgment embody frightening principles of choice and bias. Marcus's final speech, meant to 'teach you how to knit again / This shattered [scattered] corn into one mutual sheaf,' is notably one-sided, and macabre after the repeated 'chopping, and changing the best into worst' exemplified in the play" (403). Dickson notes that "imitation, whether precise translation or emulative patterning, fails to teach social codes of behavior, because it does not offer an apparatus able to judge texts, to weigh their applicability, or to guide their repetition. In *Titus*, where imitation is linked to revenge and justice—and not, as Tamora pleads, to mercy and forgiveness—rivalry leads to escalating violence only slightly worse than the simply repetitive quid pro quo of attempting exact retribution" (402–403).

Dickson's reading of *Titus Andronicus* raises some important issues for narrative ethics in general. What narratives do we choose? How do we interpret them, on what grounds? Does narrative ethics necessarily lead to a vicious circle? Shakespeare, we suggest, offers a solution to these problems. Shakespeare depicts Titus as demanding revenge rather than showing pity. Titus's decision to sacrifice Tamora's eldest son leads inexorably to what Topher in *Dollhouse* calls "blood, screaming, dying" ("The Target" 1.2). In his book, *The Shakespearean Ethic*, John Vyvyan suggests that a momentous decision of this sort is always at the root of tragedy in Shakespeare's writing. As we demonstrate in Chapter Two in a play like *The Tempest* revenge is resisted and pity prevails, thus averting tragedy. We argue, following Vyvyan: "*The Tempest* ... shows us the regeneration sequence set out completely as the tragic pattern reversed.... It is one of Shakespeare's fundamental propositions that tragedy begets tragedy, for ever and ever, until someone has the strength, the courage and the understanding to say, Enough!" (161–163). No one in *Titus Andronicus* has the "strength, courage, and understanding to say, Enough." The audience is well aware why this play is a tragedy and thus a cautionary tale. We regard this approach as a form of "enactive" narrative ethics, to borrow a term from Francisco Varela and Evan Thompson, which we explained above.

The enactive approach can be understood through Joss Whedon's literalization of the metaphor in "Normal Again," episode 6.17 of *Buffy the Vampire Slayer*. The metaphor, it will be remembered, is based on the enacting of legislation by a parliament or governing body. The law is created by the enactment of the legislation, brought forth or made real. What are created here are still words on a page, even though these words have some effect on our lives, since they are laws that usually have specific punishments built in to them for violation of said laws. In "Normal Again," Whedon takes legislative enactment one step further by having Buffy's choice result in the creation of Sunnydale and her life as a Slayer. A concerned psychiatrist keeps informing her that vampires and vampire slayers don't exist: "none of that's real, none of it. You're in a mental institution. You've been with us now for six years" (6.17). We the viewers do not really know whether Buffy is in a mental institution because she is under the delusion that she is a superhero killing vampires and saving the world, or whether she really is the Slayer having disturbing dreams about being placed in a mental institution. The episode opens with Buffy fighting a monstrous demon. During the fight, she is stabbed in the arm by a retractable spike, which suddenly protrudes from the monster's fist. She is presumably injected with something, which causes the delusion that she is in a mental institution. However, the scene immediately switches to the mental institution, where we see an extremely agitated Buffy being held down while the medical personnel administer an injection in the same place penetrated by the monster's spike. Throughout the episode, the transitions between the psychiatric hospital and the Slayer's life in Sunnydale are seamless, giving neither the audience nor Buffy any grounds for deciding which is the delusion. Things are complicated by the fact that Buffy actually did spend what she thought until now were only a few weeks in a mental institution, as she confesses to Willow: "Back when I saw my first vampires ... I got so scared. I told my parents ... and they completely freaked out. They thought there was something seriously wrong with me. So they sent me to a clinic.... I was only there a couple of weeks. I stopped talking about it, and they let me go. Eventually ... my parents just ... forgot.... What if I'm still there? What if I never left that clinic?" (6.17). As we noted above, the psychiatrist told Buffy that she has been in the mental institution for six years. We the viewers know that this is the sixth Season of *Buffy*, which gives some credence to the psychiatrist's claim. Even Buffy isn't sure. She explains to her friends: "I was like ... no. It, it wasn't 'like.' I *was* in an institution. There were, um ... doctors and ... nurses and, and other patients. They, they told me that I was sick. I guess crazy. And that, um, Sunnydale and, and all of this, it ... none of it ... was real." Xander responds in mock amazement: "Oh, come on, that's ridiculous! What? You think this isn't real just because of all the vampires and demons and ex-vengeance demons and the sister that used to be a big ball of universe-destroying energy?" Buffy continues: "I know how this must sound, but ... it felt so real. Mom was there.... Dad, too. They were together ... like they used to be ... before Sunnydale" (6.17).

Thanks to Willow's research, they learn that an antidote can be made from the monster's "pokey stinger" (6.17). Thanks to the helpful vampire Spike, we learn that the monster is a Glarghk Guhl Kashma'nik demon. Spike and Xander capture the demon and Willow makes the antidote. Before Buffy can take it, Spike confronts her, with his impeccable sense of timing, and threatens to tell everyone that they have been having an affair, if Buffy is too ashamed of him to tell them herself: "I hope you don't think this antidote's gonna rid you of that nasty martyrdom. See, I figured it out, luv. You can't help yourself. You're not drawn to the dark like I thought. You're addicted to the misery. It's why you won't tell your pals about us. Might actually have to be happy if you did. They'd either understand and help you, god forbid ... or drive you out ... where you can finally be at peace, in the dark. With me. Either way, you'd be better off for it, but you're too twisted for that. Let yourself live, already. And stop with the bloody hero trip for a sec. We'd all be the better for it. You either tell your friends about us ... or I will" (6.17). After Spike's depressing speech, it is apparent that Buffy really doesn't want to confront Spike and her increasingly miserable life in Sunnydale. Instead of taking the antidote, she pours it out. This we see as enacting the reality of the asylum, bringing it forth and reducing Sunnydale to the delusion: "I don't wanna go back there. I wanna be healthy again. What do I have to do? Oh ... please, help me." The psychiatrist responds, "It's not gonna be easy, Buffy. You have to take it one step at a time. You have to start ridding your mind of those things that support your hallucinations. You understand? There are things in that world that you cling to. For your delusion, they're safe-holds, but for your mind they're traps. We have to break those down.... I'm talking about those things you want there. What keeps you going back" (6.17). So Buffy sets out to rid herself of her Sunnydale friends and loved ones, Willow, Xander, and Dawn. She ties them up in the basement where the monster has been chained. The scene shifts to the asylum, where a tormented Buffy is being told "take your time. Make it as easy on yourself as possible. There's nothing wrong with that" (6.17). The scene then shifts back to the basement in Sunnydale, where Buffy releases the demon from its chains and stands back to let the monster take care of her friends, which she now believes are "just ... tricks [of the mind] keeping [her] from getting healthy" (6.17). Buffy cowers under the basement stairs, watching her friends attempting to fight off the monster. The scene shifts back to the asylum again, where Buffy is cowering in a corner supported by her mother: "I-It's gonna be okay, sweetheart. Whatever it is, it's not real, remember? Just keep concentrating. I'm right here, sweetie.... I believe in you. You're a survivor, you can do this ... fight it. You're too good to give in, you can beat this thing. Be strong, baby, ok? I know you're afraid. I know the world feels like a hard place sometimes, but you've got people who love you. Your dad and I, we have all the faith in the world in you. We'll always be with you. You've got ... a world of strength in your heart. I know you do. You just have to find it again. Believe in yourself." Buffy does take strength from her mother's assurances, but back in Sunnydale uses this strength to save her friends by fighting and killing the monster. Back in the asylum, she says to her mother, "You're right. Thank you. Good-bye" (6.17). By saving her friends, Buffy is enacting, bringing into being, the Sunnydale/Slayer reality. In *The Existential Joss Whedon*, we describe this as an existential choice, the ultimate Either/Or (55). There we discuss "Normal Again" in considerably more detail, comparing it with, among other things, the *Angel* episode "Birthday" (3.11) in which Cordelia must choose between two realities, two narratives of self. In one of these she is a famous television star with her own sitcom entitled *Cordy!* In the other she is the underpaid secretary for Angel Investigations, where she assists Angel in helping the helpless, having become an essential conduit for extremely painful and life-threatening visions from the Powers-That-Be. These supernatural visions tell them who they need to help. Ultimately, Cordelia, like Buffy, through her free existential choice, enacts that reality where she is of most help to others and most true to herself (see Richardson and Rabb 2007, 58–62).

In both "Normal Again" and "Birthday" the choice between two realities is in actual fact a choice between competing narratives. These narratives play a role in the kind of persons the protagonists turn out to be and allow them to contemplate imagined goals and roles, the goals which they think they want as opposed to the kind of characters they ought to be. They are, in effect, trying out, though under admittedly traumatic circumstances, various narratives of themselves. What readers of stories and viewers of plays, television shows, and movies can experiment with as vicarious experiences, Buffy and Cordelia must endure as painful situations requiring choices to be made with some urgency. Fortunately for them, they are fictitious characters. The actors of these dramas are bringing to life, or enacting, the situations, characters, and choices which otherwise exist only as scripts, words on paper.

William Shakespeare often deals with competing narratives through disguise motifs. For example, in *Twelfth Night* Viola's disguise as the page boy (actually as a eunuch), Cesario, forces her to live out two narratives simultaneously. In one she is a young woman who has just survived a shipwreck, washed up on the shores of a foreign country, Illyria, and hopes to find her twin brother who had been on the same ship. This narrative is shared only with the viewing audience and one minor character who helps her assume the disguise and then is absent from the play. In the other narrative, she becomes in effect a writer/ director/actor creating the role, and whole life history, of the page boy Cesario, and the opportunities, confusions, complications, and misunderstandings that role generates. In this role, she must deal with working for the Duke, Orsino, as a go-between in his futile wooing of the Countess, Olivia, while becoming his confidante; falling in love with Orsino while Olivia falls in love with her, thinking she is male; and being trapped into a swordfight with a foolish knight, who despite being male is no more competent in swordplay than she is. This narrative is the one she presents to all the other characters in the play as well as to the audience, who because they share knowledge of both narratives, are placed in a position of considerable intimacy with Viola, so that her asides and soliloquies have the effect of being confidences shared with the audience. Viola shares with us as Orsino shares with her. As Peter Hyland argues in his article "Shakespeare's Heroines: Disguise in the Romantic Comedies": "In a very real sense the disguised girl is the audience's representative on the stage. Shakespeare was the first dramatist to see the possibilities of a genuine distinction between the primary and the secondary persona and to manipulate this distinction so that the actor is playing two parts, one for the other characters onstage, and one for the audience" (28). This, in effect, makes the audience complicit in the disguise scenario. This was a cunning and daring move on Shakespeare's part, since cross-dressing and cross-class dressing, violating the sumptuary laws, were frowned upon in his day. As Susan Baker explains, in her article, "Personating Persons: Rethinking Shakespeare's Disguises": "Renaissance clothing participated in an elaborate system for signifying rank, gender, occupation, allegiance (household)—in sum, one's place in the social order ... [these sumptuary laws] are perhaps most interesting as symptoms of anxiety about stability in the social hierarchy, particularly about a disjunction between rank and income, about the possibility of social mobility" (313). And, as M.C. Bradbrook notes, in her article "Shakespeare and the Use of Disguise in Elizabethan Drama": "As the body revealed the soul, so appearance should reveal the truth of identity. A character could be really changed by the assumption of a disguise" (166). Baker's concept of "personation" reactivates an Elizabethan term "for the activity we designate as *acting a part* or *creating a role*" and has the advantage of suggesting "'character' as activity" (303). Viola, disguised as a boy, would be looked upon very differently, and would thus interact with those around her in ways she could not have done dressed as herself. Orsino shares confidences with her as his page boy that he would not share with a woman. Yet he is strangely attracted to his page boy and is more than happy to marry her when her true identity is revealed. Stephen Greenblatt, in his "Introduction" to the Norton edition of the play, draws our attention to the fact that "it would have been simple for Shakespeare to devise a concluding scene in which Viola appears in women's 'habits,' but he goes out of his way to leave her in men's clothes and hence to disrupt with a delicate comic touch the return to the 'normal.' The transforming power of costume unsettles fixed categories of gender and social class and allows characters to explore emotional territory that a culture officially hostile to same-sex desire and cross-class marriage would ordinarily have ruled out of bounds" (1762). Shakespeare is living on the edge here. As Peter Hyland concludes, "bearing in mind the dramatic tradition inherited by the Elizabethans that disguise suggests evil and deceit, and the contemporary attacks on transvestite fashions, it seems reasonable to conclude that the dramatist had to contend with a certain resistance in his audience to accepting his disguised heroines" (25).

Given today's attitudes towards human rights and the equality of women, Joss Whedon, too, is living on the edge with his oppressive treatment of the Actives in *Dollhouse*. Seeing how characters in Shakespeare can enact disguise scenarios, writing new stories to create new selves, helps us to imagine how characters like Echo in *Dollhouse* utilize and integrate multiple downloaded personalities. By integrating all the narratives in these downloads, and focusing them on the single goal of bringing down the Rossum corporation, Echo is, to use Baker's reactivated Elizabethan concept, personating herself.

Six

The Moral Imagination in Shakespeare: Pre-Modern and Early Modern Ethics

Citing Lily B. Campbell's *Shakespeare's Tragic Heroes: Slaves of Passion*, the entry on tragedy in Paul Edwards' eight volume *Encyclopedia of Philosophy*, states that "English Renaissance tragedy, including that of Shakespeare … constitutes a shift from the mere presentation of the fall of princes to the justification of evil in the retribution of God against those who bring evil upon themselves in their exercise of passion. Tragedies thus become *exempla* of moral philosophy, admonishing men to attend to the lessons of the consequences of evil in order to avoid ruin and misery" (Vol. 8, 157). While we do not disagree with this standard interpretation, we think Shakespeare offers a very much more complex form of narrative ethics. We utilize and extend the insightful study by James A. Knapp titled, *Image Ethics in Shakespeare and Spenser*. Knapp allows that "Shakespeare's plays invite characters and audience alike to draw on certain principles that govern appropriate moral judgment. Thus, we learn from Shakespeare that tyranny (*The Winter's Tale*), overwrought ambition (*Macbeth, Coriolanus*), inaction (*Hamlet*), etc., are wrong, and that mercifulness (*The Merchant of Venice, Measure for Measure*), forgiveness (*The Tempest*), loyalty to just authority (*King Lear, 1 Henry IV*), etc., are right. Arguments that derive these principles from the plays can be convincing, and they have the added appeal of providing a rationale for Shakespeare's ongoing popularity because his plays demonstrate universal human values" (20). However, the real importance of Shakespeare lies in the particularity of the embodied action of his characters on the stage, which suggests that ethical decisions can be hindered rather than helped by such moral precepts or principles. As Knapp himself argues, "ethical situations in Shakespeare regularly hinge on visual images that cannot be distilled into moral precepts. To make the point clear ... morality can produce stable precepts that are often useless or unmanageable in actual situations" (24–25). Hence, the moral imagination becomes more important than rational precepts and principles. Shakespeare's literary imagination thus becomes the moral imagination.

Macbeth's reasoning concerning his murder of Duncan is a case in point. Macbeth's ambition to be king has been fueled by the prophecies of the witches on the blasted heath: "All hail, Macbeth, that shalt be King hereafter!" (1.3.50). J. Gregory Keller's analysis of the crucial Act 1, Scene 7 of the play, in his "The Moral Thinking of Macbeth," explores in some detail Macbeth's cogent reasons for not murdering his king. They are considerably more particular than the precepts "regicide is wrong" and "thou shalt not kill." Keller argues that an "evil action is in part known as such for its power to rebound upon the doer. In one sense, Macbeth names an antecedent to [Kant's] categorical imperative: by acting he would assign to his act, to the maximum of his will, both a commendation to others and a universal value. He also anticipates Sartre's idea that in choosing, one chooses for all humanity" (43–44). As Macbeth himself puts it: "we but teach / Bloody instructions, which, being taught, return / To plague th'inventor. This even-handed justice / Commends th'ingredience of our poison'd chalice / To our own lips" (1.7.8–12). As Keller puts it: "To do this deed is to declare it worth doing; to declare it worth doing is to imply that others may, and perhaps even ought to, follow one's example" (43).

It is also to violate various relations of trust on which civil society depends. Macbeth says of his king, "He's here in double trust: / First, as I am his kinsman and his subject, / Strong both against the deed; then, as his host" (1.7.12–14). As Keller explains, "Social groupings depend upon the loyalty of group members. Social systems cannot stand without loyalty. Like kinship, trust forms a substratum of every social structure.... When Macbeth contemplates killing the king, removing himself from the kingship-subject relation, he kills more than the king. This deed rends the fabric on which kingship depends. Anarchy results. When anyone may kill the king, there can be no king (as when one kills one's kin, kinship crumbles). To kill the king to become king is to erode what one wants in the process of trying to reach it" (45). Macbeth has invited Duncan into his castle and thus has freely undertaken the obligations of host. As Keller puts it, "To play host is to take upon oneself a protective concern for the guest" (45). Macbeth himself notes that, as host, he "should against his murtherer shut the door, / Not bear the knife myself" (1.7.15–16).

Macbeth adds to these considerations an assessment of King Duncan himself: "Besides, this Duncan / Hath borne his faculties so meek, hath been / So clear in his great office, that his virtues / Will plead like angels, trumpet-tongu'd, against / The deep damnation of his taking-off" (1.7.16–20). As Keller explains, "the final consideration raised by Macbeth against the deed he contemplates is the worth of the other. Decisions involve more than personal consequences and the web of relationships. They involve the concrete other toward whom they are directed.... Whomever one would kill ... the other faces one as potentially worthy of notice and care" (46). Having reviewed the main issues involved in killing the king, and admitting that he has "no spur / To prick the sides of [his] intent, but only / Vaulting ambition" (1.7.25–27), Macbeth resolves that he "will proceed no further in this business" (1.7.31).

His reasoning has been set forth in a soliloquy which in this case represents his internal thinking unaffected by any external interference and thus represents the harmony of his soul, a rather Platonic consideration. Aristotle too lurks in the background. Shakespeare and much of his audience would be well aware of Aristotle's teaching that the conclusion of a "practical syllogism," or moral reasoning, is an action, not a mere proposition, e.g., "we will proceed no further in this business." Shakespeare is going against Aristotle here as Macbeth's reasoning does not ultimately guide his action. As soon as he shares his conclusion, but not the reasoning that led to it, with Lady Macbeth, she immediately starts to convince him that their ambition should not be thwarted by what she sees as his cowardice, an accusation that she throws fiercely in his face. She demands of him: "Art thou afeard / To be the same in thine own act and valor / As thou art in desire?" (1.7.39–41). To this accusation of cowardice, she adds an assault upon her husband's masculinity: "When you durst do it, then you were a man" (1.7.49). Keller speculates that "the difference between the earlier ethical thinking of Macbeth and his explanation to Lady Macbeth may be an example of the difference between private and public reasons for action, the difference between the inner dialogue and what one is willing or able to state publicly of the conclusions of that dialogue" (47). Lady Macbeth in usurping "the role of a dialogue partner ... voices the other side of the ethical debate" (Keller 47). By appealing to emotion, she convinces him to "screw [his] courage to the sticking place" (1.7.60) and continue with the plan. Courage is a virtue according to Aristotle, as well as to a seasoned warrior such as Macbeth, and such an appeal to virtue in this context is ironic. The act they are contemplating is clearly wrong and Macbeth knows it as his soliloquy so eloquently confirms.

Shakespeare is not only challenging Aristotle here, but Socrates as well, as Socrates taught that man never knowingly does wrong. Shakespeare has Macbeth doing just that. Shakespeare's argument against these Greek philosophers is in the form of narrative presented visually and powerfully on the stage. As Knapp argues in *Image Ethics in Shakespeare and Spenser*, "Literature provides a particularly interesting perspective on the relation of ethics to vision because poets have the luxury of placing images before the eyes of their characters in the safe place of the fictive. The literary artists ... recognize the same power in images as did Protestant iconophobes and Catholic iconophiles, but they were a great deal less certain about the ethical balance of the responses this power would elicit" (4). Shakespeare as a dramatist had the added advantage of placing images before the eyes of his audiences, as well as of his characters, in the safe place of the theater.

The famous "air-drawn dagger" speech (2.1.33–64), dramatically confirms that Macbeth knows that stabbing his sleeping king to death is morally wrong. Though he has now resolved to go ahead with the crime, his conscience is bothering him even before the deed is done: "Is this a dagger which I see before me / The handle toward my hand? ... Art thou not, fatal vision, sensible / To feeling as to sight? Or art thou but / A dagger of the mind, a false creation, / Proceeding from the heat-oppressed brain?" (2.1.33–39). Vision is not always reliable, and neither Macbeth nor we in fact ever receive an answer to any of these questions. In any case, the dagger that appears in Macbeth's vision soon develops drops of blood that signal the "bloody business" (2.1.48) in which Macbeth intends to use another, undoubtedly real, dagger that he holds in his hand. He concludes the speech by likening his progress towards regicide to Tarquin's striding towards his rape of Lucrece. Penetration is involved in both crimes. Macbeth asks the earth to not hear *his* footsteps lest the "very stones prate of [his] whereabout" (2.1.54–58). He clearly knows that what he is about to do is evil in the extreme. Although his mind may be led in the direction of this crime, his body and, we would say, his brain, has rebelled against it from the very instant that the thought enters that mind. Immediately upon hearing the prophecies of the witches, Macbeth cannot decide whether what they impart to him is good or ill. He asks himself that if their messages are good, "why do I yield to that suggestion / Whose horrid image doth unfix my hair / And make my seated heart knock at my ribs, / Against the use of nature?" (1.3.134–137). He experiences an embodied revulsion at the thought of accelerating fate by killing Duncan. Shakespeare is showing the beginnings of an awareness of a truly embodied ethics. Macbeth and Lady Macbeth choose ultimately to ignore such bodily admonitions against their crime, and eventually are punished in bodily ways: Macbeth cannot sleep properly, he sees a ghost, and becomes emotionally numb; Lady Macbeth faints upon hearing that Macbeth has murdered the guards they were to pin the blame on, sleepwalks, sees and smells the blood of Duncan indelibly staining her hands, and is thought to have committed suicide. You ignore the imperatives of your body at considerable risk.

Shakespeare is very much aware of the impact of this kind of visual image portrayed upon his stage. At the end of *Othello*, when Othello, having murdered Desdemona and committed suicide, falls by her on the bed, Lodovico commands Iago, but also the audience, to "Look on the tragic loading of this bed" and then, countermanding his first command, says, "The object poisons sight, / Let it be hid" (5.2.363–365). As Knapp points out, "Lodovico is confused over the value of the images here: is it better to look and learn the lesson that the image embodies or hide it from sight in order to protect the viewer from the risk of the visual?" (4). Shakespeare here is raising a rather Whedonesque meta-narrative question concerning the moral impact of the visual stage upon the audience. As we explained in Chapter Two, at this time the theater was looked upon with some skepticism and equated with bear-baiting and houses of prostitution. All were considered entertainments with dubious moral value, which stricter moralists thought should be outlawed completely. Although, as we have seen above, Keller suggests that Shakespeare anticipates the moral theories of Kant and Sartre, Shakespeare really represents a transition from the medieval to the very early modern. Kantian ethics, utilitarian ethics, and contractarianism do not appear until much later in the modern period, with philosophers like Bentham, Mill, Hobbes, and Locke, the seventeenth/eighteenth-century moralists. Shakespeare is writing in what Knapp calls "postmedieval, Reformation England" (5). The Protestant Reformation introduced what was called above an iconophobic religion as opposed to the Catholic iconophiles. Of course, Protestant churches contained visual images, including stained glass windows, but their function was to tell a story. It is the narrative that was important. Catholic churches contained many statues of saints, the mother of God, and so forth. They even had images of Christ on the cross, suffering for our sins. Generally speaking, Protestant churches displayed an empty cross, which was symbolic of more abstract doctrine, including the risen Christ and his moral teachings in the New Testament. The Christian love ethics—love your neighbor as yourself—was, paradoxically, seen to both supersede and fulfill the commandments of the Old Testament, such as "You shall not commit adultery, You shall not kill, You shall not steal, You shall not covet." Romans 13.8–10 suggests that these and "any other commandments are summed up in the sentence 'you shall love your neighbor as yourself'" (quoted by Badiou, 89).

Alain Badiou, in his book *Saint Paul: The Foundation of Universalism* suggests that this passage expresses St. Paul's attempt "to reduce the multiplicity of legal prescriptions.... A single affirmation ... is required. One that will not arouse the infinity of desire through the transgression of the prohibition" (89). Badiou, being a postmodern philosopher, is much closer to Shakespeare's premodern or very early modern position. It is the concrete particulars of the narrative that are important rather than abstract principles or precepts, Kant's Categorical Imperative, for example. When Badiou writes about arousing "the infinity of desire through the transgression of the prohibition" he is making use of what cognitive scientist George Lakoff calls "frame-based" thinking (Lakoff 2008, 119). The commandment "You shall not kill" employs the narrative frame "killing." When Macbeth reasons that killing the king would make him a poor kinsman; killing the king would make him a disloyal subject; and killing the king while he is visiting would make him a terrible host, what is he thinking about? He is thinking about "killing the king!"—the very thing prohibited by the commandment "You shall not kill." Lakoff's favorite example is "Don't think of an elephant" (Lakoff 2004). Of course the only thing you can think of when hearing such a command is an elephant. Shakespeare's insight is that since Macbeth is already thinking about killing the king, even though he has decided not to, it would be relatively easy for Lady Macbeth to change his mind by reframing the thought in a more positive manner—be a man, have the courage to become king.

We believe that Shakespeare's insight here is confirmed or corroborated by recent studies in cognitive science. In the 2005 multi-authored study titled "The Framing Effect and Risky Decisions: Examining Cognitive Functions with fMRI," functional magnetic resonance imaging (fMRI) was used to assess the mental effort involved in choosing "between one certain alternative and one risky alternative in response to problems framed as gains or losses" (Gonzalez et al. 2005, 1). They conclude that "activity in the frontal and parietal cortices suggests that working memory and imagery mechanisms are involved differentially in choosing risky versus sure options. Individuals considering potential gains display risk aversion that manifests itself as significantly higher brain activity during the selection of risky versus guaranteed responses" (17). When Lady Macbeth reframes their contemplated regicide positively in terms of becoming king, it is little wonder that Macbeth seizes the opportunity to relieve the mental stress he has created for himself through his negative framing. However, once the deed is accomplished and Macbeth has been named king, he finds that his relief from psychological stress was only temporary, as doubts and fears descend upon him yet again, first of all because of the continued existence of Banquo and his son Fleance. Part of the witches' prophesies is that although Banquo will not become king, he will beget kings. Since Banquo is still very much alive at the beginning of Act Three, Scene Two, Lady Macbeth says, "Nought's had, all's spent / Where our desire is got without content" (4–5). This moment quite probably marks the beginning of Lady Macbeth's descent into guilt and madness, aided by Macbeth's earlier unplanned killing of Duncan's guards. For Macbeth himself, the presence of Banquo is the spur to further mental torment and fruitless efforts to quiet it by more definitive action, less accompanied by negatively framed contemplation. He tells Lady Macbeth "O, full of scorpions is my mind, dear wife! / Thou know'st that Banquo and his Fleance lives" (3.2.36–37). Lady Macbeth tries to dissuade him from further acts of homicidal violence, by telling him "You must leave this" (3.2.35) and reminding him that Banquo and Fleance are mortal: "in them nature's copy's not eterne" (3.2.38). Macbeth frames this assurance of mortality in what for him are now positive terms: Banquo and his son "are assailable" (3.2.39). Lady Macbeth does not get a chance to reframe the situation in a way that would not involve more murder, because Macbeth refuses to confide in her any further: "Be innocent of the knowledge, dearest chuck, / Till thou applaud the deed" (3.2.45–46).

Shakespeare uses framing and reframing extensively and effectively in many of his plays. As we discussed above, Othello murders his wife Desdemona and then commits suicide. He had been convinced that she had been unfaithful to him. Indeed, he believed he had irrefutable evidence of this infidelity, "ocular proof" as he puts it himself (3.3.360). This ocular proof is provided by his evil ensign, Iago. Iago is, among other things, extremely jealous of Cassio whom Othello has named his lieutenant, passing over Iago who seems to have more military experience and who had therefore expected the promotion. So Iago is also angry and bitter towards Othello. However, he decides to conceal these hostile emotions and instead frame himself as the "honest" Iago who always looks out for the best interests of both Cassio and Othello. In reality, of course, he has determined to use Othello's wife, Desdemona, as the tool for destroying both Cassio and Othello. As we noted in Chapter Four, because Othello is old and racially Other, he is vulnerable and easily susceptible to Iago's insinuations that Desdemona has been sleeping with Cassio. Nonetheless, although his suspicions are easily aroused by Iago, Othello endeavors to be as ethically responsible as he possibly can, and will not proceed against his wife without what he would consider to be stronger evidence than mere hearsay: "Nor from my own weak merits will I draw / The smallest fear or doubt of her revolt, / For she had eyes, and chose me. No, Iago, / I'll see before I doubt; when I doubt, prove; / And on the proof, there is no more but this— / Away at once with love or jealousy!" (3.3.187–192). Iago attempts to provide the "ocular proof" when he serendipitously comes into possession of a hand-kerchief that Othello had given Desdemona as a gift. Iago constructs a story around the handkerchief, thus reframing the handkerchief in order to frame Desdemona. As George Lakoff explains: "Complex narratives—the kind we find in anyone's life story, as well as fairy tales, novels, and dramas—are made up of smaller narratives with very simple structures. Those structures are called 'frames'" (2008, 22). Iago makes certain that Cassio finds the handkerchief in his lodging and proceeds to feed Othello's visual imagination with a lurid story about Cassio's having an erotic dream about Desdemona. Having worked Othello into a frenzy ("I'll tear her all to pieces!" [3.3.431]), Iago, feigning the innocent, asks: "Have you not sometimes seen a handkerchief / Spotted with strawberries in your wife's hand?" (3.3.434–435). Upon confirmation that such a handkerchief was Othello's first gift to Desdemona, Iago tells Othello that he has seen Cassio wipe his beard with that very handkerchief. This is the beginning of Iago's new narrative framing of the handkerchief. The handkerchief will soon be no longer the symbol of the mutual devotion of Othello and Desdemona. When Othello sees it in the hands of Cassio's whore, Bianca, the handkerchief becomes, in Othello's eyes, the sign of Desdemona's deep betrayal of him. It is the "ocular proof" he has been seeking, but Othello is completely unaware of the extent to which his vision has been corrupted by Iago. As Robert B. Heilman explains: "when Othello is being conspicuously deceived by the seeming, he is under the illusion that he is seeing particularly well, for Iago has tutored his vision" (58). Iago's tutoring Othello's vision is, in effect, framing his perceptions so that in seeing the handkerchief, he will automatically see it as evidence of Desdemona's infidelity, rather than, as he once did, as a sign of their love for each other. Knapp, drawing on phenomenologist Merleau-Ponty's contention that all seeing is "seeing as," concludes that "ultimately Shakespeare presents us with an object (the handkerchief) so unstable that it becomes emblematic of the flaws endemic to empiricist (materialist) epistemologies, flaws that become even more pronounced when such epistemologies guide human ethical action" (153).

Othello is a good example of Shakespeare's use of framing in a tragedy. His use of it in a comedy is best seen in *Much Ado About Nothing*, especially Joss Whedon's 2012 film adaptation of the play. In *Much Ado*, we see the same kind of deceptive framing of the virtuous woman as we saw in *Othello*, and for much the same reason, to destroy the marriage before it really has a chance to commence. Just as Iago hates Othello, and will stop at nothing while stooping to everything to undo him, so Don John the Bastard similarly detests Claudio and will do all he can to make his life miserable: "That young startup hath all the glory of my overthrow. If I can cross him in any way, I bless myself every way" (1.3.65–66). Anne Barton, in her introduction to *Much Ado* in *The Riverside Shakespeare*, notes that Shakespeare makes little attempt to provide Don John with any significant motivation for the kind of havoc he intends to inflict on all around him. Don John the Bastard "has no interest whatever in Hero herself. A man incapable of any genuine human relationship, he is not even Claudio's friend, let alone his rival in love. Don John is a malcontent pure and simple.... He has nothing to gain ... except the pleasure of annoying his brother, grieving Claudio, turning laughter to tears, and reducing everyone around him to ... misery and gloom.... A plot mechanism more than a complex character in his own right, Don John appears in the play as a kind of anti-comic force, the official enemy of all happy endings" (Barton 362).

Just as in *Othello*, the deception unfolds in two phases, one primarily verbal and one decidedly visual. In the first phase of the duping of Claudio, Don John pretends to think that Claudio is Benedick, and tells him that Don Pedro (Don John's brother and Claudio's friend) is wooing Hero for himself, not for Claudio, and that they are in fact to be married very shortly (2.1.155–170). Claudio swallows the bait, as he cynically notes that "'Tis certain so; the prince woos for himself. / Friendship is constant in all other things, / Save in the office and affairs of love ... for Beauty is a witch / Against whose charms faith melteth into blood" (2.1.174–180). Claudio discovers a mere 125 lines later in the same scene that Don Pedro has in actual fact, wooed and won Hero for Claudio, as promised. This ruse having failed, Don John and his associate Borachio now switch tactics and proceed to enact an elaborate slander of Hero, which, just like Iago's slander of Desdemona, commences with verbal accusations. But Borachio knows that more than words are required, that Claudio and Don Pedro "will scarcely believe this without trial" (2.2.40–41). And so Borachio, like Iago, prepares what Othello called "ocular proof," here in the form of having Hero's maid Margaret dress in Hero's clothes, appear in the window of Hero's bedchamber the night before the wedding in a compromising position with Borachio, and thus "there shall appear such seeming truth of Hero's disloyalty, that jealousy shall be call'd assurance, and all the preparation overthrown" (2.2.47–50). Don John has arranged for Claudio, Don Pedro and himself to witness this scene of supposed infidelity, from "afar off in the orchard" (3.3.151): "Go but with me to-night, you shall see her chamber window enter'd, even the night before her wedding-day" (3.2.112–114). In Whedon's staging of this, his directions include "*Margaret up against the door-frame in the wedding dress as Borachio is up against her, moving rhythmically, mouthing 'Hero'*" (125, emphasis in original). Borachio, with Margaret's help, is framing Hero. Whedon literalizes the framing by actually mentioning the doorframe, which frames the supposed act of infidelity. Borachio in later bragging about his villainy tells Conrade: "I have to-night woo'd Margaret, the Lady Hero's gentlewoman, by the name of Hero. She leans me out at her mistress' chamber-window, bids me a thousand times good night" (3.3.143–148). In Whedon's staging of this, Borachio's bragging is given partly in voice over, so that, unlike in Shakespeare where the encounter is only reported, the visual dominates. Whedon's stage direction reads: "*As tells it, we see it: Margaret and Borachio. She is putting on one of Hero's dresses, laughing, nervous about being caught. He holds up another for her to try on—one she means to be married in. Margaret looks uncertain—do they really want to do this?*" (124, emphasis in original). The next morning, when dressing for her wedding, Whedon's Hero is preparing to wear the very dress that Margaret had worn for the previous night's deception, and Margaret somewhat guiltily tries to persuade her to wear a different one: "Troth, I think your other gown were better" (Whedon

127). The line in Shakespeare reads, "Troth, I think your other rebato were better" (3.4.6). A rebato is a stiff collar or a ruff. The passage is still open to Whedon's interpretation. Hero does wear the article of clothing she wants, despite Margaret's alternative suggestion: "No, pray thee good Meg, I'll wear this" (3.4.8). When Claudio spurns Hero at the altar, in Whedon's staging at least, the gown would function as a further visual confirmation for Claudio of her supposed infidelity. It functions much like Desdemona's handkerchief in *Othello* in being made part of a conflicting set of narratives, one signifying love and loyalty and one signifying infidelity. In both plays, the reframed object is manipulated by villains right at the beginning of what was intended to be a happy marriage, of a perfect couple. In *Othello*, of course, the repurposed handkerchief ultimately leads to the death of Desdemona, while in *Much Ado* the abused garment contributes to the apparent death of Hero, who falls down in a faint upon being so falsely accused. That faint is reframed, on the advice of the Friar, as her actual death. This is a deception practiced in order to buy time to get at the truth behind the slander: "Come, lady, die to live; this wedding-day / Perhaps is but prolong'd" (4.1.253–254).

And prolonged it is. This is, after all, a Shakespearean romantic comedy. It is expected that the principal characters will marry in the end and everybody will dance. When Borachio was bragging to Conrade about taking a thousand ducats from Don John to deceive Claudio about Hero's fidelity, they were overheard by two members of the watch and arrested: "We charge you, in the Prince's name, stand! ... Call up the right Master Constable. We have here recover'd the most dangerous piece of lechery that ever was known in the commonwealth" (3.3.164–168). They are taken to headquarters to be examined by the Master Constable, Dogberry, who, in his own way, eventually sorts things out. However, the clarification does not appear in time to prevent the fiasco at the wedding, with Claudio spurning Hero and, accompanied by Don Pedro and Don John, exiting and leaving her for dead. When Borachio, believing that his deception has been responsible for Hero's death, is brought before Don Pedro and Claudio, he confesses to Don Pedro, "how Don John your brother incens'd me to slander the Lady Hero, how ... you saw me court Margaret in Hero's garments" (5.1.235–238). Claudio is devastated that his questioning of Hero's virtue also contributed to her death. He says to Leonato: "I know not how to pray your patience, / Yet I must speak. Choose your revenge yourself, / Impose me to what penance your invention / Can lay upon my sin; yet sinn'd I not, / But in mistaking" (5.1.271–275). As penance, Leonato instructs Claudio to clear Hero's name by proclaiming her innocence, and then to marry his niece, who looks very much like her cousin Hero: Claudio is to "possess the people in Messina here / How innocent [Hero] died" (5.1.281–282), and then "to-morrow morning come you to my house, / And since you could not be my son-in-law / Be yet my nephew. My brother hath a daughter, / Almost a copy of my child that's dead, / And she alone is heir to both of us. / Give her the right you should have giv'n her cousin, / And so dies my revenge" (5.1.286–292). Claudio, amazingly enough, accedes to this odd request: "I do embrace your offer, and dispose / For henceforth of poor Claudio" (5.1.294–295). It turns out, of course, that the look-alike cousin is none other than the very un-dead Hero herself. This is a romantic comedy after all. But this is not the only happy wedding at the end of the play.

The love story *Much Ado* is most noted for is not that of Claudio and Hero, but rather that of Hero's cousin Beatrice and the young lord, Benedick. Leonato notes that "there is a kind of merry war betwixt Signor Benedick and [Beatrice]; they never meet but there's skirmish of wit between them" (1.1.60–64). During the fancy dress party Leonato is hosting, Benedick says of Beatrice, "She speaks poniards, and every word stabs" (2.1.247–248), and then adds, right out of the blue, "I would not marry her, though she were endow'd with all that Adam had left him before he transgress'd" (2.1.250–252). When Beatrice's uncle, Leonato, says he hopes to see her "one day fitted with a husband" (2.1.58), she responds, "Not till God make men of some other mettle than earth.... No uncle, I'll none" (2.1.59–62). It seems like Beatrice and Benedick are constantly proclaiming that they will never marry, and most especially not each other. She declares she has no need of a husband; he affirms that he is happy to remain a bachelor. Yet, the first thing Beatrice asks about as the men return from the war at the beginning of the play is whether Benedick is among them. A bit later Benedick tells Claudio that Beatrice far exceeds Hero in beauty (1.1.191). It seems the only thing this pair thinks about is each other and marriage. Remember our discussion, in the context of Macbeth's thoughts of regicide, of Lakoff's "don't think of an elephant." Beatrice and Benedick are constantly thinking of marriage and each other, although they tend to frame such thoughts negatively. Everyone around them can see that they are attracted and well-suited to each other, something neither Beatrice nor Benedick are willing to admit to themselves, much less to each other. Some of their friends decide to rectify the situation by conspiring to get Beatrice and Benedick to fall in love with each other. Don Pedro spearheads this conspiracy: "I will ... undertake one of Hercules' labors, which is, to bring Signor Benedick and the Lady Beatrice into a mountain of affection th'one with th'other. I would fain have it a match, and I doubt not but to fashion it, if you three will but minister such assistance as I shall give you direction" (2.1.364–370). Leonato, Claudio and Hero are quick to agree to this conspiracy. Thus we have two parallel conspiracies in *Much Ado*: first, Don John's attempt to falsely frame Hero as a "contaminated stale" (i.e., common prostitute, 2.2.25), thus breaking up her impending marriage to Claudio; and second, the more positive deception designed to bring Beatrice and Benedick together as something more than sparring partners. This is a deception intended to bring out the truth. In Whedon's version, we have Don Pedro, Claudio, and Leonato in the dining room talking about Beatrice while Benedick is outside listening, framed by a window. Don Pedro, obviously aware that Benedick is eavesdropping, says: "Come hither, Leonato. What was it you told me of to-day, that your niece Beatrice was in love with Signor Benedick?" (2.3.89–91). They are obviously framing the way Benedick will perceive Beatrice in the future. Whedon literalizes this framing by having Benedick hop up behind a window frame to listen. Don Pedro, Leonato and Claudio wander about the dining room while talking, forcing Benedick to move from window to window if he wishes to continue eavesdropping. At one point, we see him diving to the ground behind French doors in order to keep up with the conversation. The windows in the French doors are, of course, made up of multiple small frames. Thus the literal framing becomes very apparent. The trio walk from window to window just to mess with him, as Whedon's stage directions make perfectly clear (105). When they return to the French doors, Benedick is holding a small shrubbery branch which hardly conceals his body hugging the ground. We take this shrubbery as a subtle reference to Kenneth's Branagh's film adaptation of *Much Ado*. Branagh misses the literal framing scenario altogether, having Benedick hiding behind high hedges while eavesdropping.

In Whedon's version, Beatrice too is literally framed while she eavesdrops on Hero conversing about Benedick and his love for her. Hero's servant, Ursula, asks, "Are you sure / That Benedick loves Beatrice so entirely?" (3.1.36–37). Hero tells her that she has heard this from unimpeachable sources: "So says the Prince and my new-trothed lord" (3.1.38). Beatrice, her attention captured by what is being said, hesitates while carrying a basket of laundry downstairs. When she hears Ursula ask, "Are you sure that Benedick loves Beatrice so entirely?" she misses a step and falls out of sight. What better metaphor for falling in love? Whedon's stage directions read: "Beatrice, on the stairs, falls right out of sight. A few nasty thumps and crashes ... and she appears peeping up just over floor level" (109). Here her head is framed not only by the stairwell but also by the bars of the railing. This we see as a visual echo of or parallel to Benedick framed by the multiple window panes in the French doors, while he eavesdrops on the conversation about Beatrice. Beatrice is so intrigued that she crawls on her hands and knees further into the kitchen where Hero and Ursula are conversing. To avoid being seen, she hides in a niche under an island counter. Here while listening she is framed by the side and top of the counter, another visual echo of Benedick in the window frames. Just as there was considerable physical comedy in the tricking of Benedick, so there is in the tricking of Beatrice, as she not only takes the tumble down the stairs but also bumps her head on the underside of the counter top. The metaphorical re-framing works in both cases. It permanently affects how they see each other, and they are finally able to admit their love. Hence, the double wedding at the end of the play, giving everyone even more reason to dance.

Framing and deception are not always used for evil purposes. They are used in Shakespeare as mini-dramas, almost as plays-within-the-plays, to change the characters' perceptions, influence their evaluation of the given situation, and hence their behavior. Shakespeare may be using them to raise issues about how the play as a whole might affect the audience, influencing their perceptions, evaluations, and moral judgments. This was the very thing that the puritan objectors to the theater feared. Even Elizabeth I herself expresses something of this view. As Katharine Eisaman Maus notes, the Earl of Essex in his 1601 rebellion against Elizabeth "paid Shakespeare's company to perform a play [about the reign of Richard II, which ended in the deposing of the king]—almost certainly Shakespeare's play—in an attempt to rally supporters to [his] cause. 'I am Richard II,' snapped the furious queen. 'Know you not that?'" (943–944). Elizabeth clearly did not like that way of framing her reign, and Essex was shortly thereafter beheaded for treason. A little theater is a dangerous thing! The literary imagination can and does influence the moral imagination.

We suggested above that in spite of being a tragic hero, Othello at least attempts to act ethically: "I'll see before I doubt; when I doubt, prove; / And on the proof, there is no more but this— / Away at once with love or jealousy!" (3.3.190–192). Othello will not pass judgment on his wife on the basis of mere hearsay. Knapp compares him favorably to a character in *Measure for Measure* by the name of Angelo. Citing Othello's comments upon kissing Desdemona before killing her, "O balmy breath, that doth almost persuade / Justice to break her sword!" (5.2.16–17), Knapp argues that "unlike Angelo's cold willingness to execute the law (regardless of his personal failings), Othello's hesitation suggests that his effort to act ethically is authentic throughout. Of course, its authenticity is of little solace, considering that his intuition only 'almost' persuades him to change his mind" (160). On the basis of this, Knapp explains how we should understand ethical subjectivity in Shakespeare: "For Shakespeare, the fraught relationship between what we see (how we experience seeing) and what we do is a condition of ethical agency. Recourse to moral law or reason does not ease the difficulties that arise at the moment of ethical decision" (160). In *Measure for Measure,* Shakespeare tells us what is wrong with recourse to moral law in pursuit of justice. Shakespeare reveals a finer justice discovered through love, as Walter Pater suggested in his 1874 essay on *Measure for Measure* (cited in Bate xvii).

In *Measure for Measure,* the Duke of Vienna admits, "We have strict statutes and most biting laws / (The needful bits and curbs to headstrong weeds), / Which for this fourteen years we have let slip" (1.3.19–21). The laws include the prohibition of adultery, but since they have not been enforced for fourteen years, Vienna has many houses of prostitution and practically everyone ignores such laws. The Duke, claiming to be going on a trip, appoints Angelo to rule in his stead. Angelo, as we noted above, has a reputation for a "cold willingness to execute the law." As Angelo puts it, "We must not make a scarecrow of the law, / Setting it up to fear the birds of prey, / And let it keep one shape, till custom make it / Their perch and not their terror" (2.1.1–4). To enforce laws that have been ignored for so long would require Angelo to arrest practically everybody in Vienna. He therefore singles out one Claudio to serve as an example and deterrent by having him arrested and punished severely. Claudio had impregnated his love, Juliet, without benefit of the bonds of holy matrimony. For this, Angelo condemns him to death. Angelo is not a merciful fellow, though the Duke had told him, "In our remove be thou at full ourself / Mortality and mercy in Vienna / Live in thy tongue and heart" (1.1.43–45). The mercy part Angelo seems not to understand. He tells Claudio's sister, Isabella, who has come before him to plead for her brother's life, "It is the law, not I, condemn your brother. / Were he my kinsman, brother, or my son, / It should be thus with him: he must die tomorrow" (2.2.80–82).

John Vyvyan, in *The Shakespearean Ethic*, argues that throughout his plays Shakespeare "lays emphasis increasingly on the ethics of the New Testament and repudiates those of the Old" (83). Vyvyan regards *Measure for Measure* as essential for understanding Shakespeare's ethics, devoting more than two chapters to the play: Chapter Six, "*Measure for Measure*: Resolving Tragedy"; Chapter Seven, "*Measure for Measure*: Creative Mercy"; and much of Chapter Eight, "The Plays as Allegory," as well as other references throughout the book. Angelo, with his strict adherence to the letter of the law, obviously represents Old Testament principlistic legalism. Mention is made in passing of "the sanctimonious pirate, that went to sea with the Ten Commandements, but scrap'd one out of the table" (1.2.6–9). The one scraped off is, of course, "Thou shalt not steal," the commandment that, if actually followed, would make pirates cease to be pirates. For these "sanctimonious" pirates, moral principles are not written in stone, and they seem to be free to choose which commandments they wish to obey. But wait. The commandments referred to are practically the prototypes of commandments written in stone, the Decalogue, the word of God handed down to Moses and engraved on the stone tablets. Shakespeare's pirates do not seem to be treating them with the reverence they deserve. As we noted above, in the New Testament the multiplicity of these commandments (most of which are expressed or framed negatively) is reduced (elevated) to the single affirmation "Love your neighbor as yourself." In *Meas-*

ure for Measure, Claudio's love, Juliet, is asked: "Love you the man that wrong'd you?" She replies in true Christian spirit: "Yes, as I love the woman that wrong'd him" (2.3.24–25). Here Juliet is in conversation, in confession, with the Duke, who has returned disguised as a friar. As we noted above, he only "said" he was going away. The disguise he adopts is significant in that it aligns him with Christianity, the New Testament, and the Christian love ethic. Juliet tells her father confessor (the Duke) that she repents of her sin, whereupon he points out that if she repents from fear of punishment, it is not true repentence: "Which sorrow is always towards ourselves, not heaven, / Showing we would not spare heaven as we love it, / But as we stand in fear—" (2.3.32–34). At this point Juliet interrupts, saying, "I do repent me as it is an evil, / And take the shame with joy" (2.3.35–36). According to Vyvyan this answer is the perfect one: "The duke's theory of government is that his subjects should be brought to do right not from fear of the law but from love of heaven—meaning, of course, a state of divine harmony in their own souls" (72). But how does one show Christian mercy without falling back into complete indulgence, the lawlessness from which Vienna was suffering at the opening of the play?

According to Paul N. Siegel in "*Measure for Measure*: The Significance of the Title," *Measure for Measure* "refers not only to the opposite of Angelo's procedure, the Christian forgiveness of the Sermon on the Mount, with the Christian meaning superseding the Mosaic one, mercy being returned for severity; it refers also to the retribution, ironically and sometimes humorously appropriate, which is visited upon each of the misdoers even though mercy is granted to him" (1953, 318). This he calls "the law of comic justice, a retaliation which makes the audience feel that the punishment has been made to fit the crime and yet that justice has been tempered by mercy" (318). We do not regard this as comic justice. Vyvyan calls it "creative mercy" (55, 68). Siegel argues that Shakespeare "was attempting to produce not a coherent and consistent doctrine but an effective play" (319). This is because he does not realize that the play is an exercise in narrative ethics, which, given his date of publication (1953), should not be surprising. The moral significance of creative mercy is brought out in the story, or rather, it is there in the story to be worked out by the audience.

When Isabella intercedes with Angelo on behalf of her brother Claudio, Angelo begins to fall in love with her. She becomes his temptation. This is doubly ironic because she was about to give herself to the church, take holy orders, and become a nun. Angelo propositions her, offering to spare her brother if she will give herself to him. Ironically, this would have him committing an even greater crime than that of Claudio, adding a gross abuse of authority onto the sexual offence. What is even worse is that Angelo has no intention of sparing Claudio, even if Isabella acquiesces to his lewd request, fearing that Claudio would seek revenge for the defilement of his sister, not to mention for the time spent on "death row." The Duke, still in his disguise as friar, becomes aware of Angelo's temptation, and, having discovered an old love of Angelo's, Mariana, conspires with Isabella to have Mariana, disguised as Isabella, fulfill Angelo's licentious and coercive request. The Duke/friar justifies this sexual trick on the grounds that Mariana was already, in a sense, married to Angelo: "He is your husband on a pre-contract: / To bring you thus together, 'tis no sin, / Sith that the justice of your title to him / Doth flourish the deceit" (4.1.71–74). In silence and in the dark, it is plausible, a variation on the "bedtrick" used to convince *Much Ado*'s Claudio that his betrothed, Hero, was unfaithful on the very eve of their wedding. Angelo is thus made to believe that he has had his way with Isabella and that his unrescinded order to execute Claudio has been carried out. When the Duke is finally revealed as the friar who knows about Angelo's crimes and his failure to temper justice with mercy, Angelo confesses all to him: "O my dread lord, / ... But let my trial be mine own confession. / Immediate sentence then, and sequent death, / Is all the grace I beg" (5.1.366–374). At least Angelo is consistent here. Having sentenced Claudio to death for lesser crimes, he in effect sentences himself to death as well. But the Duke's response is to ask him if he were once contracted in marriage to Mariana. Mariana has already revealed that she, pretending to be Isabella, had slept with Angelo: "Tuesday night last gone, in's gardenhouse, / He knew me as a wife" (5.1.229–230). On the basis of this and of Angelo's admission of its truth, the Duke orders him to marry Mariana here and now: "take her hence, and marry her instantly" (5.1.376). The Duke tells Friar Peter, "Do you the office, friar, which consummate, / Return him here again" (5.1.377–378). Once Angelo returns married to Mariana, the Duke immediately sentences him to death in retribution for Claudio's execution. This is the Old Testament eye-for-an-eye style of justice, and one meaning of the title of the play: "'An Angelo for Claudio, death for death!' / Haste still pays haste, and leisure answers leisure; / Like doth quit like, and *Measure* still *for Measure*" (5.1.409–411). The Duke has not yet revealed that Claudio's execution has not actually been carried out. Mariana is not pleased with this sudden turn of events and pleas for her new husband's life. The Duke's responds to her, explaining why he thought the marriage fit: "Consenting to the safeguard of your honor, / I thought your marriage fit; else imputation, / For that he knew you, might reproach your life, / And choke your good to come. For his possessions, / Although by [confiscation] they are ours, / We do enstate and widow you with all, / To buy you a better husband" (5.1.419–424). Mariana does not want to buy a better husband. She loves Angelo. She implores Isabella to plead on his behalf. Amazingly, Isabella does so, manifesting the Christian love ethic of turning the other cheek, in marked contrast to the Old

Testament's eye-for-an-eye. She kneels and addresses the Duke: "Most bounteous sir: / Look, if it please you, on this man condemn'd / As if my brother liv'd. I partly think / A due sincerity govern'd his deeds, / Till he did look on me. Since it is so, / Let him not die. My brother had but justice, / In that he did the thing for which he died" (5.1.443–449). Angelo himself is repentant and once again asks that the death penalty be imposed upon him: "I am sorry that such sorrow I procure, / And so deep sticks it in my penitent heart / That I crave death more willingly than mercy: / 'Tis my deserving, and I do entreat it" (5.1.474–477). James A. Knapp, in his chapter on "The Ethics of Temporality in *Measure for Measure*," suggests that a penitential ethics can be found at the very core of the play: "Christian virtue is predicated on a penitential orientation toward the world. Importantly, the relation of God's atemporal truth to the temporally bound individual is conceived in spatial terms: the true (penitent) Christian has turned toward God, the heathen has turned away, and thus the penitential plea is always a call to 'turn' and face the penitent sinner" (135). Knapp draws our attention to what he calls a "pivotal moment in *Measure for Measure*" (135), the scene in which Isabella first pleads with Angelo for Claudio's life. Angelo has dismissed her plea and is about to leave when she says, "Gentle my lord, turn back.... Good my lord, turn back" (2.2.143–145). Angelo has already recognized that "she speaks, and is 'tis / Such sense that my sense breeds with it" (2.2.141–142). He is being seduced not only by her beauty, but also by her speech. He finds that he is enjoying arguing with her. If he turns back now, he may be turning his back on the letter of the law, on the principles that have guided his life until now. Knapp argues that this represents "a 'turning point' in the play, as well as in the ethical life of the character in question. Angelo does turn back—to invite Isabel for another interview—but in turning back, he has turned his back on the word (or the letter) of the law that was his world up to this moment in the play" (136). This represents a crucial, potentially tragic, choice for Angelo. It leads to his propositioning and attempted seduction of Isabella, to the breaking of his promise to pardon Claudio, and to his attempting to hasten Claudio's execution. As Knapp argues: "the ethical dilemma that Shakespeare stages in this scene is not whether Angelo should or should not proposition Isabella (or even whether he should or should not pardon Claudio).... Reasoned discourse on the application of the law crosses over into the living flesh, emphasizing that the law never exists outside individuals—singular embodied experiences; in other words, Jesus' claim in the Sermon that he has come to fulfill rather than destroy the law (that he is the word become flesh)" (136). The Sermon here is, of course, the Sermon on the Mount, which, as Knapp rightly points out, is the "central scriptural reference" of the play (137). Jonathan Bate, in his introduction to the Royal Shakespeare Company edition of *Measure for*

Measure, notes that "the most widely read book in Shakespeare's England was the 'Geneva' translation of the Bible. Because of this, the title of *Measure for Measure* would have been readily recognized by the play's original audience as an allusion to the opening verses of the seventh chapter of St. Matthew's Gospel" (vii). Knapp also quotes the passage, using *The Geneva Bible: A Facsimile of the 1560 Edition*: "Judge not, that ye be not judged. For with what judgment ye judge, ye shal be judged: And with what measure ye mette, it shal be measured to you againe. / And why seest thou the mote that is in thy brothers eye, but perceiuest not the beame that is in thine owne eye? / Or, how saist thou to thy brother, Suffer me to cast the mote out of thine eye, and behold a beame is in thine owne eye? / Hypocrite, first cast out the beame out of thine owne eye, and then shalt thou see clearly to cast out the mote out of thy brothers eye (Matt. 7:1–5)" (quoted in Knapp, who modernizes some of the spellings, 137). Jonathan Bate notes, "The Geneva Bible included interpretive glosses in its margins. Beside the 'measure for measure' verses appeared the admonition 'hypocrites hide their own faults, and seek not to amend them, but are curious to reprove other men's.' That could well be an instant character sketch for Angelo" (viii). As we noted above, in the play, the Duke has arranged for Angelo to be judged and convicted of much the same crime for which Angelo himself has previously convicted and sentenced Claudio. Angelo was tricked into sleeping with his former fiancée, Mariana. He sentenced Claudio to death for sleeping with his fiancée, Juliet. John Vyvyan, in his chapter "*Measure for Measure*: Creative Mercy," argues that "Angelo must be sentenced to die. Isabella has yet to be redeemed; but there is no redemption without forgiveness. Shakespeare has placed her morally in the dock beside Angelo; and now, though she does not suspect it, she is on trial with him. Angelo is her enemy. If she forgives him and intercedes for him, she will be saved" (77). Isabella, of course, hates Angelo, believing that he is responsible for the execution of her brother and disrespectful treatment of herself. She has even proclaimed, "O, I will to him, and pluck out his eyes!" (4.3.119). The fact that she can, on Mariana's entreaty, turn the other cheek and plead that his life be spared underlines the Christian love ethic which the play enacts. Because the title of the play refers the audience to Jesus' Sermon on the Mount, Knapp's emphasis on the word made flesh is more than apt. Shakespeare is showing us how the actors on the stage are, in a sense, his own words (the written script) made flesh. In *Measure for Measure* Shakespeare is giving us a key to the interpretation of his plays as performed on stage. The tragedies can be seen as cautionary tales as we illustrated above with *Macbeth* and *Othello*. Comedies and romances like *Much Ado About Nothing* and *The Tempest* show how tragedies can be averted. Speaking of the ethical unity of Shakespeare's work as a whole, Vyvyan argues that "it is a principle with Shakespeare that if the hero's actions are right, the tragic ending does not take place" (30). This he works out in some detail in *Measure for Measure*, arguing in effect that forgiveness and love win out over revenge and hate. This is the Christian ethics of love. Though one cannot be ordered to love one's neighbor, the Duke does somewhat humorously seem to command Angelo to love his new bride Mariana: "Look that you love your wife; her worth worth yours" (5.1.407). In the Christian love ethics, it is the life of Jesus that illustrates what love and forgiveness really mean. We would call it today a kind of narrative ethics. This is also what *Measure for Measure* and, by extension, Shakespeare's other plays turn out to be.

In *Measure for Measure*, a number of humorous subplots serve to underline the pervasiveness of this ethic. There is, for example, a Mistress Overdone who runs one of Vienna's many brothels. Her name itself is humorous, with a play on the word "done" in the sense that Angelo really wanted to "do" Isabella. This vulgar sense of "do" may well have originated with Shakespeare; it certainly has survived from his time to ours. One of Mistress Overdone's servants, by the name of Pompey, is asked, "How would you live, Pompey? by being a bawd? What do you think of the trade, Pompey? Is it a lawful trade" (2.1.224–226). Pompey answers rather humorously, "If the law would allow it, sir" (2.1.226). He is told, "But the law will not allow it, Pompey; nor it shall not be allow'd in Vienna" (2.1.228–229). Pompey responds incredulously, "Does your worship mean to geld and splay all the youth of the city?" (2.1.230–231). This response, along with the story we discussed earlier of the pirates scraping "Thou shalt not steal" off the tablet containing the Ten Commandments, suggests that human behavior cannot really be regulated by moral rules, or even laws with provision for the punishment of their transgression. This supports the anti-principlist narrative ethic enacted in the play as a whole.

In a second subplot, Claudio's friend Lucio not only confesses to the Duke disguised as a friar that he has fathered an illegitimate child, but he also tells this friendly friar in most unflattering terms what he really thinks of the Duke. The Duke as friar responds by saying, "I protest I love the Duke as I love myself" (5.1.341). This, of course, is a humorous play on "love your neighbor as yourself," though it also serves to underline the Christian love ethic embodied in the play. At the end of the play, the Duke treats Lucio in much the way he treats Angelo. He orders him to marry the woman who bore his child, and then, "the nuptial finish'd, / Let him be whipt and hanged" (5.1.512–513). Lucio seems more concerned about the marriage than about the whipping and hanging: "I beseech your Highness do not marry me to a whore.... Marry a punk, my lord, is pressing to death, whipping, and hanging" (5.1.514–523). The Duke proclaims, "Upon mine honor, thou shalt marry her. / Thy slanders I forgive, and therewithal / Remit thy other forfeits" (5.1.518–520). Shakespeare's tragedies typically end with a stage littered with corpses, while his comedies usually end with marriages, feasting, and dancing. *Measure for Measure* does not end with either corpses or dances. It does, however, end with multiple weddings. The Duke even proposes to Isabella. However, the weddings are performed off-stage, some with reluctant partners. There is no festive dinner and dance. That is why this is one of the problem plays. Though neither an obvious tragedy nor a comedy, as we argued above, *Measure for Measure* does serve as a guide for understanding Shakespeare's comedies, tragedies, and histories as forms of narrative ethics.

SEVEN

The Moral Imagination in Whedon: Post-Modern and Post-Christian Love Ethics

In Chapter Four, "Shakespeare and Popular Culture," we suggest that *Much Ado*'s Beatrice might well be the Shakespearean forerunner of Whedon's Buffy. Both are fiercely independent and quick with verbal putdowns. In response to one such remark on Buffy's part, the übervamp called the Master proffers the following metatextual comment, "Oh, good. The feeble banter portion of the fight" (1.12), which confirms that this is something that audiences have come to expect from Buffy. Similarly, in *Much Ado About Nothing*, Beatrice's uncle, Leonato, remarks of his niece that "there is a kind of merry war between Signior Benedick and her; they never meet but there's a skirmish of wit between them" (1.1.61–64), which is confirmed with practically every confrontation between Beatrice and Benedick. Beatrice is quite likely an inspiration for Buffy's character.

We suggest that Buffy's 250-year-old vampire with a soul "boyfriend," Angel, also has Shakespearean roots. A source for *Buffy*'s Angel could well be *Measure for Measure*'s Angelo. Both present an attractive, almost angelic, persona concealing dark undercurrents. Or, as the Duke in *Measure for Measure* notes: "O, what may man within him hide, / Though angel on the outward side!" (3.2.271–272). As we explain in the last chapter, in *Measure for Measure* the Duke of Vienna appoints Angelo to rule in his absence. At the outset of the play, the Duke asks Escalus, one of his advisors, what he thinks of this plan, to which Escalus replies, confirming Angelo's reputation for virtue and honest visage: "If any in Vienna be of worth / To undergo such ample grace and honor, / It is Lord Angelo" (1.1.22–24). In *Buffy* episode 1.7, "Angel," when Buffy discovers that Angel is in fact a vampire, Giles her watcher finds that although the old texts contain no information about anyone called Angel,

"There's mention some two hundred years ago in Ireland of, of Angelus, the one with the angelic face" (1.7). Buffy responds, "They got that right," showing that she is still attracted to him despite the fact that she now knows he is a vampire.

As for the dark undercurrents in both *Measure for Measure*'s Angelo and *Buffy*'s Angelus, Angelus is, of course, much worse. He is a vampire after all: "For a hundred years I offered ugly death to everyone I met, and I did it with a song in my heart" (1.7). Angelus, of course, has had his soul restored and now regrets his life as a murderous vampire. As he explains to Buffy, "Fed on a girl about your age ... a favorite among her clan.... Romany. Gypsies. The elders conjured the perfect punishment for me. They restored my soul.... When you become a vampire the demon takes your body, but it doesn't get your soul. That's gone! No conscience, no remorse.... It's an easy way to live. You have no idea what it's like to have done the things I've done ... and to care" (1.7). Much of Angel/Angelus' life from this point on is spent making amends for the harm he caused as a soulless vampire. *Measure for Measure*'s Angelo also becomes a penitent, making up for the evil ruler that he became. The parallels with Angelus are quite startling. Enamored by her virtue, Angelo attempts to have sex with Isabella by promising to spare her brother Claudio, but after the bedtrick that makes him think he has actually had sex with her, he orders the immediate execution of Claudio, which he falsely believes gets carried out. Ironically, Angelo's turn to evil was brought on by Isabella's virtue. Isabella was about to take her vows as a nun. Angelus turns Drusilla into a vampire, after making her watch him kill her entire family. Drusilla was about to take her vows as a nun (2.7 "Lie to Me"). Both Shakespeare's Angelo and Whedon's Angel fall in love with women they cannot have. For Angelo, it is Isabella, the woman he attempts to wrong, who apparently does not return to the nunnery, as we are left to believe that she is to accept the Duke's proposal of marriage. For Angel, it is not Drusilla but his natural enemy, the vampire slayer herself, Buffy. It was her purity of heart that made him love her and want to help her (see "Becoming, Part 1"), but as a nasty trick of fate (or of curses), true happiness with Buffy turns him evil again. In both Angelo's and Angel's cases there is a link between the woman's virtue and the man's turn to evil. The diabolical thing about the gypsy curse that restored Angel's soul is the provision that if he experiences a moment of perfect happiness he will lose his soul and revert to the evil vampire Angelus. As matters transpire, Angel does in fact experience a moment of pure happiness with Buffy as she has sex for the first time, and with a much older man at that. He loses his soul as a result and reverts to Angelus for a short time, but still long enough to wreak considerable havoc, especially in killing Jenny Calendar, Giles' Romany girlfriend. Eventually, Angel's soul is returned to him when Willow performs the restoration spell that Jenny Calendar had discovered just before her death. The newly re-ensouled Angel feels even guiltier than before, if that is possible, for he has harmed Buffy and her friends. Still attracted to Buffy, he later moves away from Sunnydale to Los Angeles, where he carries on her work protecting the inhabitants from vampires, demons, monsters, and other supernatural threats. Before his move to L.A., plagued with even more guilt, Angel wants death and actually attempts to commit suicide by waiting outside for the sun to rise and make him burst into flames. Rejecting her pleas that he get inside to avoid the sun, he confesses to Buffy, "I can't do it again, Buffy. I can't become a killer.... I want you so badly! I want to take comfort in you, and I know it'll cost me my soul, and a part of me doesn't care.... It's not the demon in me that needs killing, Buffy. It's the man" (3.10 "Amends"). Shakespeare's Angelo also seeks death as a punishment for his sins. He pleads with the Duke: "O my dread lord, / ... No longer session hold upon my shame, / But let my trial be mine own confession, / Immediate sentence then, and sequent death, / Is all the grace I beg" (5.1.366–374). Eventually the Duke does sentence him to death; however, he is saved by Isabella's surprising intercession. She exhibits a good deal of miraculous Christian charity, pleading for mercy in spite of the fact that she believes at this point that Angelo is responsible for the death of her brother Claudio. The Duke gives in to Isabella's pleas in spite of the fact that Angelo in effect rejects them, just as Angel rejects Buffy's pleas to go inside: "I am sorry that such sorrow I procure, / And so deep sticks it in my penitent heart / That I crave death more willingly than mercy: / 'Tis my deserving and I do entreat it" (5.1.474–477). Whedon's Angel is saved by a Christmas miracle. As a television weather report puts it: "while most of Southern California is enjoying a balmy Christmas, an extreme cold front has sprung up out of nowhere around Sunnydale, where they are reporting heavy snowfall for the first time in, well, ever.... Sunnydale residents shouldn't expect to see the sun at all today" (3.10). Both Shakespeare's Angelo and Whedon's Angel are, in effect, saved by a Christian miracle.

Both Angel and Angelo are subjected to "marriages" not entirely of their own choosing. The evil law firm Wolfram and Hart magically restore from death Angel's sire, Darla, in the hopes that she will again seduce him, give him that moment of pure happiness, and thus turn him back into the soulless Angelus. Sex with Darla does not produce the moment of perfect happiness. What it does produce is Angel's troublesome son Connor. Angel becomes a single father as Darla, in an act of conversion, actually stakes herself to save the child she is carrying. Shakespeare's Angelo is ordered by the Duke of Vienna to marry his former fiancée, Mariana: "Go take her hence, and marry her instantly" (5.1.377). Angelo had earlier broken his engagement to Mariana, when she lost her fortune and could not pay her dowry. When Angelo was pursuing Isabella, the Duke arranged for Mariana to substitute for Isabella in a silent liaison in a darkened room. He counsels Isabella: "Go you to Angelo ... agree with his demands ... only refer yourself to this advantage: first, that your stay with him may not be long; that the time may have all shadow and silence in it; and the place answer to convenience" (3.1.243–248). Not only does Angelo believe that his orders to execute Claudio have been carried out, he also believes that he has actually slept with Isabella. No wonder he feels guilty when the Duke confronts him with his crimes. When he learns that it was Mariana not Isabella in the liaison, he is more than aware of the irony that sleeping with his fiancée without the sanction of marriage is the very crime for which he had sentenced Claudio to death. It is little wonder that his guilt compels him to obey the Duke's command to wed Mariana. It is only apt that after this marriage the Duke then sentences him to death, which would leave Mariana a widow holding Angelo's property and fortune. As the Duke points out, this would put her in an ideal position to "buy" herself "a better husband" (5.1.425). But Mariana still loves Angelo and does not want a better husband. It is she who prevails upon Isabella to plead that mercy be granted to Angelo. The Duke grants this mercy as well as commanding Angelo to wed Mariana, but he also commands him to love her: "Well, Angelo, your evil quits you well. / Look that you love your wife.... Love her, Angelo!" (5.1.496–497, 526).

Shakespeare's audiences both of his own time and of ours would not miss the comic irony of the Duke's commanding Angelo not only to marry Mariana but to love her. Of course, love is not something that can be commanded. As we explain in the previous chapter, Shakespeare's *Measure for Measure* moves from the Old Testament ethics of commandment and an eye for an eye, to the New Testament ethics of love and turn the other cheek. Love thy neighbor as thyself is not an alternative commandment; rather, it points to the story of Jesus as moral exemplar. To live a life in imitation of Christ is not to go about creating miracles, but rather turning the other cheek and forgiving one's enemies. Isabella, in pleading for Angelo's life, is, in effect, forgiving her enemy. Love is involved here, but it is Mariana's love for Angelo, which makes her plead for Angelo's life and ask for Isabella's help in doing so. As we argue in the previous chapter, *Measure for Measure* is in fact the measure of all Shakespeare's plays, suggesting that all can and should be read as forms of narrative ethics.

We think it is significant that the *Buffy the Vampire Slayer* episode in which Angel is saved by a Christmas miracle is entitled "Amends." Just as Angelo in *Measure for Measure* calls himself a penitent and seeks to make amends for his past crimes and sins by asking the Duke to impose the death penalty upon him, as required by the laws of Vienna, so *Buffy*'s Angel seeks his own death as the appropriate penalty for his numerous and horrific crimes.

In both narratives, as we have seen, mercy wins out over retribution. In the early modern Shakespeare the move is from the principlism of the Old Testament to the narrative love ethics of the New Testament, while in the postmodern Whedon the parallel move is from the rational principlism of the Enlightenment to a post–Christian narrative love ethic. Whedon actually admits that "the Christian mythos has a powerful fascination to me, and it bleeds into my storytelling" (cited in Anderson 2003, 213).

One of the most Christian-sounding passages in Whedon's work occurs in *Buffy the Vampire Slayer* when Xander stops Willow, who has crossed over to the dark side of witchcraft, from destroying the world: "You're not the only one with powers, you know. You may be a hopped-up über-witch, but ... this carpenter can dry-wall you into the next century.... You've been my best friend my whole life. World gonna end ... where else would I want to be? ... You're Willow.... First day of kindergarten, you cried because you broke the yellow crayon, and you were too afraid to tell anyone. You've come pretty far. Ending the world, not a terrific notion. But the thing is? Yeah. I love you. I loved crayon-breaky Willow and I love scary veiny Willow. So if I'm going out, it's here. If you wanna kill the world? Well, then start with me. I've earned that" (6.22, "Grave"). Xander here is literally offering to sacrifice himself, using love to save the world. When he succeeds and Willow collapses crying in his arms, we hear in the background Sarah McLachlan singing the Prayer of Saint Francis. The prayer itself is to sow love where there is hatred. This is certainly an example of a Christian love ethic, especially with Xander referring to himself as a carpenter, the secular profession of Jesus himself. As Jana Riess explains in her book *What Would Buffy Do? The Vampire Slayer as Spiritual Guide*, "Each time Xander declares his love for his friend, her power to harm him diminishes, until finally Willow is unable to injure him and she crumples to the ground in tears. Xander, the show's gentle carpenter, has saved the world with his demonstration of unconditional love, echoing the sacrifice of another gentle carpenter of another time" (11).

Riess cites Whedon's address to fans in 2003: "We don't need heroes so much as recognizing ourselves as heroes" and concludes "For Xander, Angel, Buffy, and other characters, self-sacrifice is not a sign of weakness but of strength: their altruism extends from a desire to see justice accomplished for others as well as themselves. It's not a heroism that is out of reach but an everyday heroism borne of compassion" (11). As Giles tells Buffy in episode 2.19 ("I Only Have Eyes for You"), "To forgive is an act of compassion, Buffy. It's, it's not done because people deserve it. It's done because they need it." Heroes not only risk self-sacrifice, they also offer forgiveness.

Riess is fond of adding marginal quotations from famous authors to supplement her text. In the context of becoming our own heroes, she cites William

Shakespeare's *All's Well That Ends Well*, "Our remedies oft in ourselves do lie / Which we ascribe to heaven" (11). This quotation also applies more generally to any narrative ethics. The story itself is never going to explicitly tell you what to do. The solution lies in ourselves. The best that narrative can do is help us in our search. Not all characters are moral exemplars. Some story arcs are cautionary tales. In *Buffy*, even some moral exemplars do not exhibit compassion and Christian forgiveness for example. In Season 7, the new principal of Sunnydale High School, Robin Wood, himself the son of a Slayer, is most certainly a moral exemplar, unlike some earlier principals, two of whom were eaten by demons or students possessed by demons. Principal Wood even hires Buffy to work as a student liaison counselor for troubled students, as part of the school's community outreach program ("Lessons" 7.1). Given his background as the son of a Slayer, he knows Buffy's "secret" identity as the Slayer, and eventually becomes a trusted and crucial member of the Scooby gang, an honorary Scooby so to speak, in the fight against the First Evil, the Big Bad of Season 7, the Biggest Bad of the entire series. Wood is well-trained, very disciplined, and enormously determined. Nonetheless, he has one major flaw that threatens to compromise his status on the team and his usefulness in the upcoming battle. Thanks to the First, he discovers that the vampire Spike, the strongest warrior the Scoobies have at this point, killed his mother the Slayer, Nikki Wood, and he wants to get his revenge for that. Wood, in collusion with Giles, sets up a trap for Spike, with the intention of torturing and eventually killing him. Giles is to keep Buffy out of the way during this, but Buffy eventually figures out what is happening and rushes to stop Wood from completing his vengeance. Wood lets his powerful desire for revenge, in effect a vendetta, as Buffy calls it, interfere with their mission of defeating the First. By the time Buffy gets to them, Spike has been able to escape from Wood's imprisonment, to turn the tables on him, and very nearly kill Wood. Interestingly enough, Spike could easily have killed Robin Wood at this point, and had a powerful motivation to do so, but restrained himself: "I gave him a pass. Let him live. On account of the fact I killed his mother. But that's all he gets. He even so much as looks at me funny again, I'll kill him" (7.17 "Lies My Parents Told Me"). Spike, a vampire with a soul, shows more forgiveness, or at least tolerance, than the supposed moral exemplar, Robin Wood.

We think it is significant that Whedon chose the name Robin Wood for this character. Robin Wood is, in actual fact, a famous film critic much admired by Whedon. He is responsible for the critical concept "incoherent text," which can, as it turns out, have a positive connotation. Even before introducing Principal Wood into the series, Whedon discussed the critic Wood's notion of "incoherent text" on the *Buffy the Vampire Slayer* discussion board, The Bronze, May 22, 2002: "Now there's also people preaching one thing while glorifying another, there's what Robin Wood calls the 'Incoherent Text' of so many seventies movies, where peace and understanding may be the underlying desire, but horror and violence is the structure—or the fun ... the point is, the best texts are incoherent. They EMBODY the struggle you describe. Horror is reactionary. I'm liberal. But we get along" (quoted in Loftis, par. 9). In *Buffy the Vampire Slayer*, for example, vampires, demons, and other monsters are personifications of evil, allegories or metaphors. We experience the horror, as Whedon would say, the fun, of these monsters terrorizing their victims. We also get the violence of Buffy punching, kicking, staking and thus dusting these vampires in her fight against evil. But, as we said, these are metaphors for evil in a narrative, which is dominated by a kind of Christian love ethic. These metaphors are further complicated by the fact that not all vampires and demons are evil. Angel, for example, had his soul restored, and, as we noted above, experiences guilt and seeks redemption. Spike, thanks to the military organization, the Initiative, has had a computer chip implanted in his head, which causes him intense pain whenever he attacks a human. He finds he can attack fellow vampires with impunity and begins to help Buffy and the Scooby gang in their fight against evil vampires. He keeps telling everyone that he's evil, but this just contributes to the humor of the show, since he is quite incapable of causing harm to humans, though he does occasionally plot against them. Still, Buffy avoids staking him because he is not really much of a threat, and in fact proves helpful on several occasions. Working with Buffy and the Scooby gang fighting against evil starts to change Spike and he eventually goes in search of a soul. But even acquiring a soul does not put Spike on the side of the angels. At least in Season Seven, the First Evil gains control over him to such an extent that he can no longer be trusted. His actions are not his own. Buffy has faith in him, and he ends up loving Buffy and sacrificing himself to save the world. The moral ambiguity of the show does not mean that there is no distinction between good and evil, just that in particular situations it may be difficult to decide which is which. Gregory Stevenson, in *Televised Morality: The Case of* Buffy the Vampire Slayer, describes *Buffy* as "an incoherent text in the best tradition" (16). Matthew Pateman, in *The Aesthetics of Culture in* Buffy the Vampire Slayer, also maintains that the "inconsistent moral universe is one of the show's greatest strengths" (87). Robert J. Loftis, in "Moral Complexity in the Buffyverse," argues that "*Buffy* as an incoherent artwork offers us an interesting variation on Wood's incoherent texts. It specifically asks us to imagine an alternate world.... Yet the fictional world we see presents in a fresh way the moral dilemmas of the real world. It is a world that cries out for moral judgments but resists making them coherently. Thus we know that there are some true moral statements, we have several good candidates for true moral statements, but we cannot always reconcile them and should be prepared to revise them in light of future experience" (par. 34). This is exactly what is required in narrative ethics. Stories, unlike moral principles, do not tell us what to do, but rather, recognizing the moral complexity of the real world, they invite moral agents to work things out for themselves. Such real world moral complexity is captured metaphorically in the seven seasons of *Buffy*, and other works by Joss Whedon.

Even *Marvel's The Avengers* contains stories of self-sacrifice though it is a little light on the redemption narrative. Whedon succeeds in bringing a number of radically individualistic egotist superheroes together working as a team: Thor, Iron Man, the Hulk, Black Widow, Hawkeye, and Captain America. They are used to saving the world on their own, with help from no one and it is a large sacrifice to work with other superheroes. After all, they each have their own films or comic book series in which they star. It can be argued that S.H.I.E.L.D. Agent Phil Coulson's death is what finally forced this unlikely team to cooperate with one another. Coulson willingly confronts the Asgardian god Loki, knowing that he is risking his life. Loki is the evil adoptive brother of Thor, intent on taking over a source of unlimited power being developed by S.H.I.E.L.D. and dominating earth. He is thus this movie's Big Bad. Coulson is killed by Loki, thus making the ultimate sacrifice, though he does appear again in Whedon's television spinoff, *Marvel's Agents of S.H.I.E.L.D.*, where he is very much alive. *S.H.I.E.L.D.* incidentally, stands for the Strategic Homeland Intervention, Enforcement and Logistics Division.

During the early episodes of *S.H.I.E.L.D.*, Coulson keeps trying to discover how they brought him back from the dead. It seems to be a secret beyond his security clearance. He seems to remember waking up in Tahiti. At one point, lying on a lounge under the thatched roof of a beach-side gazebo, he asks "Did I fall asleep?" and is given the reply, "For a little while." Whedon fans will be reminded of *Dollhouse*. When the actives have their memories wiped, they have a very similar conversation upon awakening from the procedure. Coulson eventually gets memory flashes of lying on an operating table with electrodes probing his exposed brain. In the episode "Seeds" he complains, "They changed my memories. Whose to say they didn't change more?" (1.12). Coulson seems to be worried that he has become something like a Doll or an Active, as we know it from Whedon's show *Dollhouse*. We know that in *Dollhouse* agent Ballard was saved by having his memories and personality downloaded into his own brain. We discuss *Dollhouse* in more detail in Chapter Five. Here it is enough to know that Coulson is worried about his origins, at least in this life, i.e., life after *The Avengers*.

In the same episode, "Seeds," one of the subplots involves Skye, who is constantly worrying about her origins. She has discovered that a S.H.I.E.L.D. agent had left her at an orphanage and she knows that as a child she was bounced around from foster home to foster home. Coulson's team seems to have adopted her after they caught her hacking into the S.H.I.E.L.D. computer system in search of her parents or any further information about her origins. They have been keeping her around because of her superior computer skills, which they find useful in illegally hacking into otherwise inaccessible computers, using "the backdoor" as she likes to put it. In this episode we discover that a large S.H.I.E.L.D. team and an entire village had died trying to protect her, because as an infant she was known to have special powers, though what they are at this point remains a mystery. She was moved from foster home to foster home for her own protection. Though Coulson does not tell her about her presumed special powers, he does let her know that many S.H.I.E.L.D. agents died trying to protect her. He is surprised by her response to this devastating information: "all that time it was S.H.I.E.L.D. protecting her, looking after her. That's what she took away from the story. Not the family she'll never have, but the one she's always had. Here I am telling her something that could destroy her faith in humanity, and somehow she manages to repair a little piece of mine. The world is full of evil and lies, and pain and death, and you can't hide from it. You can only face it. The question is: when you do, how do you respond? Who do you become?" Here the transformative nature of narrative, which we discuss in Chapter Five, comes to the surface, in this almost metanarrative moment.

Agents of S.H.I.E.L.D. and *The Avengers*, as well as *Buffy the Vampire Slayer* and *Angel*, are, in essence, about saving the world (again). After all, it's in *Buffy* that we discover that "apocalypse" needs a plural (4.12 "A New Man"). With his movie, *The Cabin in the Woods*, Whedon, in a truly apocalyptic act of moral imagination, raises the question: "Is the world worth saving?" He helps us to imagine a situation in which the answer could well be NO! Human sacrifice to pacify the Ancient Ones has become commonplace, mechanized, and trivialized. On one level the film is a teenage zombie massacre movie in which college kids go off to a cabin in the woods for a holiday and are attacked by zombies. But these zombies are being manipulated, as are the college kids themselves. The cabin is full of hidden electronic surveillance equipment. Doors can be opened and locked remotely. Even the atmosphere of the grounds around the cabin can be altered with the introduction of mood-altering mists, such as pheromones. The control room, deep below the cabin in the woods, is full of computer screens and technicians in white lab coats, watching their victims in the cabin, electronically pulling the puppet strings, and indeed frivolously betting on the outcome. From the standpoint of narrative ethics and metaphor, Whedon tells us that what he is getting at here is that "we are all controlled, we are all experimented upon, and we are all dying from it" (Whedon and Goddard 19). The real horror in this movie is not the zombies, but the technicians in the white lab coats, and their banal attitude toward what they are doing. And what they are doing is preparing and offering blood sacrifices to the Ancient Ones, to appease them and prevent them from awakening and returning to the surface of the earth where they would destroy humankind. Saving the world has not only become a technological commonplace, but also an international competition, as the same thing seems to be going on in Japan, for example. As Gerry Canavan, in his *Slayage* article, "'Something Nightmares Are From': Metacommentary in Joss Whedon's *The Cabin in the Woods*," astutely observes: *The Cabin the Woods* "is a film that paradoxically insists on the moral and political *unacceptability* of horror fantasy at the same time that it asserts its timeless *inescapability,* leaving its unsettled audience no choice but to hover quite uncomfortably between these two interpretative poles" (par. 10). What really makes the audience uncomfortable is the conclusion of the story. One of the victims, Marty, thanks in part to the amount of marijuana in his bloodstream, is immune to the chemicals used to control these kids and begins to see how they are being manipulated, discovering some of the hidden cameras and microphones. Breaking into the underground control room on a glass-walled elevator discovered in one of the empty zombie graves, he and Dana, the only other surviving teen, discover that they are part of a ritualized human sacrifice. On their elevator ride, as they pass multitudinous glass-walled prison cells containing practically every monster that has ever appeared in a horror movie, they begin to realize that in the cabin they had been inadvertently choosing which monsters would be sent to the surface to hunt and kill them as part of this ritual sacrifice. Marty and Dana fill the roles of the fool and the virgin. The athlete, the scholar, and the whore have already been sacrificed, in accordance with the logic of teen horror movies. However, this particular selection of teens does not quite fit the ideal template: Marty is really no fool, and Dana is certainly no virgin. But, as the Director of operations (Sigourney Weaver) tells Marty and Dana, they make do with what they've got, and if Marty and Dana sacrifice themselves, the world would be saved, the Ancient Ones would be appeased. Marty doesn't think the world is worth saving under these conditions. This is truly a cautionary tale. But what is it cautioning against?

We are looking at the works of Joss Whedon from the point of view of a narrative ethics which privileges literature over logic, and favors metaphor over formal premises and conclusions, story over ethical rules and moral principles. Closing the Hellmouth in *Buffy* can be read as preventing evil from entering the world. A similar device is used in the Whedon *Avengers* movie as well, though there evil in the form of an invading force is streaming in through a portal in the sky, rather than from below. The Avengers team, not unlike Buffy, risks life and limb to seal this version of the Hellmouth. The metaphorical message is clear. One is obliged to fight evil, to stop evil from entering our world, to seal the Hellmouth or to prevent it from opening. However, in the Whedonverses, just as in real life, it is often difficult to identify the evil, to distinguish wrong from right. As we noted above, vampires and demons, for example, *can* be metaphors for evil, but in *Buffy* not all vampires and demons *are* evil. At the end of *The Cabin in the Woods* the question is raised whether allowing the Ancient Ones to take over the world, destroying humankind, is any more evil than performing ritual sacrifices to placate them. The mythology of the Ancient Ones appears near the beginning of the Whedon canon, in fact as early as the second episode of *Buffy the Vampire Slayer*. There, Giles explains to Buffy and the Scoobies: "This world is older than any of you know, and contrary to popular mythology, it did not begin as a paradise. For untold eons, Demons walked the earth; made it their home, their ... their Hell. In time they lost their purchase on this reality, and the way was made for mortal animals. For Man. What remains of the Old Ones are vestiges: certain magicks, certain creatures..." (1.2 "The Harvest," shooting script, p. 74). Giles goes on to explain that the various demons and demon/human hybrids such as vampires are "Waiting for the animals [including us] to die out, and the Old Ones to return" (p. 75). This mythology of the Ancient Ones can be read on many levels. After all, it was Whedon himself who invited viewers to bring their own subtext. Certainly *The Cabin in the Woods* raises once again the question of sacrificing the one to save the many. This is a recurring theme in Whedon's work: e.g., Wesley's willingness to sacrifice Willow to stop Mayor Richard Wilkins III's ascension (*Buffy* 3.19), and thus the end of the world; Giles' willingness to kill Ben to prevent the Hellgod Glory from destroying the world (*Buffy* 5.22); and Jasmine's scary offer to murder "thousands to save billions" (*Angel* 4.21). We discuss this issue of sacrificing "thousands to save billions," in considerably more detail in the following chapters. Here it is enough to note that no one followed Wesley's advice, and that Giles, although killing Ben, said in effect that we shouldn't have to do this sort of thing, that the world ought not to be this way. Angel also rejected Jasmine's better world: "The price was too high, Jasmine. Our fate has to be our own, or we're nothing" (4.21). It is only in *The Cabin in the Woods* where the many no longer deserve to be saved. At the conclusion of the film, we see Marty and Dana huddled together, smoking a joint, as the ancient chamber they are in starts to crumble around them. Their unauthorized arrival and Marty's pushing the iconic Big Red Button released all the caged monsters who then attack the underground control facility, which is now starting to shake as the Ancient Ones awaken. Marty says casually to Dana: "I'm sorry I let you get attacked by a werewolf and then ended the world." He then takes a drag on the joint he is smoking, passes it to her and she takes a drag too, and replies: "Nahh, you were right. Humanity ... Pfft. It's time to give someone else a chance" (*The Cabin in the Woods: The Official Visual Companion* [151]). One way we like to take the issues raised in *The Cabin in the Woods* is as a metaphor for becoming complacent about the dangers of using nuclear technology, both for peaceful and for military purposes. As Drew Goddard, Whedon's co-author, explains: "I grew up in Los Alamos, New Mexico, this town that exists only because it's where they set up the lab to design and build the atomic bomb. It's strange. I feel, as much as anything, that seems like *Cabin in the Woods*, particularly the downstairs aspect, because it involves very, very smart people designing weapons that are going to destroy the world. There's something fascinating about that area to me, and every war, at the end of the day, is really just a history of sending kids to be slaughtered. Because that's still going on in our culture, I think that as much as anything influenced *Cabin in the Woods* and where our heads were at" (quoted by Cooper, par. 25). Extending Goddard's metaphor, L. Andrew Cooper, in his *Slayage* article, "*The Cabin in the Woods* and the End of American Exceptionalism," takes the film more generally as an allegory of the "establishment that would sacrifice the young to maintain its own comfortable, privileged existence" (par. 14). While we do not quarrel with readings that see the film as about the exploitation of the younger generation by the older, we wish to extend the allegory to encompass the peaceful as well as the military uses of nuclear technologies. Just as Goddard sees the human sacrifice competition control room, with its banks of computers and monitors and technicians in white lab coats, as reminiscent of the nuclear research labs in Los Alamos, we see the control room as eerily similar to the depiction of the nuclear generator control room in the movie *The China Syndrome*. The complacency of the operators is almost identical, at least until things start to go horribly wrong. In *The Cabin in the Woods*, the trivializing and normalization of human sacrifice and the cavalier attitude of everyone in the control room, including betting on which monster will kill who first and manipulating what has now become an elaborate game, can certainly be seen as a metaphor for our cavalier attitude towards environmental issues, including the use of nuclear technology and the burial of nuclear waste. The monstrous grotesque hand of an Ancient One thrusting up out of the earth at the end of *The Cabin in the Woods* to destroy humankind with an apocalyptic slap (cf. Cooper, par. 24) could certainly be taken for this buried nuclear waste coming back to bite us. As Whedon is fond of saying, "From beneath you it devours" (7.2, "Beneath You").

In our contribution to Wilcox and Cochran's *Investigating Firefly and Serenity* (2008), entitled "Reavers and Redskins: Creating the Frontier Savage," we argued that from the perspective of a Native American respect for "land, boundary and sacred places," the concept of Earth-That-Was makes the space westerns "*Firefly* and *Serenity* every bit as much horror-comedies as *Buffy* ...

or even *Angel*" (p. 132) and, we would now add, *The Cabin in the Woods* as well. We see the Initiative in *Buffy*, the Alliance in *Firefly/Serenity*, and the Rossum Corporation in *Dollhouse*, as parallel to the sacrifice-control technicians in *The Cabin in the Woods*. All are misusing reason and technology and are punished for doing so, with dire consequences for the rest of humanity. As philosopher James South noted early in the creation of the Whedon canon, back in 2001, well before *Buffy* ended its television run, "There is present in *Buffy the Vampire Slayer* a real worry about the uses of technology and the ways in which it can dehumanize humans" (98).

The terraforming technologies depicted in *Firefly/Serenity* go badly awry and lead to the death of almost all the population of the planet Miranda. And the 0.1 percent that weren't killed, were turned into Reavers, which we take as metaphors for the "savage redskin" of Hollywood B-movies. *Firefly/Serenity* should be read as suggesting that we (i.e., Euroamerican colonists) are responsible for creating and perpetuating this dehumanizing stereotype. When this revelation of the Reavers' origins dawns upon River, she is shown falling to her knees vomiting: "We suggest that this reaction is due partly to River's being raised under the Alliance ... just as the young River told her teacher what is wrong with the Alliance is that 'We meddle.... We're meddlesome,' so, though she probably could never articulate it, River has now come to realize that 'Reavers. *We* made them.' Her reaction is due in part to cultural guilt, a concept, again, Whedon explores in depth in 'Pangs'" (Rabb and Richardson 2008a, 135).

In "Reavers and Redskins," we cite a number of contemporary Native American thinkers (Mi'kmaq, Chickasaw, Lakota, etc.) to the effect that "protecting ... ecologies and ... biodiversity is an integral part of protecting Indigenous spirituality" (131, Battiste and Henderson 107). Indigenous identity is connected to the land, as are Indigenous stories and narratives. *The Cabin in the Woods* gives us a stark contrast to this notion of the importance of place. As Katherine A. Wagner points out in her *Slayage* article "Haven't We Been Here Before?" "*The Cabin in the Woods* ... highlights a significant, albeit infrequently analyzed, element within horror: placelessness" (par. 1). She defines placelessness "as an internal response to a personal or social detachment from place. It occurs through the intentional or unintentional eradication or erosion of the diversity, distinctiveness, and identities of a place or places ... placelessness will ultimately undermine and destroy cultural and individual identities" (par. 1). On their way to the cabin, the teens, in trying to find their way, note that it does not even show up on a GPS, that "it is unworthy of global positioning." As Wagner observes, "Their route to the cabin takes them through a wooded area that could be nearly any forested space in America" (par. 7). The fact that the scene was filmed in Canada, in the province of British Columbia, only serves to underline Wagner's point. She argues, "Placelessness ... is the result of casual, superficial, or partial interactions and experiences with a place or places. Such experiences often create impersonal, inaccurate, or incomplete relationships that hamper both conscious and unconscious efforts to understand, perceive, and appreciate the significance of places, their roles in societal and individual development, and their complex identities" (par. 5). This sense of placelessness captures the horror of a Western non–Indigenous attitude toward land and the environment, a complete lack of respect for place. On the basis of this, we argue that in *Firefly/Serenity*, Whedon's reference to Earth-That-Was also displays his environmentalism. Citing Russell Means' claim that "if the feminist movement ... is to stop violence against women, it will first have to stop the initial rape and violence against our Mother Earth," we show "how the feminist Whedon of *Buffy* leads inevitably to the more environmentalist Whedon of *Firefly/Serenity*" (Rabb and Richardson 2008a, 132). The whole concept of terraforming is a kind of neat encapsulization of some forms of colonialism: the desire to remake everything in our own image, hence not rendering a given planet simply inhabitable, but rather making it a "new Earth," so you get all the arrogance and recklessness that one could expect with such a project. Terraforming, after all, rides roughshod over the environment, including the flora and fauna, if any, that were already there (like introducing rabbits and cane toads to Australia). In *Firefly/Serenity*, we don't see signs of that kind of ecological disaster, but terraforming does not sound like a nice friendly working with the current environment; it sounds much more invasive and brutal, a form of environmental assimilation, with all the ignorance and disrespect that implies, the attitude of placelessness. It actually makes *Serenity* a kind of horror film. As Whedon says in his "Afterword" to *The Cabin in the Woods: The Official Visual Companion*:

> Why do we need horror movies? And I don't mean enjoy, I mean NEED. Because we do. We revel in them. And maybe that's a response to the darkness of the world (or an inoculation against it), or maybe it really is why we need to be gotten rid of.... I think, and I hope this movie conveys, that it's a bit of both. If there's one constant I've found in my work, it's the devastating and necessary human capacity for conflict of interest. We are always at war with ourselves. Our darkness and our better angels. Our desire to achieve and our desire to succumb. Our capacity for self-destruction, or at least self-sabotage. Watching horror, identifying and objectifying, rooting for and against both sides, is a particular thrill, a sleigh ride into that inner conflict.... Here's to the end of the world [172–173].

From an environmental standpoint, in *The Cabin in the Woods* the world does not really end. It is preserved, by eliminating us. From beneath us it devours.

The Cabin in the Woods can also be seen as a metaphor or critique of American exceptionalism, its place, or rather placelessness, in the global community (see both Cooper and Wagner). With Berlin, Stockholm, Rangoon, Buenos Aires, Madrid, and finally Japan failing to appease the Ancient Ones, one of the technicians in the control room, "in an attempt to reclaim a sense of place within this situation, declares: 'I'm telling you, you want good product, you gotta buy American'" (Wagner par. 19). Given the ending of the movie, it demonstrates "the consequences of a false understanding of America's place in the global landscape" (Wagner par. 19). Such sensitive issues are best explored metaphorically, since American exceptionalism involves, at least in part, sacrificing American youth to preserve a standard of living enjoyed by a very small percentage of the global population, or for that matter, even of the American population. Narrative ethics allows us to explore in story issues which we would be reluctant to contemplate and express in a more direct format. It is not just narrative that can help us approach the unapproachable; poetry can do so as well. We end this chapter with a poem inspired by T.S. Eliot and Joss Whedon.

<blockquote>
This is the way the world ends
This is the way the world ends
This is the way the world ends
Not with a bang
But a gigantic, monstrous hand
Thrust out of the hole in the earth left by
The complete collapse of the cabin in the woods.
</blockquote>

EIGHT

Reason and Rules in Ethics: The Parfit Pathology

To better understand the narrative ethics we find in Shakespeare and Whedon it is useful to look at alternative ethical theories, ones based more on reason and rules rather than emotion and imagination. We will discuss the three major rational theories of objective ethics as they have actually been applied to Whedon's work. The three theories are often thought to be competing, but recent scholarship suggests otherwise. Philosopher Derek Parfit in his major study, titled significantly *On What Matters,* famously concludes that "it has been widely believed that there are ... deep disagreements between Kantians, Contractualists, and Consequentialists. That, I have argued, is not true. These people are climbing the same mountain on different sides" (Vol. 1, 419). Parfit's 1365-page two-volume study, incidentally, is widely believed to be one of the most important works in the field of ethics since the writings of Immanuel Kant (1724- 1804). We see it as a very Kantian work bringing Contractualism and Consequentialism/Utilitarianism under what amounts to a Kantian Categorical Imperative or Supreme Principle Morality. "An act is wrong just when such acts are disallowed by some principle that is optimific, uniquely universally willable, and not reasonably rejectable" (Parfit 2011, Vol. 1, 413). As Parfit explains, optimific principles are those, which "would make things go best" (Vol.1, 410). As we will see, this constitutes the Consequentialist or Utilitarian portion of the supreme principle, just as the inclusion of the phrase "not reasonably rejectable" is intended to cover the Contractualists. The "universally willable" criterion is very Kantian as can be seen in Scott R. Stroud's "A Kantian Analysis of Moral Judgment in *Buffy the Vampire Slayer,*" a contribution to James B. South's 2003 collection Buffy the Vampire Slayer *and Philosophy* (185–194). This is one of the earliest philosophic analyses of the Whedonverse. Stroud notes quite correctly, that "Kant holds that humans and their duties (of virtue) are commanded by one fundamental categorical imperative—one should *'act only in accordance with that maxim through which you can at the same time will that it should become a universal law.'*... This version of the 'moral law' is often referred to as the Formula of Universal Law (FUL)" (Stroud 2003, 186, emphasis in original). Stroud also considers Kant's "Formula of Humanity as an End in Itself (FHE), *'So act that you use humanity, whether in your own person or in the person of any other, always at the same time as an end, never merely as a means'*" (186, emphasis in original). Stroud's quotation of the various formulas of the categorical imperative (FUL and FHE) are English translations from Kant's *Groundwork of the Metaphysics of Morals* originally published in 1785 as *Grundlegung zur Metaphysik der Sitten* (Kant 1996). Both this and Parfit's extensive use of the Kantian model we believe constitutes corroborating evidence for Mark Johnson's observation that Western moral thought is still stuck in the 18th century (Johnson 1993, 15). As Lakoff and Johnson have shown, "As difficult and complicated as Kant's moral theory is, its conceptual structure is actually Strict Father family morality (1) tied to rationality by faculty psychology, with Reason playing the role of the Strict Father, and (2) universalized to all human beings via the Family of Man metaphor" (1999, 416–417). This is certainly evident in Stroud's Kantian analysis of *Buffy the Vampire Slayer*.

With specific reference to the TV series *Buffy the Vampire Slayer* Stroud asks "what kind of moral system could be brought to bear on this show to highlight some of the tensions and dimensions of Buffy's struggle against evil" and suggests as an answer that "we can use the thought of the German enlightenment philosopher Immanuel Kant to analyze the various levels of moral judgment within this epic story of good vs. evil vs. teenage impulses" (185). In fairness to Stroud, it should be noted that he says that Kant can "be brought to bear" on *Buffy*, but he does not really ask what kind of moral system is suggested by the show, or explicitly used, defended, or attacked in *Buffy*. Rather, he chooses to impose a moral system on the show, primarily as an explanatory device, or a means of justifying certain moral choices the characters make. For example, Stroud notes: "one theme of Seasons Five and Six has been the Slayer's reluctance to be a Slayer. Instead, she wishes for a normal life and normal college experience and normal experiences at her place of work" (188). Ignoring the fact that normality has been one of Buffy's desires since Season One, Stroud goes on to argue "if Buffy shirks her duties as the Slayer, she will be acting on maxims that privilege her inclinations and desires, and not her rational side. For instance, if Buffy retreats from the role of the Slayer, the results will be disastrous for the community—innocent lives will perish because of her abdication of duty, and one can say that she is not willing to treat others as ends in themselves [the FHE Kantian imperative]" (189). Apart from the fact Stroud seems to be slipping into a non–Kantian consequentialist analysis—the results would be disastrous—his attempt to argue that Buffy in doing her duty is "acting on maxims that privilege her ... rational side" (189), seems strained at best and just plain contrary to the text at worst. Buffy is not shown to be using reason and principles to determine where her duty lies. For example, in 1.2 "The Harvest," when Jesse, a friend of Xander's, is held captive by vampires as Buffy-bait, Buffy explains why she is going to his rescue, and she does not explicitly appeal to rules or rational principles, even though Giles has just finished saying, in his attempt to keep the budding Scooby gang in the loop, "For as long as there have been vampires, there's been the Slayer. One girl in all the world, a Chosen One." Buffy interrupts, "He loves doing this part," and goes on to say, "Jesse is *my* responsibility. I let him get taken." Here she is responding neither to moral principles nor to Giles' orders.

Her excellence of character (moral virtue) is even more apparent in both "Prophecy Girl" (1.12) and "Anne" (3.1). In both cases Buffy wants to lead a normal life instead of being the Slayer, and has, in fact, resigned from slaying. In both cases she ultimately discovers that the Slayer is who she truly is and wants to be. In "Prophecy Girl," Willow is traumatized by the especially invasive attacks of vampires, tearfully telling Buffy, "I thought I could take anything. But, Buffy, this ... this was different.... I knew those guys. I go to that room every day. And when I walked in there, it ... it wasn't our world anymore. They made it theirs. And they had fun. What are we gonna do?" To which Buffy replies, "What we have to" and acts like the Slayer again going off to confront the übervamp Master, knowing that there is prophecy which says that she will fight the Master and she will die.

In the episode "Anne," Buffy has not only given up slayage, she has actually left town and changed her name in an effort to get away from it all, to become invisible, to be no one. This is the episode in which Whedon metaphorically explores the effects of homelessness on teenagers, suggesting how the lack of nurturance leads to premature aging and lack of both purpose and identity. Many are captured and taken to a hell dimension where they are forced, under the strictest of discipline, into slave labor until they are too old to work. They are then spit back onto the streets as hollow wrecks of who and what they once were. Although a lifetime has passed in the hell dimension, the time in our reality has been but a few days at most, suggesting how living on the streets can really age people and strip them of identity. They tend to wander about in a daze muttering, "I'm no one." In order to rescue one of these homeless teens, Buffy allows herself to be captured and taken to this hell dimension. There each of the new captives is asked, "Who are you?" and forced to reply, "No one," under threats of the severest punishment. This is a parody of strict father morality, without the morality, discipline for discipline's sake. When Buffy/Anne is asked who she is, she replies defiantly "I'm Buffy, the Vampire

Slayer. And you are?" She then leads the captives in a rebellion against their monster masters and helps these teens escape from this hell dimension. Its link with our reality closes once the final prisoner escapes. Buffy once again has chosen to become who she truly is. During the episode, when she was reluctant to be the Slayer, and was seeking anonymity, she was nonetheless recognized by a girl she had helped earlier in Sunnydale, and was told things like "But ... but that's who you are and stuff. I mean, you help people, and, you know ... how to do stuff." Being who you are and excellence of character seems to be the emphasis here. There is no suggestion that Buffy is acting on orders or following Kant's categorical imperative, as Stroud suggests.

Stroud analyzing Oz's attempt to control his inner monster, the werewolf, seems to be drawing on the outmoded faculty psychology so apparent in Kantian accounts of morality. Stroud describes Oz's werewolf form as "his natural side" (189). "Here we have a case of the natural side, exemplified by the inclinations and cravings of animalistic desire, overcoming the rational side of human nature; instead of a balanced control of the inclinations, they are running wild in Oz's case" (189). Stroud concludes, "the lesson of this character is ... that the moral judgments about what an individual is to will should stem from their rational nature" (189). For Kant and other principlists, of course, this faculty of reason provides the principles which help to control our desires and selfish inclinations. But this not how Oz goes about controlling his werewolf nature, which, incidentally, is not his natural side as Stroud contends, but was forced upon him when bitten by another werewolf. Oz goes about controlling his monster within by traveling to Tibet and learning Eastern meditation. As Oz explains to Willow, upon his return to Sunnydale, "This warlock in Romania sent me to the monks [in Tibet] to learn some meditation techniques. Very intense. All about keeping your inner cool ... there's more. I take some herbs and stuff. Some chanting. A couple of charms" and he shows some beads on a string wrapped around his hand (4.19 "New Moon Rising"). None of this, of course, has anything to do with the rational principles of 17th–18th-century Western philosophy exemplified by Kantian ethics. Oz is simply trying to regain the person he was before being bitten by a werewolf. Metaphorically, he is trying to control the monster within in order to become the person he truly is. He is not doing this, as Stroud would have it, through a rational appeal to rules or principles, an approach we like to call the Parfit pathology for reasons, which will become apparent. Given the early publication of Stroud's essay it deals only with the first six seasons of *Buffy*. Stroud therefore did not have access to Buffy's famous anti-principlist declaration from 7.5 "Selfless": "There's no mystical guidebook, no all-knowing council—human rules don't apply.... There's only me. I am the Law." The shooting script version of this speech is even more explicit in rejecting a strict father family morality: "There's no mystical guidebook, no all-knowing council—human rules don't apply and Father doesn't know best. There's only me. I am the Law" (http://www.buffyworld. com/buffy/scripts/127_scri.html).

In the more recent study, *The Philosophy of Joss Whedon* (2011), although Kant is mentioned a number of times, what is emphasized is moral development rather than adherence to rules or the categorical imperative. Stroud does not even appear in the index. Jason D. Grinnell's contribution to this volume, "Aristotle, Kant, Spike, and Jayne: Ethics and Character in the Whedonverse," traces the character development and the development of character in Jayne and Spike. In the *Firefly* episode "Ariel," Jayne starts to develop a conscience after turning in the fugitives Simon and River Tam to the Alliance for a reward. He shows he cares about what kind of person he has become when he asks Mal not to tell the others what he has done. Mal is about to shoot him into the vacuum of space through an open airlock, but changes his mind on hearing this. As Grinnell argues, "The kind of character excellence emphasized by Aristotle and Kant is starting to take root in Jayne. Mal seems to recognize change, and Whedon leads us to believe that this is what causes him to spare Jayne" (98).

Spike develops from a selfish vampire into a person who can show genuine love for Buffy and, like the Slayer, a willingness to sacrifice himself to save the world from the First's army of übervamps, by helping to close the hellmouth. Grinnell argues: "He has become, in Aristotle's language, a person who is affected when he should be, at the things he should be, in relation to the people he should be, for the reasons he should be, and in the way he should be.... Kant, too, would approve for Spike is not acting out of selfishness or treating others as tools [means] to reach his own goals" (99–100). There is no emphasis on the commands of strict father morality or following moral rules, consequentialist or otherwise. Grinnell concludes, "Whedon shows us that ethics isn't about merely producing good consequences or following the rules to meet some minimum threshold of good-enough behavior. It is, rather, about developing the wisdom and excellence of character that will allow us to be genuinely good. Spike and Jayne reveal the many layers of ethics and the important differences between the moral correctness of acts and the moral goodness of persons" (100).

We now turn to two papers which take a consequentialist or utilitarian approach in discussing the Whedonverses. The first is Jacob Held's article, "Justifying the Means: Punishment in the Buffyverse," which, like Stroud's paper, also appeared in South's 2003 collection Buffy the Vampire Slayer *and Philosophy* (227–238). The second is Steven Harper's article, "Jasmine: Scariest Villain Ever," which appeared in the 2004 anthology, *Five Seasons of Angel: Science Fiction and Fantasy Writers Discuss Their Favorite Vampire,* edited by

Glenn Yeffeth (49–55). Consequentialism attempts to evaluate the rightness or wrongness of an action or type of action in terms of its consequences or results. A type of action which has optimific consequences or "makes things go best," as Parfit might put it, is obviously right. Optimific principles, it will be remembered, are those, which "would make things go best" (Parfit 2011, Vol. 1, 410). An act, or kind of act, which has bad consequences would, of course, be wrong. The utilitarian version of consequentialism, which stems from the British philosophers Jeremy Bentham (1748–1832) and John Stuart Mill (1806–1873), spells out the relevant consequences in terms of "the greatest happiness of the greatest number." Since it is difficult to foresee all the possible long-term consequences of any given action, it is considered more rational to judge kinds of action or principles of action since, as Mill famously noted, we have had the whole history of humankind to discover which sorts of actions generally make things go best, or lead to the greatest happiness of the greatest number. This evaluation of moral principles in terms of their consequences is known as Rule Utilitarianism as opposed to Act Utilitarianism (which attempts to judge actions themselves rather than principles).

We will begin with Harper for, though he is obviously sympathetic to the utilitarian approach to ethics, not only does he not argue that such can be found in the *Buffy*verse, he actually finds himself confronted with a Whedon narrative which shakes his faith in utilitarianism to its very foundations. The narrative in question is from season four of *Angel* ("Peace Out," *Angel* 4.21). There we meet the beautiful goddess Jasmine who promises "the best of all possible worlds, without borders, without hunger, war, or misery. A world built on love, respect, understanding, and, well, just enjoying one another" (*Angel* 4.21). Following the title of Harper's article, we should ask why is Jasmine the "Scariest Villain Ever?" Well according to Harper this "best of all possible worlds," all this "bliss doesn't come without a price. Once you see Jasmine, you lose all will to do anything but serve her" (Harper 2004, 51). Harper is genuinely troubled, and as the narrative makes clear, rightly so, by the kind of world Jasmine offers. We may achieve world peace and crime-free loving societies, but Jasmine has deprived her followers of freedom in the process. As Angel puts it, "The price was too high, Jasmine. Our fate has to be our own, or we're nothing" (4.21). As Harper himself observes, "Jasmine's followers take on a wild-eyed fanaticism similar to the kind that powered the Inquisition … they see unbelievers as dangerous" (54). But even this is not what really troubles Harper.

Jasmine is not the beautiful loving goddess she appears to be. She needs to eat people, but not that many (between eight and twelve people a day). But what Harper finds truly frightening is that he feels almost willing to pay this price for what she offers, "an end to death by violence … no wars, no genocides, no holocausts, no murders, no spouse abuse, no child abuse, no drive-by shootings, and no suicides" (51). As Jasmine herself says, "I murdered thousands to save billions" (4.21). Harper is genuinely troubled by Jasmine's offer because, as we said, he seems to accept the viability of a utilitarian cost-benefit approach to moral decision making. So, for Harper this does constitute a genuine moral dilemma. As Harper perceptively puts it: "She offers a better world at an affordable price. Scary to the marrow" (51). Whedon, without discussing the arguments of philosophers like Bentham, Mill or Parfit, indeed, without presenting formal rational arguments at all, but simply by telling a story has exposed what is wrong with the utilitarian, cost-benefit approach to ethics. He has used narrative and imagination to refute a rational ethical theory! Of course Parfit's famous triple theory, "An act is wrong just when such acts are disallowed by some principle that is optimific, uniquely universally willable, and not reasonably rejectable," can be used to show just why what Jasmine offers is wrong (Parfit 2011, Vol. 1, 413). The thousands could quite reasonably reject being murdered in order to save billions of others. The principle, if there were one, would not be "universally willable." The thousands would find it difficult to will their own murder. Nor would they consent to being used merely as a means to achieve a better world for others. Both forms of Kant's categorical imperative (FUL and FHE) as well as some form of contractualism are needed to supplement the utilitarian approach to ethics. Parfit would be wrong to claim that "[t]hese people are climbing the same mountain on different sides" (Vol. 1, 419). At least, if they are doing so separately and independently. Consequentialism or utilitarianism, Kantian Principlism and Contractualism all need one another, as the Jasmine story arc demonstrates, much to the horror of Harper. Of course, if stories or narratives can demonstrate such things, do we really need the moral principles? It is, in part, to deal with this very question that we are writing this study of the moral imagination in Shakespeare and Whedon. The foundational assumption that an objective ethics can only be justified through these three rational moral theories using principles and premises is, of course, what we are calling the Parfit pathology.

Before we discuss contractualism in relation to the Whedonverses we need to deal with the consequentialism in Jacob Held's article, "Justifying the Means: Punishment in the Buffyverse" (in South 2003, 227–238). Held takes what he calls a utilitarian approach to interpret *Buffy* 5.22, "The Gift," where Giles takes it upon himself to kill the character Ben, who unwittingly is the vessel which the Hellgod Glory (Glorificus) must use in order to manifest herself and destroy the world. Glory has proved to be invincible, and Ben seems to be her only weak spot in that she needs him in order to become embodied and wreak destruction upon the world. Held argues that Buffy should have killed Ben when she had the opportunity: "[M]y contention is that we should admonish Buffy and maintain that if she truly wants to protect the welfare of the people, that is, if her goal is the security and freedom of all the people, then this goal dictates that she should kill Ben" (237). Buffy recognizes Ben as an innocent bystander and refuses to kill him. It is thus left to Giles to confront this choice between two evils, killing an innocent person or allowing the destruction of the entire world. The sacrifice of the individual in this case would certainly seem to be the lesser of the two evils. As Held puts it: "I think Giles was justified in killing Ben.... Utilitarian equations for maximizing whatever end is proposed are always fallible or troublesome, but whether to trade one life for six billion has an obvious answer" (238). What about Jasmine's justification for eating people: "I murdered thousands to save billions" (*Angel* 4.21)? Harper, as we have seen, is both tempted and deeply troubled by her offer: "She offers a better world at an affordable price. Scary to the marrow" (51). Angel, as we know, did not accept her offer: "The price was too high, Jasmine. Our fate has to be our own, or we're nothing" (*Angel* 4.21). And Buffy did not kill Ben. As Held understands it: "She simply reasons that Ben is innocent and so should not be killed. By way of explaining her decision, Giles points out that Buffy is a hero and thus could not kill Ben even though she was aware of the dire consequences. Giles, though, takes the utilitarian view and makes short shrift of Ben, strangling him to death" (237). Though Held seems to understand that Giles is not happy about being forced into the position of choosing the lesser of two evils, what Held fails to comprehend is why this troubles Giles so. He cites Giles "justification": "I've sworn to protect this sorry world and sometimes that means saying and doing what other people can't. What they shouldn't have to" (*Buffy* 5.22 "The Gift"; Held 2003, 237). We argue that Giles' speech makes it quite clear that the world ought not to be this way. Being forced to choose evil is wrong. It is certainly not the ethical ideal. In our book *The Existential Joss Whedon*, we put it this way: "People should not have to choose between evils, lesser or otherwise. It constitutes a lack of freedom as the ethical ideal in *Buffy* makes perfectly clear, since freedom involves preventing evil from entering the world. Being forced to choose between evils is what makes the existentialist tragic hero tragic, because it is still choosing evil, allowing evil to enter the world" (137–138). Held, on the other hand, gives a strictly utilitarian interpretation: "The only way to guarantee a positive outcome is to kill Ben. Yes it is unfair to kill an innocent. Yes, it seems repugnant and brutal. But if it saves the universe then we need to overcome our disgust and do what only Giles was strong enough to do: kill Ben" (237). Held then quotes Giles' "protect this sorry world speech" introducing it with the words "As Giles himself notes" (237). But this utilitarian interpretation misses the larger point the narrative is making, that this is not how things ought to be. As we have said many times and will continue to repeat: the ethical ideal in *Buffy* involves preventing evil from entering the world, as is illustrated metaphorically by the many attempts to close the Hellmouth or to prevent it from opening. But to see this, it is necessary to look at the entire narrative as a whole and not get bogged down on individual episodes.

In the graphic narrative continuation of the *Buffy*verse stories, the writers occasionally have fun with the metaphorical nature of ethical references like the Hellmouth. For example, In *Spike: A Dark Place* (9.2) the leader of "the fighting demon sturgeons" assures Spike that he was at the Hellmouth, the hole in the ground that is all that remains of Sunnydale: "Oh, I was there mister ... when the Slayer shattered that thing all Hell broke loose.... Uh ... so to speak." Adding "so to speak" is an amusing way of letting us know that the writers are playing with the literalization of metaphor. An explicit and amusing in-text reference to metaphor appears in *Angel and Faith* Season 9 "Family Reunion." Angel and his now adult son Connor, together with Willow and Faith, find it necessary to explore the hell dimension in which Connor was raised, Quor'toth. Connor is their guide as he is one of the few people ever to have survived in this place. He even discovers there a group of loyal followers who rejoice in his return. Connor now feels guilty about having inadvertently taught them what amounts to a kind of Whedonian love ethic: "I inspired them to practice love mercy and compassion in a world where they're punishable by death.... The way time passes here its been centuries.... How many died because of me? Hundreds of thousands?" (*Angel and Faith* 9.13). Quor'toth is a place where hate and fear may well be appropriate survival strategies and love and trust will get you killed. Indeed, here love is described as "the most reviled of all emotions, punishable by death" (*Angel and Faith* 9.12). Willow describes Quor'toth as "the embodiment of the most Hellish of all Hell dimensions" (*Angel and Faith* 9.14). Quor'toth is certainly a hell of a Hell dimension. But it is something more as well. Willow's use of "embodiment" turns out to be more literal than metaphorical. When Faith asks one of Connor's followers: "Hey, little guy, when you said we'd have to fight 'Quor'toth itself' what did you mean?" she receives the following answer: "The Old One who gives this world its name. Why?" As this huge monster descends upon them knocking over tall buildings demanding, "WHO DISRUPTS MY FEAST," Faith allows that "I kinda thought it was a metaphor" (*Angel and Faith* 9.13). Given Whedon's proclivity toward the literalization of metaphor, this reference to metaphor by one of the characters in the text is humorous enough. But the writers don't stop there. To Faith's "I kinda thought it was a metaphor," she receives as a response from Connor's disciple the following question: "What is a metaphor?" (*Angel and Faith* 9.13). It is left ambiguous whether metaphor does not exist in this particular hell dimension, or if it is just this one follower of Connor who does not grasp the concept. But this doesn't matter. Nothing hangs on it so far as the story is concerned. Given that writing credit (script) for this issue goes to Christos Gage, with Whedon listed as "Executive Producer," it is likely that Gage is having some fun at the expense of Whedon's extensive use of metaphor. The fact that the "Executive Producer" kept it in the script not only attests to Whedon's own sense of humor, but also tends to confirm that finding moral metaphors in the subtext is not something imposed on it by readers, or fandemics like ourselves. This point also holds, of course, if Whedon himself introduced the reference to metaphor. Hence, our use of "the writers" above. Of course Quor'toth really is the literalization of a metaphor. It draws upon the well-known metaphor that Evil feeds on anger, hate, fear, and other such negative emotions. As one of Connor's followers explains to his returned savior: "For ages Quor'toth has slumbered, sustained on hate and death. It is you who have caused it to rise. You, and we who follow you.... Your compassion ... your love ... are as knives in its belly.... It will end us all" (*Angel and Faith* 9.13). This explains why its first words upon awakening were "WHO DISRUPTS MY FEAST" (*Angel and Faith* 9.13). Given the large print and shaky font, it certainly looks like these words are shouted in rage and hate. The "knives in its belly" symbolism is put in proper perspective by Willow as she attempts to use her magic to fight Quor'toth. "Angel, we're like a mild case of food poisoning to that thing, warm fuzzy feelings aren't going to let us beat an old one" (*Angel and Faith* 9.13). Notice how the feeding on emotions metaphor is extended here. As we noted above, positive emotions like love, compassion, and trust have no place in this dog-eat-dog hell dimension. Yet Connor's followers, though bipedal demons, are fur covered and look very much like dogs with large floppy ears and cute puppy dog snouts. The words "dog-eat-dog world" do not appear in the text, yet that is the kind of world it is, and the art by Rebekah Isaacs suggests as much. But though Connor's followers look like dogs, they have rejected the dog-eat-dog philosophy in favor of what they believe Connor has brought to their world.

Whedon is always very careful in his selection of names. Angel's son Connor is no exception. "Connor" is an Anglicization of the Gaelic Conchobhar which is said to mean "lover of hounds," from the Gaelic *con*, meaning "wolf or hound," and *cobhair, "aid or desiring"* (http://genealogy.about.com/od/sur name_meaning/p/connor.htm). This may well have influenced Rebekah Isaacs' artwork on Connor's followers. They certainly have a hound dog snout. "Connor" could also mean strong leader from the Gaelic *conn*, meaning "wisdom, strength, counsel" plus, of course, *cobhair*. Connor is leading his dog-like disciples away from the dog-eat-dog world of Quor'toth through a philosophy of love and compassion.

We suggested above that this is a challenge to Whedon's own love ethic, showing some of its limitations. It is actually portrayed as a kind of spoof on a Christian love ethic, which as we have said, is very close to that of the atheist Whedon. Connor has returned to this Hell dimension where he had lived for seventeen years. He had obviously learned how to defend himself from the constant onslaught of demons. His followers call him the Destroyer. This is the second coming "The Destroyer has returned" (*Angel and Faith* 9.12). On his first visit he was kidnapped and brought here by Holtz, an ancient vampire hunter, seeking revenge for the killing of his family by Angelus. But he raised Angel's son as his own, and was overheard by the dog-like demons telling Connor, "You did well today son. I'm sorry you had to fight alone. I know it's hard. It will continue to be. But remember this and draw strength from it. I love you. I will **always** love you" (*Angel and Faith* 9.12). Connor's followers take this as "the source of his unparalleled might" (*Angel and Faith* 9.12). As one of them explains to Connor, "Hallellujah! **Love!** The most reviled of all emotions, punishable by death! **This** is the key to the Destroyer's Power! In the Days since, a small but devoted flock has arisen, following your ways. Practicing love, mercy, and compassion. Awaiting your inevitable return to deliver us all" (*Angel and Faith* 9.12). Upon hearing this, Faith says to Connor, "Look at you, Hipster Jesus" (*Angel and Faith* 9.12). By this point in the story we have also seen a religious icon resembling Connor hanging on the wall of an abandoned house. Upon encountering it Faith asks, "So Connor's what, some wrath-of-god thing here?" to which Angel replies, "More like their devil" (*Angel and Faith* 9.12). The words "second coming" actually appear in the text. A flying demon they are fighting recognizes Connor and flees in fear saying, "No. In the name of all that's damned, no! ... The second coming! The Wrath of the Destroyer! **Woe upon us all!**" (*Angel and Faith* 9.12). There can be no doubt that the Christian mythos is bleeding into Whedon's work again. We are tempted say "hemorrhaging." Connor refers to himself as the "worst messiah ever" after he attempts to counsel his followers: "You don't need me. Just ... y'know, be good to each other. Do unto others as you'd have them do unto you. And uh ... the force will be with you ... always" (*Angel and Faith* 9.14). His followers seem to have accepted a Jasmine-like offer. They are willing to die for Conner and what they believe he stands for, love and compassion. As we have seen, these are punishable by death in Quor'toth. Unlike Jasmine, Connor does not regard his followers as a food source, nor does he expect them to die for him.

Both the followers of Connor and those of Jasmine exhibit a kind of blind fanatical faith in their respective leaders and their supposed teachings of love, respect, and compassion. We have argued that "Jasmine also raises difficulties for the kind of love ethics Whedon seems to favor" (Richardson and Rabb 2007, 148). This is also the case for the story arc involving Connor's followers in Quor'toth. Love is indeed seen as very powerful in the Buffyverse.

Xander for example, in the sixth season of Buffy, is able to control the Dark Willow and thus save the world by drawing on his love for her. "You may be a hopped-up über-witch, but ... this carpenter can dry-wall you into the next century.... You've come pretty far. Ending the world, not a terrific notion. But the thing is, yeah. I love you.... If you wanna kill the world, well, then start with me. I've earned that" (6.22 "Grave"). As Jana Riess confirms, in *What Would Buffy Do? The Vampire Slayer as Spiritual Guide*, Xander here is playing the role of Christ saving the world through love: "Xander, the show's gentle carpenter, has saved the world with his demonstration of unconditional love, echoing the sacrifice of another gentle carpenter of another time.... In one of the show's most explicitly Christian references, the Prayer of Saint Francis of Assisi is sung [by Sarah McLachlan] after Xander's moving display of heroism" (Riess 2004, 11). As we ourselves have argued in the *Existential Joss Whedon*: "Xander is certainly performing the Christ-like role. His reference to himself as a carpenter confirms this, as, we suggest, does his name. The normal short form of 'Alexander' is, of course, 'Alex,' not 'Xander,' just as the usual short form for Abraham is 'Abe,' not 'Bram,' as in Bram Stoker, the author of Dracula. The short form 'Xander,' we contend, conjures 'Christ' in much the same way as 'Xmas,' the short form for 'Christmas' does. 'Xander' is then 'Christ-ander,' from 'andros,' the Greek for 'man.' Thus 'Xander' is 'Christ-man'" (86). Our interpretation, and that of Riess, is, we believe, corroborated by the treatment of Connor as a Christ-like figure in the *Angel and Faith* graphic narrative. It is significant that Dark Willow appears in both. Quor'toth tends to bring out the dark side of anyone in this hell dimension. And Willow in using all her magic to fight the embodiment of Quor'toth succumbs to her dark side. In this case she is rescued by Angel who himself has to risk succumbing permanently to his dark side (Angelus) in the attempt. As he explains later: "I took a calculated risk. A vampire bite stimulates the brain's pleasure centers. I figured it would calm her down" (*Angel and Faith* 9.14).

Though in the *Existential Joss Whedon* we argued that Whedon supports a kind of post Christian love ethic, given both the Jasmine and Quor'toth narratives we now believe that in many cases love is not enough. It is the story that counts. Whedon is presenting us with a narrative ethic pure and simple. Moral imagination is more important than love. In some situations, Quor'toth for example, love and trust may get you killed. Whedon does not turn love into a universal principle.

The blind faith of Connor's followers in Quor'toth raises another interesting question as well. They, presumably, are freely giving up their autonomy and, if required, even their lives to serve him. Is it morally responsible, or even philosophically possible, to freely give up your autonomy? There is something philosophically odd and morally suspect about freely giving up one's freedom.

This is something that, from a moral perspective, would seem to be "reasonably rejectable," to use Parfit's famous way of putting it (Parfit 2011, Vol. 1, 413). This brings us to the third of the three moral theories we are concerned with in this chapter, namely Contractualism. Again we will discuss this theory using two papers that relate it directly to the Whedonverses. Both appear in *The Philosophy of Joss Whedon* edited by D. A. Kowalski and S. E. Kreider (2011). The paper most relevant to the question of freedom we posed above is "Dollhouse and Consensual Slavery" by S. Evan Kreider, one of the editors of *The Philosophy of Joss Whedon*. Though, as the title of the paper suggests, it is primarily about Whedon's television series *Dollhouse*, Kreider does touch on the Jasmine story as an afterthought: "Jasmine (the Big Bad of season four of *Angel*) robs her followers of their autonomy, though in return for (supposed) happiness" (Kreider 2011, 68, note 15). Contractualism does maintain that it is permissible to give up some of your autonomy (usually to the State or Government) in return for something considered to be of greater value, such as security or protection. Kreider cites the 17th-century philosopher John Locke (1632–1704) to illustrate: "According to Locke, many of the moral rules that we live by can be conceived of as a system of agreements—that is, a social contract. Prior to such a contract, humans could be thought of as living in a state of nature [which] ... is in constant danger of degenerating into a state of war, a state in which people violate the rights of others by acts of violence (violating the right to life), enslavement (violating the right to liberty), and theft (violating the right to property)" (64). According to contractualism, then, the social contract gives us a system of rules "not reasonably rejectable" (Parfit 2011, Vol. 1, 413). Such rules are designed to protect our natural rights to life, liberty and property. In return for such protection we give up much of our freedom to a government whose role it is to enforce these rules. Kreider's discussion of contractualism in the context of Whedon's *Dollhouse* is revealing because there we find an actual contract signed by the "Dolls" giving up five years of their lives to the Dollhouse. This is, in typical Whedonesque fashion, an extreme form of contractualism since the Dolls' memories and identities are wiped clean and other skills and identities imposed upon them as the need arises, and Dollhouse customers require. Kreider cites Ballard, the FBI agent who infiltrates the Dollhouse in an attempt to rescue one of the Dolls, Echo (formerly Caroline): "I don't care that these people signed themselves over to you. There is no provision for ... for consensual slavery. It is wrong. You know it's wrong. You feel it in your bones" ("Briar Rose"; Kreider 2011, 62). From a Lockean perspective, Kreider argues: "Slavery involves the violation of another person's natural right to liberty. Legitimate social contracts are designed to protect natural rights, and so slavery could never be part of a legitimate social contract" (64). Kreider then tentatively concludes that, "Locke's view seems closest to Joss's own focusing as it does on the impossibility of a legitimate slavery contract" (65). Kreider goes on to argue that Whedon actually improves on Locke's position: "It is not merely that such contracts place the slave and the master in a state of war, as Locke argues, but also that any legitimate contract must still leave all parties involved with some rights including the option to default on the contract; the slave giving up all his rights, has no such option" (67). Since the "Dolls" have had their original memories and identities erased, they have no such option. Echo, who not only finally retrieves her original self as Caroline, but also retains some of the memories and skills of all the personalities programmed into her, puts it this way: "I have thirty-eight brains, and not one of them thinks you can sign a contract to be a slave" ("Omega," cited in Kreider 2011, 65 and 67). As Kreider is at pains to point out, in this quotation "Echo says 'can,' not 'should,' emphasizing the point that such a contract is not just immoral, but impossible—there is no such contract" (65). We agree, Whedon's narrative imagination is an improvement over Locke's Contractarian arguments.

It has also been argued that Whedon's television series, *Firefly,* and spin-off movie, *Serenity,* taken together as "*Firefly/Serenity* serves as a microcosm for Whedon's pervasive commitment to Lockean ideals of government and individualism" (Foy 39). The argument appears in the first of the two papers on contractualism published in *The Philosophy of Joss Whedon*; namely, Joseph J. Foy's "The State of Nature and Social Contracts on Spaceship *Serenity*." Foy compares Locke's notion of the social contract with that of Thomas Hobbes (1588–1679) while making specific reference to *Firefly/Serenity*. The Alliance, a totalitarian government, which seems to combine the worst features of China and the United States, has complete control over the core planets in this new solar system (e.g., Ariel, Shinon and Londinium) while the planets and habitable moons further out in the system are far less developed, and as Foy notes: "struggles for survival among various colonies are marked by greed, corruption, and lawlessness, not unlike the American frontier during the days of Westward expansion" (40). This, Foy suggests, calls to mind Thomas Hobbes' description of a State of Nature where everyone is "fending for themselves and their own interests.... Without a common power to deter our selfish impulses, competition results in violent clashes, making life in such a state [as Hobbes himself famously put it] 'solitary, poor, nasty, brutish, and short'" (Foy 2011, 40). Think of the dog-eat-dog world of Quor'toth. Foy wants to argue that "Whedon suggests, as does Hobbes, that some form of common authority is necessary in order to provide order and peace" (41–42). Foy rightly notes that Whedon diverges from Hobbes in the kind of authority required: "Hobbes advocates a limitless government of unchecked authority to maintain order and peace.... Whedon ... as demonstrated by his depiction of the Alliance ...

implicitly shows that such an illiberal concentration of power leads to unacceptable tyranny that is destructive to the ends of a good life" (Foy 43). This is, of course, much closer to Locke's conception of the social contract. Locke argued that even in the state of nature we have certain natural rights to, for example, life, liberty, and property, as we noted above. If, therefore, the government itself violates these natural rights (as the Alliance did) we have a right, if not a duty, to break the social contract and attempt to change said government. As Foy puts it, "Acts of disobedience against the illiberal state are warranted" (50). We agree with Foy, that Mal and his crew are engaged in just such acts. However we have some difficulty with Foy's further suggestion they have somehow formed their own mini social contract among themselves. Locke allowed that if you cannot fight the government, or commonwealth as he put it, under whose rule you feel oppressed, you can under some circumstances sell what property you have and seek some other commonwealth under whose protection you wish to live. According to Foy "that's exactly what Mal does when he purchases *Serenity* and hires his crew. With the all-encompassing rule of the Alliance, there is no other commonwealth outside of the jurisdiction of the state, and so they have to form their own. They enter into a new form of commonwealth together aboard the ship, defined by the principles of the Lockean social contract" (Foy 49). We really don't see how imposing contractualism, i.e., "principles of the Lockean social contract," on this narrative helps to illuminate the story. Foy tries to use the Jayne story arc to support his case. We discussed the relevant part of Jayne's story above in reference to Jason D. Grinnell's article "Aristotle, Kant, Spike, and Jayne: Ethics and Character in the Whedonverse," which interestingly enough also appears in *The Philosophy of Joss Whedon*, the same anthology as Foy's paper. The story involves Jayne's attempt to turn in Simon and River Tam for a reward from the Alliance. We have argued in support of Grinnell's conclusion that the only reason Mal did not shoot Jayne out of his airlock prison into the vacuum of space was that Jayne showed some development of moral character. But Foy wants to argue using the principles of the Lockean social contract: "Jayne is a member of the crew only insofar as he is willing to abide by the commitment to the common defense and protection of the rights and security of all. When he threatens to endanger others, Mal similarly threatens to terminate the implied contract that affords Jayne protection and membership within the community" (Foy 48). On the basis of his interpretation of Jayne's story, Foy concludes that "this example reveals that the Lockean form of social contract exists among those on board *Serenity*" (48). But Foy's interpretation misses the whole point of the story concerning character development and the use of the moral imagination to show that even hired guns like Jayne can and do change for the better, even if only just a little better. There is really no need to appeal to Lockean contractualism in order to understand Jayne's story. Even Derek Parfit, after taking more than 400 pages to develop his triple theory, his principle combining Kantianism, Consequentialism, and Contractualism, actually admits that "in explaining why many kinds of act are wrong, we would not need to claim that such acts are disallowed by some triply supported principle" (Parfit 2011, Vol. 1, 414). In some cases such an appeal would not only be obviously unnecessary, but also both puzzling and indeed offensive. As Parfit explains: "This is like the fact that, after some rape or murder, we ought not to say 'What if everyone did that?' or 'What if everyone believed such acts to be permitted?'" (414). He rightly concludes, and we think this is the most important statement in his entire two-volume study, "Some acts are open to objections that are both clearer and stronger than the objections to these acts that are provided by Kant's formulas [e.g., FUL and FHE], or by any version of Contractualism or Rule Consequentialism" (414). Of course we are arguing that it is the narrative or story surrounding such acts which reveals such clear and strong objections to them. We know, for example, that Jayne was wrong to turn in Simon and River Tam to the Alliance, especially after seeing Simon risk everything to rescue his sister from the Alliance training facility, and Mal and his crew doing everything in their power to keep them safe while on the run. That is why we feel such relief when Jayne finally begins to realize that what he did was wrong, and pleads with Mal not to let the Tams know who it was that turned them in. Parfit argues that in more difficult or dubious cases "it may help to ask whether some act is permitted or disallowed by some triply supported principle" (414). We are arguing, on the other hand, that such dubious or difficult cases require a moral imagination, which is often aided by the literary imagination in the form of narrative or story. Moral principles alone, without detailed stories or extended narratives to breathe life and content into them, are really rather sterile or empty, etiolated. On their own, without their surrounding narratives, they do not really help with the dubious cases, and even Parfit, the leading principlist, admits that they are not needed in the obvious ones.

In this chapter we have defended the narrative ethics we find in Shakespeare and Whedon by rejecting the Parfit pathology at the basis of the book *On What Matters* (Parfit 2011). We have done so by arguing that it's not really the rules that matter, it is, rather, the *story* that matters (see Charon and Montello 2002).

Conclusion: Narrative Ethics in Action

As we have argued at some length in the previous chapters, recent findings in the relatively new field of cognitive science are altering in fundamental ways our understanding of moral and ethical thinking. We now believe that all moral theories are metaphorical. The source domain for such metaphorical thinking has been found to be neural networks associated with the sensorimotor system of our brains. Moral thinking turns out to be primarily unconscious, and for the most part imaginative and metaphorical rather than literal. Its logic is drawn from the source domain of the metaphor and is based more on imagination and narrative than on some kind of disembodied abstract reason. It follows, we believe, that narrative plays a much larger part in moral decision-making than was once thought.

We were pleased to see that James Knapp in his study, *Image Ethics in Shakespeare and Spenser,* also draws upon recent work in cognitive science. As we have said, Knapp's book has been a guiding influence on our study of Shakespeare and Whedon. Knapp draws upon the work of psychologists like Jonathan Haidt and Stephen Pinker, while we have drawn on the studies by George Lakoff and Mark Johnson. Cognitive science is a relatively new field of study and, admittedly, Pinker and Lakoff, for example, do not agree on all aspects of cognitive theory. From the standpoint of narrative ethics this doesn't really matter; and as the discipline develops, there is every indication that cognitive science will continue to support the narrative turn in ethics. Knapp, for example, tells us that he included in his study "recent developments in cognitive psychology because they emphasize just how persistent the ethical questions raised by Spenser and Shakespeare are" (17). Knapp explains: "Recent advances in psychology and cognitive research into the genetic proclivity for moral judgment provide ... new research that suggests the brain is hard-wired for a 'moral sense' (one in which an appeal to a moral belief-instinct—rather than a reasoned argument—governs action)" (17). He goes on to argue that what psychologists like Pinker don't really come to grips with is a "fundamental difficulty with moral judgment: that while every appeal to morality feels like an appeal to a universal precept, such precepts are difficult to define outside of the particular situations in which they are invoked" (17). Some may claim that the value of literature for moral instruction lies in its ability to illustrate universal moral truths, but this ignores the "particularity of the situations found in ... poetry and plays" for example (20). Knapp finds it "impossible to accept the suggestion that the value of literature corresponds to its ability to convey uncomplicated moral precepts" (20). Knapp, shows by way of example, that "certainly a case can be made that *Measure for Measure* champions mercy over retribution, but the playwright's reflection on ethical problems in the play far exceeds any didactic moral concerning the value of mercifulness" (20). In our discussion of *Measure for Measure* in Chapter Seven, we noted that although the Duke showed some mercy toward Angelo, Claudio, and Mariana, it was what Vyvyan called "a creative mercy," in that they all experience some form of "kindly" retribution. It is the particularity of their stories that is important. As we also argued, in *Measure for Measure* Shakespeare is moving from the universal moral principles of the Old Testament to the particularities of a life in imitation of Christ in the New Testament. Although this is a Christian love ethics, the play shows the ironic humor of attempting to turn love into a commandment, when the Duke orders Angelo to love his bride, Mariana (whom Angelo had previously rejected because of her lack of a dowry).

A further example of the significance of the particularity of the story can be seen in Prince Hal's rejection of the corpulent knight, Sir John Falstaff, in the *Henry IV* plays. Knapp asks, "Do we return to *1 & 2 Henry IV* to reconfirm our understanding [of the principle that community, the commonwealth, is more important than the individual, Falstaff] or to witness the manner in which Falstaff complicates any straightforward attempt at moralizing?" (20). Falstaff is a lovable, witty, and inventive character, more than a bit of a rogue, and sometimes a downright criminal. He is a loquacious character. Indeed, Shakespeare has given Falstaff (who appears in three plays) more to say than any of his other characters. Critics have paid more attention to Falstaff, than to any other of Shakespeare's characters save Hamlet. As Jean Howard puts it, in her "Introduction" to *Henry IV, Part I* in *The Norton Shakespeare*: "Aside from Hamlet, no other Shakespearean figure has attracted as much critical attention as the fat knight" (1152). Howard describes Falstaff as Price Hal's "tutor in folly, his intimate friend, and surrogate father" (1147). Calling Falstaff "the play's most interesting and memorable character," she argues "Much of the poignancy of the play's depiction of the friendship between the two comes from the tension between their apparent intimacy and the Prince's stated intention to repudiate his companion. Falstaff's threat to monarchical values is obvious. Against the future-oriented calculations of Hal and his father, he insists on living in the present. As his huge body testifies, he demands the immediate gratification of physical desires. To eat, drink, and jest—these are pleasures that for Falstaff brook no delay. Hal can discipline himself ... and he can plot a personal reformation sometime far in the future and work toward that end. Falstaff cannot" (1152). As Charles Boyce notes, in *Shakespeare A to Z*, Falstaff is "physically huge, stunningly amoral, and outrageously funny" and "is generally regarded as one of the greatest characters in English literature. Lecherous, gluttonous, obese, cowardly, and a thief, he lies to the world but is honest to himself" (185). There is a little bit of Falstaff in all of us, which is why we are attracted to the character. As Boyce puts it, "He moves us, in a way that Hal or Hotspur ... cannot, because, like him, we all often feel irresponsible, dishonest, selfish inclinations. We know that Falstaff is part of us, like it or not. In the *Henry IV* plays he represents a childish, self-centred universe of pleasure that adults are doomed to leave and that is defeated by a harsh and demanding political ideal, insistent on duty and order" (188). Harold Bloom, in *Shakespeare: The Invention of the Human*, argues that Hamlet and Falstaff "are the most intelligent of Shakespeare's persons" (271). Bloom argues that, "the greatest of all fictive wits dies the death of a rejected father-substitute, and also of a dishonored mentor" (272). It is important to remember that, Hal, once he becomes king, banishes Falstaff, indeed, refuses even to recognize him. The impact of this rejection can only be fully appreciated by watching a good performance of the play. We would recommend the 2012 BBC series, *The Hollow Crown*, a television production of *Richard II*, *Henry IV, Parts 1 and 2*, and *Henry V*, in which Tom Hiddleston plays Prince Hal/Henry V, and Simon Russell Beale plays Falstaff. (Hiddleston, incidentally, plays Loki in Kenneth Branagh's *Thor* and Joss Whedon's *Avengers*; Beale won The British Academy Television Award for Best Supporting Actor with his portrayal of Falstaff.)

Harold Bloom argues, "To reject Falstaff is to reject Shakespeare" (278). Good theatrical presentations bring out the particularity of the ethical. As Knapp argues: "the value of examining Shakespeare and moral agency lies less in the evaluations we can make about the actions of his characters and more in the particularity of the ethical situations with which Shakespeare presents both characters and audience alike" (23). It is in this context that Knapp discusses Stephen Pinker's scientific study of a universal moral sense. He notes that Pinker uses "an important thought experiment from neuroethics, known as the Trolley Problem" (23). At first we were not altogether pleased to see the Trolley Problem turning up in Knapp's discussion of Shakespeare and Spenser. It represents the kind of short trivial "case study" which narrative ethics exposes as totally inadequate in any serious discussion of moral problems, not to mention in the understanding of moral choice.

Anyone who has studied ethics in the last few years will be more than familiar with the Trolley Problem. There are several versions. They all involve an out-of-control trolley car rushing down the track toward five workmen who are standing on the track and who, for some incomprehensible reason, are totally unaware of the danger they are in. There is a siding onto which the tram could be switched. Unfortunately, there is also a workman standing on this siding, but fortunately (fortunately?) only one workman. Should the trolley be switched onto the siding in an effort to save the five workmen by sacrificing the one? This is a version of the classic example of sacrificing the one to save the many. In another version of the Trolley Problem, usually compared to the first, instead of a siding there is a bridge crossing the tracks on which you and a fat man are standing. You know you can stop the trolley by throwing something heavy in its path, thus saving the five workmen towards which it is hurtling. The only object heavy enough to do the job is the fat man beside you. Should you throw him off the bridge? In various online surveys it has been shown that most people would switch the trolley to the siding, indeed be willing to throw the switch themselves, but most would be unwilling to push the fat man off the bridge (www.moral.wjh.harvard.edu). There is some controversy about what this difference shows about our ethical thought. According to Knapp, "Pinker sides with those who suggest that it is the active role in killing the man that makes the difference. In other words, the thought experiment allows us to glimpse a universal category of moral instinct (do not kill people with your bare hands)" (23–24). Knapp quite rightly disagrees with Pinker. He argues that "the man's particularity alters the ethical situation ... he is not simply a man but a 'fat man.' Unlike the abstract man who will die in the first example—an example that welcomes the kind of calculus that allows action to favor the benefit of the many over the one—the second example is more particular than abstract" (24). The second example, which many ethicists call "Bridge," is not all that particular, since we are told nothing more than that a fat man is standing on the bridge. Is he married? Does he have children? Does he have a job? A home? Is he suicidal? This is why we are suspicious of this kind of "case study." Knapp seems to recognize the lack of particularity, because he asks us to consider the problem in the context of Prince Hal's "sacrifice of Falstaff for the good of England" (24). Though admittedly, "Hal's rejection of Falstaff is a straightforward example of placing the commonwealth above individual interests," Knapp goes on to argue that "this particular fat man is much more compelling than that moral lesson could ever be.... I would argue that the plays raise a more interesting question for a discussion of Shakespearean ethics and morality: why is it that we are unwilling to throw Falstaff off the bridge? Rather than nod in agreement with the newly prudent King Henry we yearn for more of the jovial knight" (24). We would add that Hal, in rejecting Falstaff, actually turns him from an intimate friend into an ambiguous abstract stranger. Hal's rejection is phrased in a way that denies the particularity of Falstaff, including a refusal to even acknowledge his name—"I know thee not"—and substitutes a more abstract identity for it—"old man" (*Henry IV, Part 2*: 5.5.47). He transforms his former friend from a living, breathing, vital human being into a bad dream that he now despises: "I have long dreamt of such a kind of man, / So surfeit-swell'd, so old, and so profane; / But being awak'd, I do despise my dream" (5.5.49–51). Though, as we noted above, there is a little Falstaff in all of us, at this point in the play, there is no Falstaff left in poor Hal: "Presume not that I am the thing I was" (5.5.56).

We suggest that Hal's dismissal of his life with Falstaff as a mere dream could well be an inspiration for Joss Whedon's *Buffy* episode "Normal Again" (6.17), in which both Buffy and the viewers have difficulties in knowing what is reality and what is dream. As we explained in more detail in Chapter Five, in fighting a demon, Buffy is injected with its hallucinogenic venom, and we see her in a psychiatric hospital being held down by interns as she is being injected with a tranquilizer or an anti-psychotic in exactly the same spot that the demon's venom entered. She is told that she has been in the psychiatric hospital for six years and that her life as a vampire slayer in Sunnydale is a delusion. Since this is the sixth season of *Buffy the Vampire Slayer*, viewers are left wondering whether they have been watching a dream or a delusion for the last six years. The episode was upsetting for Buffy and viewers alike. We have argued that Buffy ultimately chooses the Sunnydale reality. But she gets the strength to do this from the psychiatric hospital reality, where her mother says, "Buffy, fight it. You're too good to give in, you can beat this thing. Be strong, baby, ok? I know you're afraid. I know the world feels like a hard place sometimes, but you've got people who love you.... You've got a world of strength in your heart. I know you do. You just have to find it again. Believe in yourself." Buffy uses this strength to fight the demon and save her Sunnydale friends. We have argued elsewhere that "not only does she save her friends, but there is a sense in which her very choice actually creates the friends that she saves, since that is the reality she chooses" (Richardson and Rabb 57). Prince Hal chooses to regard his youth with Falstaff as a mere dream and thus dismisses that part of his life, chooses instead to follow his father's lead in opting for the life of political and military responsibility. Still, as we see in the play *Henry V*, he does bring something from his life with Falstaff when he disguises himself as a commoner and walks among his troops, discussing with them what they think about the impending battle. This is something his father, like most kings in Shakespeare, would never have done because they tend to despise the common touch. So Falstaff did indeed have a positive influence in the end. The connection we find between the *Henry IV* plays and Whedon's "Normal Again" is given some corroboration from the fact that Whedon, as a youth, watched BBC productions of Shakespeare with his English teacher mother and enjoyed reading Shakespeare on his own. It is reported that "the first play that he read was *Henry IV*" (Lavery 2014, 42). Whedon's title, "Normal Again," also applies to Hal's choice of returning from Falstaff and the Boar's Head Tavern to *his* normal aristocratic life as the Prince of Wales, heir to the throne of England. His choice, as is Buffy's, is a moral choice. The moral implications of both, need to be understood in the context of long and complicated stories. Viewing such stories helps members of the audience exercise their own moral imaginations. The life of the imagination expands real life experience through vicarious moral choice. Both Shakespeare and Whedon take us to places inaccessible to us in real life and force us to confront situations, which help us, often by means of metaphor and allegory, to deal with the real choices we are forced to make. This is one reason we have argued that Whedon is the Shakespeare for our time.

Serenity, Whedon's movie extension of the *Firefly* space western narrative, raises Trolley-like questions, though in the more illuminating context of a broader story. Mal and his crew of the firefly-class spaceship, Serenity, steal the payroll of a remote Alliance outpost. This is very much like a bank robbery from a B-western, except that Mal and three of his crew are riding to the bank on a hovercraft instead of on horseback, though they do call the hovercraft "the mule." Once they have broken into the bank vault and are loading the loot onto the hovercraft, they are interrupted by a Reaver attack. Mal's first response is to ask one of the bank guards if the vault opens from the inside. When he is told that it does, he tells the guard, "You get everybody upstairs in there, and you seal it. Long as you got air, you don't open up. Understand?" (Screenplay, in *Serenity: The Official Visual Companion* 65). Mal and his companions, Zoe, Jayne, and River, exit the bank and jump onto the hovercraft followed by a young man who grabs the hovercraft and shouts "Take me with you! ... I can't stay here! Please!" (66). Mal tells him to get in the vault with the others, and tells Zoe to drive, which she does, leaving the young man in the dust. What happens next is important from an ethical standpoint. The screenplay stage directions detail it as follows: "As they move from him, four Reavers jump out of the shadows and grab the young man. Mal unhesitatingly draws his gun.... Mal fires twice. The young man takes both bullets in the chest, slumps down dead" (66). Later, back on Serenity, Mal and Zoe briefly discuss the incident. Mal says: "I had to shoot him. What the Reavers woulda done to him before they killed him..." Zoe interrupts, "I know. That was a piece a' mercy. But before that, him begging us to bring him along...." Mal then interrupts, "We couldn't take the weight. Woulda slowed us down." Zoe asks, "You know that for certain—" Mal responds, "Mule [the hovercraft] won't run with five. I shoulda dumped the girl? Or you? Or Jayne? (considering) Well, Jayne..." Zoe suggests that they might have "tossed the payload." But Mal reminds her that they were hired to do this robbery and that if they cross those who hired them, "there we are back in mortal peril. We get a job, we gotta make good." Zoe responds, "Sir, I don't disagree on any particular point, it's just ... in the time of war, we woulda never left a man stranded." To which Mal says, "Maybe that's why we lost." Zoe is obviously not happy with this reply, but this is where they part company as Mal goes into his own cabin. As the stage directions say, "Once alone, Mal lets his own disappointment show" (77). The entire bank robbery scene and its aftermath let viewers know that Mal is obviously a flawed hero, if hero at all. *Firefly* fans watching the movie will know in more detail what would have happened to the young man had Mal not shot him. In the *Firefly* episode "Serenity," Mal and his crew encounter a Reaver ship. Zoe explains what will happen if the Reavers board them: "If they take the ship, they'll rape us to death, eat our flesh and sew our skins into their clothing and if we're very very lucky, they'll do it in that order." Mal, it seems, had two reasons for shooting, or at least sacrificing, the young man. The first is to save him from an inevitable slow and horrible death at the hands of the Reavers. The second takes us back to the Trolley Problem. The mule, the hovercraft, will not fly with five, so Mal, Zoe, River, and Jayne couldn't take him along. The detailed story in *Serenity* is much more nuanced than any Trolley Problem scenario we have come across, though the basic problem is the same—sacrificing the one to save the many, in this case, the many are the four bank robbers whom we have come to know and love, rather than the five faceless (and possibly deaf) workers maintaining the trolley car tracks. Interestingly enough, we don't know very much about the young man who is sacrificed by Mal. The screenplay simply describes him as a young man. The only other time we meet him is during the robbery when, lying on the floor with the rest of the customers, he slowly starts to reach for his weapon. Zoe, having noticed this move, with the help of River, gently places her sawed-off shotgun against his cheek and asks, "You know what the definition of a hero is? It's someone who gets other people killed. You can look it up later" (63). That is all we know about this young man. He is as abstract and faceless as a solitary worker standing on a siding waiting for some moral philosopher to do him in. Yet Mal has given him every opportunity to save himself from the Reavers, as he has the other people in the bank. He has told them all to hide in the protection of the vault until the nomadic Reavers leave. We know that neither Zoe nor Mal were happy about the shooting of the young man, but there is a sense in which he brought it on himself. He could have joined the others in the vault and chose not to. It is in part that choice that led to his tragic outcome. Of course, one can argue that had Mal and crew not robbed this particular bank, Mal would not have shot this young man. On the other hand, had they not been robbing the bank during the Reaver attack, the vault would not have been open and none of the townspeople would have been saved. Saving the people in the vault is then an unintended consequence of robbing the bank. Can we credit Mal for saving the people in the bank? He didn't force the bank guards to open the vault with the intention of saving anyone. On the other hand, when he learns of the Reaver attack, the first thing he does is to tell the guards to get everyone inside the vault and lock the door, as he has learned that it can be opened from the inside. The people in the vault are likely going to be the only survivors of the Reaver attack in this remote outpost. The more telling question is "Should Mal have shot the young man?" Given our emphasis on narrative ethics, this question cannot really be answered until one has at least seen the entire movie *Serenity*, and perhaps even the short television series *Firefly*. In other words, it is important to have the whole story in order to make an informed judgment. The question—should he have shot the young man—is an important one with ramifications beyond this space western, indeed beyond science fiction. Since Mal shot him to save him from a slow, agonizing death at the hands and jaws of the Reavers, it raises serious questions in medical ethics concerning assisted suicide and other forms of euthanasia.

The classic Trolley Problem was actually first introduced to deal with some recurring questions in medical ethics. It first appears in philosopher Philippa Foot's 1967 *Oxford Review* article, "The Problem of Abortion and the Doctrine of the Double Effect." She introduces examples like the Trolley Problem in order to sidestep questions concerning the rights of the fetus and whether or not the fetus should be considered a person: "[O]ne way of throwing light on the abortion issue will be by setting up parallels involving adults or children once born" (5). The doctrine of double effect has often been used in discussing the abortion issue. For example, is it ever permissible to save the mother's life by terminating the life of the fetus she is carrying? The doctrine of double effect can be invoked in just such cases. As Foot puts it, "by 'the doctrine of double effect' I mean the thesis that it is sometimes permissible to bring about by oblique intention what one may not directly intend.... It is said for instance that the operation of hysterectomy involves the death of the foetus as the foreseen but not strictly or directly intended consequence of the surgeon's act, while other operations kill the child and count as the direct intention of taking an innocent life" (6). According to the doctrine of double effect, then, you can save the mother's life by performing a hysterectomy, which, incidentally, kills the fetus, but not by performing a craniotomy, since crushing the skull would be directly killing the fetus. In the case of the craniotomy, sometimes "it is said we may not operate but let the mother die. We foresee her death but do not directly intend it, whereas to crush the skull of the child would count as direct intention of its death" (6). In the case of the hysterectomy, we save the life of the mother; in the second case both mother and child are allowed to die. Foot finds this unacceptable. To explain why, she introduces examples like the Trolley Problem, which do not involve a fetus, though still examining the difference between killing and allowing to die.

Her version of the Trolley Problem does not really capture the distinction between direct killing and allowing to die. She has a tram driver hurtling down the tracks and discovering that his brakes have failed but there are those five workmen on the track ahead. The trolley driver can steer his tram onto a siding on which is waiting the other, solitary, workman. Should the driver, must the driver, switch the trolley onto the siding thus killing one rather than five? The principle here is that killing five is worse than killing one. In this case, if the driver does not steer the trolley onto the siding, he will be actively driving the trolley over the five. He will be killing five rather than one. Foot admits that most people would agree that the driver should switch to the siding, even though he foresees that doing so will result in the unintended death of the one. She contrasts this example with one in which "a judge or magistrate is faced with rioters demanding that a culprit be found for a certain crime and threatening otherwise to take their own bloody revenge on a particular section of the community. The real culprit being unknown, the judge sees himself as able to prevent the bloodshed only by framing some innocent person and having him executed" (8). To make the example as close to the Trolley Problem as possible, she supposes that the rioters have five hostages "so that in both the exchange is supposed to be one man's life for the lives of five" (8). This example involves the corruption of the justice system, and this in itself would be enough for the judge to refuse to convict an innocent man regardless of the negative consequences. To avoid the (distracting) appeal to the integrity of the justice system, she imagines "that some private individual is to kill an innocent person and pass him off as the criminal" (8). She still finds this horrifying. It is one thing to foresee the death of the one, but something else again to deliberately cause that death as part of some other plan no matter what the believed benefit. It is for similar reasons that a medical doctor may not kill one healthy patient in order to harvest organs to save five other patients. If that were the common practice no one would have faith in the health care system. But this is not like killing the fetus in order to save the mother in a case where doing nothing is sure to result in the death of both mother and fetus. Foot is concerned that some ethicists would actually permit this to happen because they believe that abortion is wrong, even though the death of mother and fetus would be the unfortunate foreseen result. This is why Foot is critiquing the doctrine of double effect.

To show what is wrong with allowing both mother and fetus to die using the doctrine of double effect, Foot introduces yet another example not unlike the trolley problem. Here though no trolleys are involved. Rather a group of spelunkers led by a fat man are trapped in a cave because their large leader got stuck in the only entrance as he presumably tried to back out. As Foot explains, "Obviously the right thing to do is to sit down and wait until the fat man grows thin; but philosophers have arranged that flood waters should be rising within the cave. Luckily (luckily?) the trapped party have with them a stick of dynamite with which they can blast the fat man out of the mouth of the cave. Either they use the dynamite or they drown" (7). If they don't use the dynamite they will all drown including the fat man. At this point the poor fat man is probably thinking that, instead of going spelunking with this bunch, how much safer it would be to stand on a bridge watching trolleys pass by on the tracks below. Foot introduces the spelunkers example, though she calls them "potholers," in order to show, in her words, "how ridiculous" a possible version of the doctrine of double effect would look. "[S]uppose that the trapped explorers were to argue that the death of the fat man might be taken as a merely foreseen consequence of the act of blowing him up. ('We didn't want to kill him ... only to blast him out of the mouth of the cave.') ... [T]hose who use the doctrine of double effect would rightly reject such a suggestion, though they will, of course, have considerable difficulty in explaining ... the criterion of 'closeness' if we say that anything very close to what we are literally aiming at counts as if part of our aim" (7). Foot ultimately concludes, in the case of abortion, that it would be wrong to allow both mother and child to die if it is possible save the mother by aborting the fetus. She says: "This is parallel to the case of the fat man in the mouth of the cave who is bound to be drowned with the others if nothing is done. Given the certainty of the outcome, as it was postulated, there is no serious conflict of interests here, since the fat man will perish in either case, and it is reasonable that the action that will save someone should be done" (14). Since this is exactly parallel to the abortion case, it follows that the mother's life should be saved by killing the fetus. Foot explains: "Moreover we would be justified in performing the operation whatever the method used [hysterectomy or craniotomy], and it is neither a necessary nor a good justification of the special case of hysterectomy that the child's death is not directly intended, being rather a foreseen consequence of what is done" (14). Foot goes on to ask the rhetorical question: "what difference could it make as to how the death is brought about?" (14).

We find it interesting that despite Foot's rejection of the doctrine of double effect this doctrine is used, citing Foot herself, by Arno Bogaerts in his contribution to *The Avengers and Philosophy: Earth's Mightiest Thinkers*. In applying the doctrine of double effect to *The Avengers*, he gives a nice, easy to understand, definition of the doctrine: "Simply put, the doctrine of double effect states that it is sometimes morally permissible to promote a good end even if—unintentionally but foreseeably—serious harm will result from it. It is not, however, permissible to cause the same harm intentionally" (159). He goes on to argue that "for the doctrine of double effect to be accepted and work effectively there has to be proportionality between bad effects (the means) and good effects (the ends)" (160). It seems that whenever superheroes, like the Avengers, attempt to intervene and prevent some evil from happening, the consequences are often worse than the evil they were attempting to avert. As Bogaerts puts it: "It really does seem that any time a superhero tries to be proactive, it comes back to bite him on the Asgard, almost as if the genre itself is preventing proactive superheroing" (161). Drawing on the classic distinction between negative and positive duties, which, incidentally, Foot also uses, Bogaerts argues that "violating a negative duty (by acting to kill someone, for instance) is often considered worse than violating a positive duty (by not acting to save someone in danger)" (164). From this he concludes that in the real world "negative duties almost always seem to be morally stronger than are positive ones" (164). This is not the case in the world of superheroes: "For superheroes, however, positive duties seem to be more important than negative duties" (164). He argues that "whenever superheroes act too much on their positive duty to help the world around them, they become proactive. And ... this inevitably sets them on a slippery slope toward, in essence, supervillainy" (164). Stan Lee's character Loki, adoptive brother of Thor, comes to mind. By the time we meet him in Whedon's *The Avengers* he is already a supervillain, attempting to conquer and rule the earth. Bogaerts doesn't refer to Whedon's *The Avengers*, basing his argument on the pre–Whedon Avengers narratives. Rather than looking at the pre–Whedon narratives, we will draw on an episode of Whedon's *Agents of S.H.I.E.L.D.*, since S.H.I.E.L.D. is itself a proactive agency. After all, Bogaerts' article is entitled "The Avengers and S.H.I.E.L.D.: The Problem with Proactive Superheronics."

The S.H.I.E.L.D. episode "The Asset" (1.3) actually raises Trolley-like problems, though in the much more nuanced environment of a fully developed story. It appears that Canadian physicist, Dr. Franklin Hall, has been kidnapped. Phil Coulson and his agents of S.H.I.E.L.D. are assigned to rescue him, since Hall is a "priority red protected asset." They learn that the abductor is wealthy businessman, Ian Quinn, who is a well-known philanthropist. He is also known to have created his wealth by exploiting the world's resources. In fact, it was gold ingots from one of his mines used to pay a local for the use of a front-loader found at the scene of the crime, which led S.H.I.E.L.D. to him. Quinn has a large estate in Malta, which is likely where he has taken Dr. Hall. S.H.I.E.L.D. also learns that Hall and Quinn studied together at university and were searching for a new element called gravitonium. They suspect that a small device found at the scene of the abduction in Colorado might actually be using this element, since it seems to be able to distort gravitational fields. This device, a sphere of only 2.5 cm. diameter, seems to have been responsible for lifting a semi-trailer containing Dr. Hall off the road. As a priority red protected asset, he was being secretly transported in the semi to a new location. We later learn that Dr. Hall himself had leaked the route to Quinn, suspecting that Quinn will use the information, as he did, to abduct him. Hall, it turns out, suspects that Quinn has discovered a source of gravitonium and is building a gravity generator, which would, among other things, revolutionize the transportation industry, immobilize the military, and in essence allow Quinn to take over the world. However, Hall knows that such a device would actually be extremely unstable and endanger millions of lives. Without informing S.H.I.E.L.D., he has set out to destroy this device, as it is much too dangerous and much too powerful to be in the hands of a villain like Quinn, or even in those of S.H.I.E.L.D. itself. Coulson and S.H.I.E.L.D. cannot attempt a full-blown rescue assault into Malta without creating an international incident. Quinn is hosting a world-wide annual shareholders meeting at his estate, and Skye, a S.H.I.E.L.D. apprentice, has used her superior computer hacking skills to get herself an invitation, well actually an e-vite. S.H.I.E.L.D. does need a "man" on the inside in order to disable the security perimeter and allow a couple of agents covertly to slip in to rescue Hall and, of course, retrieve Skye. We have described part of Skye's story arc in Chapter Seven and need not repeat details here. The *S.H.I.E.L.D.* episodes need to be seen in their entirety to get the full nuance of the story. Here it is enough to say that Coulson is able to break into Quinn's underground laboratory where he finds Dr. Hall powering up a large gravity generator, having, Coulson estimates, a 12-foot diameter. This is very much larger than the one they found at the scene of the abduction, which S.H.I.E.L.D. techies had described as being only 2.5 cm. in diameter. It is therefore much more dangerous, which is why Hall, it turns out, is attempting to cause it to destroy itself. The confrontation between Hall and Coulson is quite amusing, as the gravity generator distorts gravity, and Hall and Coulson find themselves standing on the ceiling, while all the furniture and lab equipment comes crashing "down" around them. We see the gravity generator protected by a large glass panel, spinning away like a huge distorted gyroscope. Hall tells Coulson that he "can't let anyone have control of this," that it is too dangerous. He means to deprive both Quinn and S.H.I.E.L.D. of this technology. He would rather let it destroy itself and the entire compound. Coulson tells him that he should have told S.H.I.E.L.D.

what he was doing, that they could have helped. But Hall believes that neither Quinn nor S.H.I.E.L.D. are capable of handling this technology. Both experiment without thought of consequences. Concerning S.H.I.E.L.D., Hall reminds Coulson: "Your search for an ultimate power source brought an alien invasion." This single sentence is an amusing, concise plot summary of Whedon's *The Avengers*. Coulson's response is even more amusing. He says: "Fair point." While both of them are fighting, Coulson is able to cut the power line to the gravity generator, but this has no effect as the machine goes right on spinning. This he tells his tech people with whom he is in constant communication. They inform him that he needs a catalyst in the center of the machine to stop the action of the gravitonium. Coulson has been pleading with Hall to stop the machine telling him that he is killing innocent people, to which Hall replies that he is saving millions. Coulson actually says, "I have good people here," which we regard as making the deaths particular. One of his people is, after all, Skye, who, it turns out, is very important to S.H.I.E.L.D. They believe she has special powers. We suspect that she may even be of Asgardian or other alien descent, at least partially. From a moral point of view, Hall's response to Coulson here is important: "We have to live with the choices we make, and sometimes we have to die with them too." So Hall is willing to die to prevent this dangerous technology from falling into anyone's hands. Coulson responds: "I understand. You made a hard call—now I have to make mine." He then fires several rounds at the window protecting the gravity generator. The glass shatters. Hall is sucked into the machine, becoming the catalyst, which brings things to a halt. We see his body becoming part of the gravitonium in an incredible spinning light display at the center of the machine. What is interesting from a moral point of view is that Coulson intends that Hall be sucked into machine. Coulson is shown as deliberately grabbing on to something to prevent being sucked into the machine himself as soon as the glass shatters. In a sense, Coulson is sacrificing one person to save those at Quinn's compound in Malta, including his agents and himself. Dr. Hall was destroying this machine in order to save millions. A foreseen consequence, of course, is that the compound and all persons present would also be destroyed along with the machine as it swallows itself and everything around it.

In the conclusion of the episode, we see Coulson in videoconference with a S.H.I.E.L.D. agent, telling him that he wants "it at the deepest level of the fridge." We eventually figure out that he is having the gravity generator put away in an unmarked vault. It is to be unlisted and no access is to be permitted. Coulson allows that this is "what Hall would have wanted." Fans of Marvel comics may suspect that Dr. Franklin Hall will return as the supervillain Graviton, his molecules having combined with the gravitonium. There is, however, no hint of any such regeneration at this point in Whedon's *Agents of S.H.I.E.L.D.*

In comparing this kind of complex story with the merely schematic ones that are found in philosophical discussions like the Trolley Problem, we believe that the more nuanced, detailed story is a closer approximation to the difficulties faced in real life situations, where ethics cannot be reduced to arithmetic, where five is not always greater than one. The Trolley Problem has become so popular that entire books have been written on the subject (see, for example, Cathcart 2013, Edmonds 2014). The trouble is that such discussions usually end up trying to decide what moral principle is at play in making the decision, as if principles tell us what to do. We have been arguing for a narrative ethics in which the moral imagination plays a greater part in ethical decisions than do moral principles. As one recent book on the Trolley Problem puts it, "Regardless of what we say our reasons are, most of us are going to judge this case by how it strikes us emotionally. And our emotional response is going to be pretty much determined by the kind of story we each tell ourselves about this case" (Cathcart 114). This kind of criticism of a principlist approach to the Trolley Problem is in essence saying, "that we are all trying to sort out who it's OK to kill or allow to die, without any information at all about who these people are. What novelists try to do is try to imagine the particulars of a situation" (Cathcart 112). Thomas Cathcart, in his amusing book, *The Trolley Problem or Would You Throw the Fat Guy Off the Bridge?*, though somewhat sympathetic to the narrative approach, does wonder just how much particular information is needed before one is in a position to make a responsible choice. He asks, for example, "Wouldn't doctors be reluctant to save the life of *anybody* for fear they might turn out to be a serial killer?" (114 emphasis in original). How much information we need before we are forced to make a decision, or feel justified in acting, can itself be an ethical choice. It is not another arithmetical problem. Cathcart, himself, attempts to put the Trolley Problem in more of a story form by imagining the trial of someone accused of homicide by diverting a trolley. Still, after all the presentations by prosecution and defense, Cathcart concludes "With apologies to Yogi Berra: When your trolley comes to a fork in the track, take it. *And* be able to say why you did" (124 emphasis in original).

The trouble with most discussions of the Trolley Problem is that they take a principlist, as opposed to a narrative, approach and are more concerned about finding a moral principle that will tell us what to do in such situations; e.g., killing five is worse than killing one. Such principles are rarely all that helpful in that they must be revised as philosophers imagine more details; e.g., innocent bystander by a railway switch, fat man on a bridge. Derek Parfit, for example, tests out the following complicated principle: "It is wrong to impose harm on someone as a means of achieving some aim, unless (1) there is no better way to achieve this aim, and (2) given the goodness of this aim, the harm we impose is not disproportionate, or too great" (Vol. I, 229). The latter qualification invokes the proportionality provision discussed above. Parfit is not really happy with this principle. It doesn't tell us "which harms would be too great. We would have to use our own judgment here" (Vol. I, 229). He criticizes Judith Jarvis Thomson's claim, in her 1985 *Yale Law Journal* paper, "The Trolley Problem," that "it would be wrong to kill or seriously injure one innocent person, however many other people's lives we could thereby save" (Vol. I, 229). Thomson is arguing that people have a right to life, indeed a right not to be interfered with by, for example, being pushed off a bridge. Thomson defends the principle that rights trump utility (Thomson 1985, 1395). Parfit admits: "Most of us would accept a less extreme view. We would believe it to be right to kill one innocent person if that were the only way in which we could prevent some nuclear explosion that would kill as many a million other people. But we may believe it to be wrong to kill one person as a means of saving only five, or only fifty other people. There would be cases in between in which this question would have no clear or determinate answer" (Vol. I, 229). We are reminded of Jasmine's claim in Whedon's *Angel* television series, "I murdered thousands to save billions" ("Peace Out" 4.21).

Judith Jarvis Thomson, incidentally, is responsible for introducing two of the most famous Trolley Problem scenarios: the innocent bystander who might throw a switch (1397), often called Bystander, and the fat man on the bridge (1409), which, as we have said, is usually referred to as Bridge. Parfit's own version of Bridge does not involve a fat man. Instead, he puts himself in the picture. "I am on a bridge above the track. Your only way to save the five would be to open, by remote control, the trap-door on which I am standing, so that I would fall in front of the train, thereby triggering its automatic brake" (Vol. I, 216). Parfit's version does have an unforeseen benefit. It does show that the reluctance to push the fat man off the bridge is not, as some have argued, because there is "a universal moral instinct (do not kill people with your bare hands)" (Knapp 23–24). As we noted above Knapp argues that "the man's particularity alters the ethical situation ... he is not simply a man but a 'fat man'" (24). We know of course that Knapp spells out the particularity in much more detail through his discussion of Shakespeare's Falstaff. Parfit makes things pretty particular by putting himself on the bridge in place of the fat man. The remote controlled trap door also avoids the messiness of pushing him off with your bare hands. Still, people are reluctant to try to save the five men down the track by dropping Parfit to his death, by opening the trap door on which he is standing. Does our reluctance, here, have something to do with treating Parfit as a means to stopping the tram? If so we would be appealing to something like a version Kant's supreme principle of morality which we discussed in the last chapter as the "Formula of Humanity as an End in Itself (FHE) '*So act that you use humanity, whether in your own person or in the person of any other, always at the same time as an end, never merely as a means'"* (cited in Stroud 2003, 186, emphasis in original). Parfit doesn't think so. He argues, "the wrongness of our acts never or hardly ever depends on whether we are treating people merely as a means" (Vol. I, 232). In order to understand what is meant by "treating people merely as a means" he examines both a narrow and a wider sense of the phrase. In the strict or narrow sense "we kill someone as a means only when this person's death is an essential part of what achieves our aim" (Vol. I, 219). Macbeth, for example murders Duncan in order to become King of Scotland. As long as Duncan lives, Macbeth cannot become king. Duncan's death is therefore an essential part of what achieves Macbeth's aim. We examined *Macbeth* in some detail in Chapter Six, "The Moral Imagination in Shakespeare," showing how Shakespeare captures the internal struggles Macbeth has with this plan to become king, and the tragedy that results from attempting to carry it out. No reference to 18th-century moral principles is required to show what is morally wrong with Macbeth's behavior. We see Macbeth asking himself what kind of subject would he be if he murders his king? What kind of kinsman would he be? Since Duncan is his guest, what kind of host would he be? We see him reason that to kill the king to become king is self-contradictory for "when anyone may kill the king, there can be no king (as when one kills one's kin, kinship crumbles)" (see Keller 45). This is captured in Macbeth's famous lines "We but teach / Bloody instructions, which, being taught, return / To plague th'inventor. This even-handed justice / Commends th'ingredience of our poison'd chalice / To our own lips" (1.7.8–12). His whole body physically rebels at the very idea, as does that of lady Macbeth. Yet she persuades him to go ahead. What follows is a series of other "necessary" murders, the decline and death of Lady Macbeth, likely at her own hand, and ultimately the death of Macbeth himself. As his severed head is carried out on stage the audience is left in no doubt that Macbeth took a wrong turn in his journey of life. Moral principles such as Kant's FHE about never treating people as mere means are hardly needed here, and would add nothing to the moral judgment toward which Shakespeare has guided his audience. If anything, Shakespeare's Scottish Tragedy provides some particular content to such abstract principles.

With Macbeth we have been discussing the strict or narrow sense of "merely as a means." Parfit prefers a wider sense. "In a wider sense ... we kill or injure someone as a means when we act in some way that involves and foreseeably kills or injures this person as a means of achieving some aim" (Vol. I, 219). Parfit explains, "in *Bridge*, you would not really be *killing* me as a means of saving the five. You would be merely using my body as a means of stopping the train, and you would be delighted if I survived" (Vol. I, 219, emphasis in original). Macbeth would not be delighted if Duncan survived. It is in the wider sense of being used as a means that Parfit thinks he could rationally agree to be used as a means to saving the lives of five strangers. If this is so, and since it is obvious that the five strangers could also rationally agree, dropping Parfit to his death through the trap door on the bridge would not be wrong. Here Parfit is appealing to another version of Kant's categorical imperative which we discussed in Chapter Eight: The Formula of Universal Law (FUL), *"act only in accordance with that maxim through which you can at the same time will that it should become a universal law"* (cited in Stroud 2003, 186, emphasis in original). We have quoted the version we used in Chapter Eight rather than that used by Parfit, as readers are already familiar with it. Nothing hangs on this because Parfit actually revises Kant's categorical imperative, distilling it to what he calls the Consent Principle: "It is wrong to treat anyone in any way to which this person could not rationally consent" (Vol. I, 181). In so far as his Bridge example is concerned, Parfit considers the following argument sound: "Since your treatment of me would be governed by the Consent Principle, you would be neither be treating me merely as a means, nor close to doing that, so no version of the Mere Means Principle would condemn your act" (Vol. I, 221). Upon further reflection, he admits that killing him as a means of saving five strangers intuitively *seems* wrong. However, he argues, "this intuition is not ... strong.... If we were choosing the principles that, in such non-medical emergencies, everyone would follow, we would have more reason, I believe, to choose principles that would require you to save the five. Though I am still inclined to believe that it would be wrong for you to kill me as a means, this intuition is not strong enough to convince me that we ought to reject the Kantian Formula" (Vol. II, 154). He seems to be using practical reason to counter an intuitive belief. While some of our former beliefs have, historically, proven to be wrong, the acceptance of slavery for example, Parfit here seems to be being hyper-rational. He cites with approval Victorian moral philosopher Henry Sidgwick (1838–1900): "I believe in Sidgwick's words, 'the real progress of ethical science ... would be benefited by an application to it of the same disinterested curiosity to which we chiefly owe the great discoveries of physics'" (Parfit Vol. II, 153). A disinterested curiosity is hardly appropriate when your life is on the line. Yet that seems to be exactly what Parfit is calling on when he concludes: "this intuition is not strong enough to convince me that we ought to reject the Kantian Formula" (Vol. II, 154). He does admit that, "there might be other cases in which this moral theory conflicts more strongly with our moral intuitions. If that were true, we might justifiably reject this theory" (Vol. II, 154). If he is willing to reconsider or reject rules and principles which conflict strongly with our moral intuitions, then we have difficulty in seeing just how moral principles help us decide difficult cases in which our moral intuitions sometimes conflict.

As we have seen in the previous chapter, Parfit presents us with a supreme principle of morality which, he argues, reconciles Kantians, Contractualists, and Consequentialists: "An act is wrong just when such acts are disallowed by some principle that is optimific, uniquely universally willable, and not reasonably rejectable" (Vol. I, 413). His discussion of the merely means principle (FHE) we see as just clearing the way for this version of the supreme principle of morality. Interestingly enough, under questioning he admits: "If there is no single supreme principle, that ... would not be a tragedy. But [he adds] it *would* be a tragedy if there was no *single true morality*. And conflicting moralities could not all be true" (Vol. II, 155, emphasis in the original). He allows that in attempting to bring together Kantians, Contractualists, and Consequentialists his "main aim was not to find a supreme principle, but to find out whether we can resolve some deep disagreements.... [I]f we cannot resolve our disagreements, that would give us reasons to doubt that there are *any* true principles" (Vol. II, 155, emphasis in the original). Parfit's darkest fear is that if there were no true moral principles then there "might be nothing that morality *turns out to be,* since morality might be an illusion" (Vol. II, 155, emphasis in the original).

As we indicated at the beginning of this chapter, throughout this book we have argued that morality turns out to be for the most part imaginative and metaphorical rather than literal. Its logic is drawn from the embodied source domain of the metaphor and is in actual fact based more on *narrative* and *imagination* than on any kind of disembodied abstract reason. Like Kantian ethics, indeed like most 17th- and 18th-century ethical theories and those derived from them, the conceptual structure of Parfit's position "is actually Strict Father family morality ... with Reason playing the role of the Strict Father, and ... universalized to all human beings via the Family of Man metaphor" (Lakoff and Johnson 1999, 416–417). We are arguing that our moral thinking is driven more by myths and metaphors than by reason and principles. This does not mean, as Parfit fears, that morality turns out to be an illusion— far from it. Metaphor can and does reveal truth.

Given, as we argued in Chapter Two, that "there is no ethical system that is not metaphorical" (Lakoff and Johnson 1999, 325). And given that all such "metaphors are grounded in the nature of our bodies and social interactions" it follows that "they are thus anything but arbitrary and unconstrained" (Lakoff and Johnson 1999, 290). As Mary Thomas Crane concludes, based of Lakoff and Johnson's application of second generation cognitive science, such meaning is "anchored ... by a three-way tether: brain, culture, discourse" (24). We need not fear that morality is an illusion. We have argued that in all his work, in all his stories, Whedon's "perspective on good and evil is not a relativistic one in which the categories of good and evil are constantly redefined based on current circumstances, but neither is it an absolute one in which good and evil are always clearly defined" (Stevenson 73). With respect to Shakespearean tragedy, following Martha Nussbaum we have argued: "A whole tragic drama, unlike a schematic philosophical example making use of a similar story, is capable of tracing the history of a complex pattern of deliberation, showing its roots in a way of life ... [a]s it ... lays open to view the complexity, the indeterminacy, the sheer difficulty of actual human deliberation" (Nussbaum 14). Neither Shakespeare nor Whedon lead us to anything like ethical relativism in which morality might well be an illusion. But, it is important to understand that the opposite of ethical relativism is not ethical absolutism; rather, the opposite of ethical relativism is, unrelativism as Whedon, someone who writes metaphorically of vampires, the undead, might put it.

We hope we have shown that there are good grounds for distrusting schematic philosophical examples like the Trolley Problem. We are in actual fact convinced that the Trolley Problem has taken moral philosophy down the wrong track. Discussion of the Trolley Problem has become so pervasive in recent years that some discussants are now calling themselves trolleyologists (Cathcart 1, Edmonds 10). We are not sure that a couple of self-declared Buffyologists like ourselves are really in any position to make fun of trolleyology. Still the suffix of both terms is "logos" the Greek term for "word" or, more generally, talk. So trolleyology is talk about trolleys, and Buffyology is talk about Buffy or *Buffy.* In defending narrative ethics, our position is that we will learn more about moral thought by talking about *Buffy* than we will by talking about trolleys. We admit that Derek Parfit has displayed a good deal of moral imagination in this discussion of the Trolley Problem with his take on what he calls *Bridge*, for example. He has displayed his towering intellect and imagination as well in his earlier work *Reasons and Persons* (1986) in which he even draws upon short science fiction scenarios. If his towering intellect had only been directed toward writing imaginative literature, science fiction and fantasy say, what a contribution he might have made to moral thought, to the revitalization of moral philosophy! We would counter Parfit's Bridge with Shakespeare's Falstaff, or even Whedon's Jasmine. By "Shakespeare's Falstaff" we mean, of course the story of this character in *1 and 2 Henry IV,* the account of his death and influence in *Henry V,* and even the Falstaff of *The Merry Wives of Windsor.* By "Whedon's Jasmine," of course we mean Jasmine's story arc in Whedon's television series *Angel.* It would have to include at least part of the story arc of Angel's son Connor and his partner Cordelia since they are, in some sense, the parents of this dubious goddess. This was, however, no virgin birth. The *Angel* series itself has to be understood in the context of *Buffy the Vampire Slayer* since it is in essence a spin off from that show. Or to speak in the narrative context, Angel moved from Sunnydale to Los Angeles to avoid losing his soul, again. Metaphors abound!

Our reference to Falstaff and Jasmine, then, is meant more broadly to refer to the works of William Shakespeare and Joss Whedon, and even more generally to imaginative literature as a whole. We have used Shakespeare and Whedon as particular illustrations of narrative ethics. Of course, we are not suggesting that when faced with a difficult moral choice we should read the entire works of Shakespeare or binge-watch seven seasons of *Buffy*, five seasons of *Angel*, and other works of Joss Whedon. However, we have argued, people familiar with Shakespeare and Whedon are in a better position to think through ethical quandaries and to make responsible moral choices. This is no different than having more lived experience, which is why wisdom is usually associated with age. Literature helps us to exercise the moral imagination, and, as we have shown, moral judgment depends more on the moral imagination than on the principles of practical reason. As Tony Adams in his 2008 "Review of Narrative Ethics," explains: "If stories remain riddled with ideas about how to live well ... we must critically evaluate these stories.... But we must not approach stories with a prescription or typology for analysis.... Every situation is different and a preformed set of principles runs the risk of doing violence to a story and its author" (Adams 179).

Some argue that the major difficulty with narrative ethics is in deciding which stories or texts to rely upon and how best to read them. We have argued that both Whedon and Shakespeare tend toward a communitarian (post)–Christian love ethics. However, what is to prevent someone who leans more toward an anti-communitarian, individualist ethics of egoism from recommending the works of Ayn Rand, for example? Rand is a good counterpoise to Whedon since her two major novels, *The Fountainhead* and *Atlas Shrugged*, have been made into movies designed to promote her ethos and her philosophy of Objectivism. One of her major characters, Howard Roark in *The Fountainhead*, proclaims, "The world is perishing from an orgy of self-sacrifice" (Rand 1993, 684). Whedon, as we have seen, looks positively on self-sacrifice. His heroes see it as a virtue. They feel a deep responsibility for other people. What grounds do we have for following Whedon rather than Rand? We read the story arc of *Firefly/Serenity*'s Jayne Cobb, as well as that of Faith, the Slayer who goes bad, as narrative answers to this difficult question. Jayne certainly lives by the "virtue of selfishness," as does the unreformed Faith, who explains to Buffy that "life for a Slayer is very simple: want, take, have" ("Bad Girls" 3.14). Jayne is originally recruited by Mal when Mal bribes him to turn on his former employer, who happens to have the drop on Mal and his crew at the time. Jayne is happy to accept a bigger cut of the payoff and his own bunk ("Out of Gas" 1.5). Jayne is certainly out for himself. In another episode, Mal asks Jayne why he didn't turn on them, and Jayne replies: "Money wasn't good enough." Mal asks "What happens when it is?" They both agree that that will be an "interesting" day ("Serenity" 53). The "interesting day" doesn't happen until the graphic narrative continuation *Serenity: Leaves on the Wind*, where, in Part 1, Jayne is offered a briefcase full of money to help someone called Bea find the fugitive Mal and his crew, now in hiding because they have been branded by the Alliance as traitors as well as thieves. Upon seeing the cash, Jayne responds: "Well, what are we waitin' for?" Fortunately, Bea and her group are not part of the Alliance. They call themselves the New Resistance, and want Mal to join their cause (Part 2).

In spite of his selfishness, in the *Firefly* episode "Jaynestown," Jayne is held up as the "hero of Canton" with a statue erected in his honor. Ironically enough, he and a partner called Stitch on an earlier visit to Canton had attempted a robbery. Things went wrong, Stitch got left behind to be arrested; and Jayne dropped the money from his ship while attempting to flee. The workers in this mining community misinterpreted the event and thought that Jayne had stolen the money from their overlords and was distributing it, Robin Hood style, to the workers as it rained down upon them. In addition to erecting a statue of their hero, Jayne, they even have a song celebrating him and his exploits. In the graphic narrative continuation, *Serenity: Leaves on the Wind*, Jayne proudly tells Bea: "There's some worlds where I'm revered as a hero." To which Bea replies: "Same worlds where siblings marry, I'm guessing" (Part 2). This suggests that Bea has the proper measure of the man. In "Jaynestown," when Mal and his crew, including Jayne himself, visit Canton, Jayne's old partner Stitch confronts him with a shotgun. One of the inhabitants, who reveres Jayne as a hero, throws himself in front of Jayne, taking the full impact of the shotgun blast. He saves Jayne's life but dies in the process. Jayne cannot understand this kind of self-sacrifice for another person. He says over and over, "Don't make no sense." Yet he also wonders, "Don't know why that eats at me so..." (32). He seems not yet to understand why rational self-interest ought not to be a guide to action, though his body seems to be telling him something his mind is not yet able to process. Jayne exhibits further progress in the episode "Ariel" after he has attempted to collect a reward for turning Simon and River Tam over to the Alliance. Mal is furious with him and seems willing to have him sucked out of an open airlock as they are taking off. Jayne, facing death, does not want to be remembered badly and pleads with Mal not to tell the Tams that it was he who had betrayed them. That Mal at least sees this as progress is shown by the fact that he closes the airlock and doesn't leave Jayne to die. We discuss this episode in more detail in Chapter Two, as well as briefly in Chapter Eight. Jayne also shows some moral progress when he agrees to the risky venture to the planet Miranda, which requires sneaking through the main Reaver fleet. Mal had given all members of his crew the opportunity to safely stay behind. Though Jayne has nothing to gain from this expedition, he joins his colleagues at some considerable risk to himself. The fact that this is seen as progress, no matter how minimal, suggests that the Jayne story arc is at least in part a narrative argument against the "virtue of selfishness." Jayne is really a parody of Rand's egoistic heroes.

The fact that Faith does not like who she finds herself becoming and, like Lady Macbeth, attempts suicide (see Chapter Four), suggests that her story arc is also a narrative argument against radical individualism. As Karl Schudt puts it, in "Also Sprach Faith: The Problem of the Happy Rogue Vampire Slayer," Faith finally comes to recognize a basic moral truth: "She has strength and the means to defend the defenseless, and therefore has the duty to do so." He concludes: "Furthermore, she must save the people because the sort of person she will be if she doesn't is unacceptable" (32).

Our reading of Whedon here is corroborated by Russell W. Dalton's treatment of Whedonesque heroes in his essay, "To Assemble or to Shrug? Power, Responsibility and Sacrifice in *Marvel's The Avengers*." Dalton compares "Whedon's approach to power in *The Avengers* with those found in the fictional work of ... Marvel Comics legend Stan Lee and novelist and philosopher Ayn Rand" (165). Noting that Whedon acknowledges his childhood reading of Marvel comics as one of many influences on his thought, Dalton argues: "Much of Whedon's work has been devoted to exploring the proper and improper use of extraordinary power, and Lee's work serves as a likely influence upon Whedon's perspective on that theme" (167). For both Lee and Whedon, "power carries with it the burden and responsibility of service and compassion to others" (167). This brings to mind the famous Spiderman slogan: "With great power there must also come ... great responsibility" (Dalton 172). Dalton quite rightly notes that these are "perhaps the most well-known words that Lee ever wrote" (172). He makes it quite clear that the responsibility is to others.

Citing Rand's "non-fiction" writings such as *The Virtue of Selfishness: A New Concept of Egoism*, Dalton captures her egoistic beliefs with the principle "people should act in their own rational self-interest and not for the sake of others" (Dalton 167). Dalton misses the point that in her fictional works, Rand turns out to be a kind of closet principlist, as she herself freely admits: "[w]ithout an understanding and statement of the right philosophical principle, I cannot create the right story" (quoted in Peikoff 1996, 6). It is narrative not "philosophical principle" that drives most literary artists. As we have shown in the previous chapters, the approach of both Shakespeare and Whedon is to develop characters, put them into difficult situations, and see how they react. This is how most great writers proceed. Their characters sometimes surprise even their authors. The transformative nature of narrative, which we discussed in Chapter Five, can sometimes affect the characters themselves. Billionaire playboy, Tony Stark, alias Iron Man (played by Robert Downey, Jr.)

is a case in point. As Dalton points out, Whedon inherited this character from Stan Lee and the Marvel franchise. In Whedon's *The Avengers* we see Tony Stark's character changing as he attempts to work with the other superheroes—Captain America, Thor, the Hulk, and so forth. At the beginning of the movie Stark appears as totally self-centered, having just completed building Stark Towers as a monument to his massive ego. As his name "STARK" lights up in large bold letters at the top of the building, he is asked how it looks and replies, "Like Christmas, only more ... me" (quoted in Dalton 172). Captain America, played by Chris Evans, true to his character, attempts to take Stark down a peg by telling him: "The only thing you really fight for is yourself. You aren't the guy to make the sacrifice play ... you should stop pretending to be a hero" (quoted in Dalton 173). As Dalton quite rightly points out, though Stark is dismissive, Captain America has clearly had an effect on him. By the time Loki, played by Tom Hiddleston, has taken over Stark Towers, and stands atop the building, looking down on the city demanding the inhabitants pay homage to him, Stark, as Dalton points out, "has an epiphany and it stops him short. He recognizes that he and Loki are not that different" (173). At this point, both Stark and Loki are parodies of Ayn Rand's ideal. As Dalton observes, "At the film's climax, Stark does make the sacrifice play. He is willing to die to save others. By the end of the film, we see that Stark is a changed man and is changing the tower's name.... Stark no longer needs his name up in lights. He is no longer using his power and privilege to build a monument to his ego but instead to build headquarters where he can work with others for the sake of others" (173).

We are arguing that this story arc, the Stark arc, along with those of Jayne and Faith, can be read as narrative arguments against Ayn Rand's ideal of rational egoism. In both Whedon and Shakespeare, the most egoistic characters turn out to be the most villainous, or at least victims of their own poor choices, though some, obviously, are given the chance to reform. Ultimately, readers themselves must choose between narratives. Given the transformative nature of narrative, this is an important choice, since it may well be choosing what kind of person, or monster, one is willing to become. It should be noted that principlists like Derek Parfit argue that "Rational Egoism is best regarded, not as a moral view, but as an external rival to morality" (vol. 1, 166). This leaves us with the question: "Why be moral?" Such questions can only be answered through story, through narrative ethics, using the moral imagination rather than moral principles.

We hope that our study of Shakespeare and Whedon with its emphasis on the moral imagination will contribute to the narrative turn in ethical theory across a wide variety of disciplines from the health and environmental sciences, through research ethics, to the discipline of moral philosophy itself.

Adams, Michael. 2003. *Slayer Slang: A* Buffy the Vampire Slayer *Lexicon*. New York: Oxford University Press.

Adams, Tony E. 2008. "A Review of Narrative Ethics." *Qualitative Inquiry* 14: 175–194. Accessed May 15, 2011. DOI: 10.1177/1077 800407304417.

"After Life." 2001. *Buffy the Vampire Slayer*. Season 6. Episode 3. Written by Jane Espenson. Directed by David Solomon. Twentieth Century–Fox Home Entertainment, Inc., 2004. DVD.

Alessio, Dominic. 2001. "'Things Are Different Now?': A Post-Colonial Analysis of *Buffy the Vampire Slayer*." *European Legacy* 6.6: 731–740.

"Amends." 1999. *Buffy the Vampire Slayer*. Season 3. Episode 10. Written and directed by Joss Whedon. Twentieth Century–Fox Home Entertainment, Inc., 2003. DVD.

Anderson, Wendy Love. 2003. "Prophecy Girl and the Powers That Be: The Philosophy of Religion in the Buffyverse." In James B. South, ed., Buffy the Vampire Slayer *and Philosophy: Fear and Trembling in Sunnydale*. Chicago: Open Court, 212–226.

"Angel." 1997. *Buffy the Vampire Slayer*. Season 1. Episode 7. Written by David Greenwalt. Directed by Scott Brazil. Twentieth Century–Fox Home Entertainment, Inc., 2002. DVD.

"Ariel." 2007. *Firefly: The Official Companion*. Volume Two. Written by Jose Molina. Directed by Allan Kroeker. Broadcast 2002.

Aristotle. 1962. *The Politics*. Trans. T. A. Sinclair. Baltimore: Penguin.

"As You Were." 2002. *Buffy the Vampire Slayer*. Season 6. Episode 15. Written and directed by Douglas Petrie. Twentieth Century–Fox Home Entertainment, Inc., 2004. DVD.

"The Asset." 2013. *Marvel's Agents of S.H.I.E.L.D*. Season 1. Episode 3. Written by Jed Whedon and Maurissa Tancharoen. Directed by Milan Cheylov. ABC Studios Production.

Atchley, Clinton P.E. 2009. "*King Lear, Buffy*, and Apocalyptic Revisionism." In Kevin K. Durand, ed., Buffy *Meets the Academy*. Jefferson, NC: 81–90.

"Bad Girls." 1999. *Buffy the Vampire Slayer*. Season 3. Episode 14. Written by Douglas Petrie. Directed by Michael Lange. Twentieth Century–Fox Home Entertainment, Inc., 2003. DVD.

Badiou, Alain. 2003. *Saint Paul: The Foundation of Universalism*. Trans. Ray Brassier. Stanford: Stanford University Press.

Baker, Lee C.R. 1986. "The Open Secret of *Sartor Resartus*: Carlyle's Method of Converting His Reader." *Studies in Philology* 83.2: 218–235.

Baker, Susan. 1992. "Personating Persons: Rethinking Shakespeare's Disguises." *Shakespeare Quarterly* 43.3: 303–316.

Banks, J.T. 2002. "The Story Inside." In R. Charon and M. Montello, eds., *Stories Matter: The Role of Narrative in Medical Ethics*. New York: Routledge, 218–226.

Barton, Anne. 1997. "Introduction" to *Much Ado About Nothing*. In *The Riverside Shakespeare*. Second Edition. Edited by G. Blakemore Evans, et al., 361–365.

Basso, Keith H. 1996. *Wisdom Sits in Places: Landscape and Language Among the Western Apache*. Albuquerque: University of New Mexico Press.

Bate, Jonathan. 2010. "Introduction." In Jonathan Bate and Eric Rasmussen, eds., *Measure for Measure*. The RSC Shakespeare. New York: The Modern Library, vii–xxv.

Battis, Jes. 2005. *Blood Relations: Chosen Fam-*

ilies in Buffy the Vampire Slayer *and* Angel. Jefferson, NC: McFarland.

Battiste, Marie, and James (Sa'ke'j) Youngblood Henderson. 2000. *Protecting Indigenous Knowledge and Heritage: A Global Challenge.* Saskatoon: Purich Publishing.

Beauchamp, Tom L., and James F. Childress. 2008. *Principles of Biomedical Ethics.* New York: Oxford University Press.

Beckwith, Sarah. 2011. *Shakespeare and the Grammar of Forgiveness.* Ithaca: Cornell University Press.

"Becoming, Parts One and Two." 1998. *Buffy the Vampire Slayer.* Season 2. Episodes 21 and 22. Written and directed by Joss Whedon. Twentieth Century–Fox Home Entertainment, Inc., 2002. DVD.

"Beneath You." 2002. *Buffy the Vampire Slayer.* Season 7. Episode 2. Written by Doug Petrie. Directed by Nick Marck. Twentieth Century–Fox Home Entertainment, Inc., 2004. DVD.

Berry, Ralph. 1978. *The Shakespearean Metaphor: Studies in Language and Form.* London: Macmillan.

Bloom, Harold. 1998. *Shakespeare: The Invention of the Human.* New York: Riverhead Books.

Boas, F.S. 1968. *Shakespere and His Predecessors.* New York: Haskell House. First published in 1896.

Bogaerts, Arno. 2012. "The Avengers and S.H.I.E.L.D.: The Problem with Proactive Superheronics." In Mark D. White, ed., *The Avengers and Philosophy: Earth's Mightiest Thinkers.* Hoboken. NJ: John Wiley and Sons, 154–168.

Boyce, Charles.1990. *Shakespeare A to Z.* New York: Bantam Doubleday Dell.

Bradbrook, M.C. 1952. "Shakespeare and the Use of Disguise in Elizabethan Drama." *Essays in Criticism* 2: 159–168.

"Briar Rose." 2009. *Dollhouse.* Season 1. Episode 11. Written by Jane Espenson. Directed by Dwight Little. Twentieth Century–Fox Home Entertainment, Inc., 2009. DVD.

Brown, Theodore L. 2008. *Making Truth: Metaphor in Science.* Urbana: Urbana University Press.

Buckman, Alyson. 2012. "'Didn't Get the Memo? Hero of the People Now': Joss Whedon, Hat Tricks, and the Complication of Viewer Responses." Feature Presentation at the *Slayage 5* Conference, University of British Columbia, July 2012.

"'*Buffy* Speak' featurette." 2003. *Buffy the Vampire Slayer.* Twentieth Century–Fox Home Entertainment, Inc. DVD. Disc 3.

"Bushwhacked." 2003. *Firefly: The Complete Series.* Written and directed by Tim Minear. Created by Joss Whedon. Twentieth Century–Fox Home Entertainment, Inc., 2003. DVD.

Bussolini, Jeffrey. 2013. "Television Intertextuality After *Buffy*: Intertextuality of Casting and Constitutive Intertextuality." *Slayage: The Journal of the Whedon Studies Association.* 10.1 [35]. 54 pars. http://slayageon line.com/essays/slayage35/Bussolini.pdf. Accessed April 2, 2013.

The Cabin in the Woods: The Official Visual Companion. 2012. London: Titan Books.

The Cabin in the Woods. 2011. Written by Drew Goddard and Joss Whedon. Directed Drew Goddard. Lionsgate, DVD.

Cahoone, Lawrence. 2010. *The Modern Intellectual Tradition: From Descartes to Derrida.* Course Guidebook. Chantilly, VA: The Great Courses.

Calvert, Bronwen. 2010. "Mind, Body, Imprint: Cyberpunk Echoes in the Dollhouse." *Slayage: The Journal of the Whedon Studies Association.* 8.2 & 3 [30 & 31]. 24 pars. http://slayageonline.com/essays/slayage30_31/calvert.pdf. Accessed August 15, 2013.

Campbell, Lily B. 1930. *Shakespeare's Tragic Heroes: Slaves of Passion.* Cambridge: Cambridge University Press.

Canavan, Gerry. 2013/2014. "'Something Nightmares Are From': Metacommentary in Joss Whedon's *The Cabin in the Woods.*" *Slayage: The Journal of the Whedon Studies Association.* 10.2/11.1 [36–37]. 40 pars. http://slayageonline.com/essays/slayage36/Canavan.pdf. Accessed January 20, 2014.

Čapek, Karel. 1921. *R.U.R.* http://www.amazon.com/R-U-R-Rossums-Universal-Penguin-Classics/dp/0141182083

Carlyle, Thomas. 1902. *The Complete Works of Thomas Carlyle.* New York: Thomas Y. Crowell and Company.

Cathcart, Thomas. 2013. *The Trolley Problem or Would You Throw the Fat Guy Off the Bridge?: A Philosophical Conundrum.* New York: Workman Publishing.

Charon, Rita, and Martha Montello, eds. 2002. *Stories Matter: The Role of Narrative in Medical Ethics.* New York: Routledge.

"Choices." 1999. *Buffy the Vampire Slayer.* Season 3. Episode 19. Written by David Fury. Directed by James A. Contner. Twentieth Century–Fox Home Entertainment, Inc., 2003. DVD.

"Chosen." 2003. *Buffy the Vampire Slayer.* Season 7. Episode 22. Written and Directed by

Joss Whedon. Twentieth Century–Fox Home Entertainment, Inc., 2004. DVD.

Coker, Catherine. 2010. "Exploitation of Bodies and Minds in Season One of *Dollhouse*." In Erin B. Waggoner, ed., *Sexual Rhetoric in the Works of Joss Whedon: New Essays*. Jefferson, NC: McFarland, 226–238.

Collins, Philip, ed. 2002. *Charles Dickens: The Critical Heritage*. London: Routledge.

Cooper, L. Andrew. 2013/2014. "*The Cabin in the Woods* and the End of American Exceptionalism." *Slayage: The Journal of the Whedon Studies Association*, 10.2/11.1 [36–37]. 25 pars. http://slayageonline.com/essays/slayage36/Cooper.pdf. Accessed January 21, 2014.

"The Core, Part Three." 2013. *Buffy the Vampire Slayer*. Season 9. Number 23. Script by Andrew Chambliss. Pencils by George Jeanty. Executive producer Joss Whedon. Milwaukee: Dark Horse Comics.

Crane, Mary Thomas. 2001. *Shakespeare's Brain: Reading with Cognitive Theory*. Princeton: Princeton University Press.

Croteau, Melissa, and Carolyn Jess-Cooke, eds. 2009. *Apocalyptic Shakespeare: Essays on Visions of Chaos and Revelation in Recent Film Adaptations*. Jefferson, NC: McFarland.

"Crush." 2001. *Buffy the Vampire Slayer*. Season 5. Episode 14. Written and Directed by Joss Whedon. Twentieth Century–Fox Home Entertainment, Inc., 2003. DVD

Crystal, David. 2008. *"Think on My Words": Exploring Shakespeare's Language*. Cambridge: Cambridge University Press.

Curry, Agnes. 2008. "'We Don't Say Indian': On the Paradoxical Construction of the Reavers." *Slayage: The Journal of the Whedon Studies Association*, 7.1 [25]. 42 pars. http://slayageonline.com/PDF/Curry2.pdf.

Dalton, Russell W. 2013. "To Assemble or to Shrug? Power, Responsibility and Sacrifice in *Marvel's The Avengers*." In Anthony R. Mills, John W. Morehead and J. Ryan Parker, eds., *Joss Whedon and Religion: Essays on an Angry Atheist's Explorations of the Sacred*. Jefferson, NC: McFarland, 165–182.

"Deep Down." 2002. *Angel*. Season 4. Episode 1. Written By Steven S. DeKnight. Directed by Terrence O'Hara. Twentieth Century–Fox Home Entertainment, Inc., 2004. DVD.

Dennett, Daniel C. 1991. *Consciousness Explained*. Boston: Little, Brown.

Dennett, Daniel C. 1993. "Review of F. Varela, E. Thompson and E. Rosch, *The Embodied Mind*." *American Journal of Psychology* Vol. 106: 121–126.

Dennett, Daniel C. 1996. *Kinds of Minds: Toward an Understanding of Consciousness*. New York: Basic Books.

Dennett, Daniel C. 2013. *Intuition Pumps and Other Tools for Thinking*. New York: W. W. Norton.

DeVoss, Danielle Nicole, and Patrick Russell LeBeau. 2010. "Reading and Composing Indians: Invented Indian Identity through Visual Literacy." *The Journal of Popular Culture* 43.1: 45–77.

Dial-Driver, Emily, Sally Emmons-Featherston, Jim Ford, and Carolyn Anne Taylor, eds. 2008. *The Truth of* Buffy: *Essays on Fiction Illuminating Reality*. Jefferson, NC: McFarland.

Dickson, Vernon Guy. 2009. "'A pattern, precedent, and lively warrant': Emulation, Rhetoric, and Cruel Propriety in *Titus Andronicus*." *Renaissance Quarterly* 62.2: 376–409.

Donaldson, Laura. 1992. *Decolonizing Feminisms: Race, Gender, & Empire Building*. Chapel Hill: University of North Carolina Press.

"Doomed." 2000. *Buffy the Vampire Slayer*. Season 4. Episode 11. Written by Marti Noxon, David Fury, and Jane Espenson. Directed by James A. Contner. Twentieth Century–Fox Home Entertainment, Inc., 2003. DVD.

"Doppelgängland." 1999. *Buffy the Vampire Slayer*. Season 3. Episode 16. Written and directed by Joss Whedon. Twentieth Century–Fox Home Entertainment, Inc., 2003. DVD.

"Earshot." 1999. *Buffy the Vampire Slayer*. Season 3. Episode 18. Written by Jane Espenson. Directed by Regis B. Kimbel. Twentieth Century–Fox Home Entertainment, Inc., 2003. DVD.

Edmonds, David. 2014. *Would **You** Kill the Fat Man? The Trolley Problem and What Your Answer Tells Us About Right and Wrong*. Princeton: Princeton University Press.

Edmondson, Paul, and Stanley Wells, eds. 2013. *Shakespeare Beyond Doubt: Evidence, Argument, Controversy*. Cambridge: Cambridge University Press.

Edwards, Paul. 1967. *Encyclopedia of Philosophy*. 8 volumes. New York: Macmillan.

Emmons-Featherston, Sally. 2008. "Is That Stereotype Dead? Working with and Against 'Western' Stereotypes in *Buffy*." In Emily Dial-Driver et al., eds, *The Truth of* Buffy: *Essays on Fiction Illuminating Reality*. Jefferson, NC: McFarland, 55–66.

"Enemies." 1999. *Buffy the Vampire Slayer*. Season 3. Episode 17. Written by Douglas Petrie. Directed by David Grossman. Twentieth Century–Fox Home Entertainment, Inc., 2003. DVD.

Espenson, Jane. 2002. Interview. The Succubus Club (Transcript). 22 May 2002. http://www.slayage.com/news/020522-je_int.html. Accessed June 19, 2013.

Espenson, Jane. 2004. *Finding Serenity: Anti-Heroes, Lost Shepherds, and Space Hookers in Joss Whedon's "Firefly."* Dallas: BenBella.

Espenson, Jane. 2006a. *Jane in Progress*, December 29, 2006. http://www.janeespenson.com/archives/00000268.php

Espenson, Jane. 2006b. *Jane in Progress*, October 3, 2006. http://www.janeespenson.com/archives/00000207.php

Espenson, Jane. 2006c. *Jane in Progress*, May 9, 2006. http://www.janeespenson.com/archives/00000095.php

Espenson, Jane. 2006d. *Jane in Progress*, May 2, 2006. http://www.janeespenson.com/archives/00000088.php

Espenson, Jane. 2006e. *Jane in Progress*, April 28, 2006. http://www.janeespenson.com/archives/00000083.php

Espenson, Jane. 2006f. *Jane in Progress*, January 19, 2006. http://www.janeespenson.com/archives/00000011.php

Espenson, Jane. 2007a. *Serenity Found: More Unauthorized Essays on Whedon's* Firefly *Universe.* Dallas: BenBella.

Espenson, Jane. 2007b. *Jane in Progress*, April 15, 2007. http://www.janeespenson.com/archives/00000337.php

Espenson, Jane. 2010. "Introduction." In Jane Espenson, ed., *Inside Joss' Dollhouse.* Dallas: BenBella, 1–3.

Espenson, Jane, ed. 2010. *Inside Joss' Dollhouse.* Dallas: BenBella.

"Faith, Hope, and Trick." 1998. *Buffy the Vampire Slayer.* Season 3. Episode 3. Written by David Greenwalt. Directed by James A. Contner. Twentieth Century–Fox Home Entertainment, Inc., 2003. DVD.

Family Reunion, Parts 1–4. 2012. *Angel and Faith.* Season 9. Numbers 11–14. Script by Christos Gage. Art by Rebekah Isaacs. Colors by Dan Jackson. Executive Producer, Joss Whedon. Milwaukee: Dark Horse Comics.

"Fear, Itself." 1999. *Buffy the Vampire Slayer.* Season 4. Episode 4. Written by David Fury. Directed by Tucker Gates. Twentieth Century–Fox Home Entertainment, Inc., 2003. DVD.

Fedderson, Kim, and J.M. Richardson. 2009. "*Liberty's Taken,* or How 'captive women may be cleansed and used': Julie Taymor's *Titus* and 9/11." In Melissa Croteau and Carolyn Jess-Cooke, eds., *Apocalyptic Shakespeare: Essays on Visions of Chaos and Revelation in Recent Film Adaptations.* Jefferson, NC: McFarland.

Fesmire, Steven. 2003. *John Dewey and Moral Imagination: Pragmatism in Ethics.* Bloomington: Indiana University Press.

Fichte, J.G. 1978. *Attempt at a Critique of All Revelation.* Trans. Garrett Green. Cambridge: Cambridge University Press. *Versuch einer Kritik aller Offenbarung,* 1792.

Firefly: The Official Companion. 2006. Volume One. London: Titan Books.

Firefly: The Official Companion. 2007. Volume Two. London: Titan Books.

"Five by Five." 2000. *Angel.* Season 1. Episode 18. Written by Jim Kouf. Directed by James A. Contner. Twentieth Century–Fox Home Entertainment, Inc., 2003. DVD.

Flaherty, K. J. 2005. "Theatre and Metatheatre in *Hamlet.*" *Sydney Studies in English* 31.1: 3–20.

"Flooded." 2001. *Buffy the Vampire Slayer.* Season 6. Episode 4. Written by Douglas Petrie and Jane Espenson. Directed by Douglas Petrie. Twentieth Century–Fox Home Entertainment, Inc., 2004. DVD.

Foot, Philippa. 1967. "The Problem of Abortion and the Doctrine of the Double Effect." *Oxford Review* 5: 5–15.

Foy, Joseph J. 2011. "The State of Nature and Social Contracts on Spaceship *Serenity.*" In Dean A. Kowalski and S. Evan Kreider, eds., *The Philosphy of Joss Whedon.* Lexington: University Press of Kentucky, 39–54.

"The Freshman." 1999. *Buffy the Vampire Slayer.* Season 4. Episode 1. Written and Directed by Joss Whedon. Twentieth Century–Fox Home Entertainment, Inc., 2003. DVD.

Frey, Charles H. 1979. "*The Tempest* and the New World." *Shakespeare Quarterly* 30: 29–41.

Frey, Charles H. 1995. "Embodying the Play." In Nigel Wood, ed., *The Tempest.* Buckingham: Open University Press, 67–96.

"The Gift." 2001. *Buffy the Vampire Slayer.* Season 5. Episode 22. Written and directed by Joss Whedon. Twentieth Century–Fox Home Entertainment, Inc., 2003. DVD.

Ginn, Sherry. 2010. "Memory, Mind, and Mayhem: Neurological Tampering and Manipulation in *Dollhouse.*" *Slayage: The Journal of the Whedon Studies Association,* 8.2 & 3 [30 & 31]. 24 pars. http://slayageonline.

com/essays/slayage30_31/ginn.pdf. Accessed August 17, 2013.

Ginn, Sherry. 2012. *Power and Control in the Television Worlds of Joss Whedon.* Jefferson, NC: McFarland.

Gonzalez, Cleotilde, Jason Dana, Hideya Koshino, and Marcel Just. 2005. "The Framing Effect and Risky Decisions: Examining Cognitive Functions with fMRI." *Journal of Economic Psychology* 26: 1–20.

Grant, Julia L. 2010. "Slaying Shakespeare in High School: Buffy Battles *The Merchant of Venice* and *Othello.*" In Jodie A. Kreider and Meghan K. Winchell, eds., *Buffy in the Classroom: Essays on Teaching with the Vampire Slayer.* Jefferson, NC: McFarland, 202–212.

"Grave." 2002. *Buffy the Vampire Slayer.* Season 6. Episode 22. Written by David Fury. Directed by James A. Contner. Twentieth Century–Fox Home Entertainment, Inc., 2004. DVD.

Greenblatt, Stephen. 1997. "Introduction" to *Twelfth Night.* In *The Norton Shakespeare,* ed. by Stephen Greenblatt, et al. New York: W.W. Norton, 1761–1767.

Greenblatt, Stephen. 2013. "On the Edge of Slander." *New York Review of Books* 26 September 2013: 50–51.

Grinnell, Jason D. 2011. "Aristotle, Kant, Spike, and Jayne: Ethics and Character in the Whedonverse." In Dean A. Kowalski and S. Evan Kreider, eds., *The Philosophy of Joss Whedon.* Lexington: University Press of Kentucky, 88–102.

Harper, Steven. 2004. "Jasmine: Scariest Villain Ever." In Glenn Yeffeth, ed., *Five Seasons of* Angel: *Science Fiction and Fantasy Writers Discuss Their Favorite Vampire.* Dallas: BenBella, 49–55.

Hart, Michael Anthony. 1996. "Sharing Circles: Utilizing Traditional Practice Methods for Teaching, Helping, and Supporting." In Sylvia O'Meara, et al., eds., *From Our Eyes: Learning from Indigenous Peoples.* Toronto: Garamond, 59–72.

"The Harvest." 1997. *Buffy the Vampire Slayer.* Season 1. Episode 2. Written by Joss Whedon. Directed by John Kretchmer. Twentieth Century–Fox Home Entertainment, Inc., 2002. DVD.

Heilman, Robert B. 1956. *Magic in the Web: Action and Language in* Othello. Lexington: University of Kentucky Press.

Held, Jacob. 2003. "Justifying the Means: Punishment in the Buffyverse." In James B. South, ed., Buffy the Vampire Slayer *and*

Philosophy: Fear and Trembling in Sunnydale. Chicago: Open Court, 227–238.

"Here's How It Was: The Making of *Firefly* featurette." 2003. *Firefly: The Complete Series.* 20th Century–Fox. Disc 4. DVD.

Hester, D. Micah. 2001. *Community as Healing: Pragmatist Ethics in Medical Encounters.* Lanham, MD: Rowman and Littlefield.

Hofstadter, Douglas, and Emmanuel Sander. 2013. *Surfaces and Essences: Analogy as the Fuel and Fire of Thinking.* New York: Basic Books.

Holland, Norman N. 2009. *Literature and the Brain.* Gainesville: PsyArt Foundation.

Howard, Jean E. 1997. "Introduction" to *1 Henry IV.* In *The Norton Shakespeare,* ed. Stephen Greenblatt, et al. New York: W.W. Norton, 1147–1156.

"Hush." 1999. *Buffy the Vampire Slayer.* Season 4. Episode 10. Written and directed by Joss Whedon. Twentieth Century–Fox Home Entertainment, Inc., 2003. DVD.

Hyland, Peter. 1978. "Shakespeare's Heroines: Disguise in the Romantic Comedies." *Ariel: A Review of International English Literature* 9.2: 23–39.

"I Only Have Eyes for You." 1998. *Buffy the Vampire Slayer.* Season 2. Episode 19. Written by Marti Noxon. Directed by James Whitmore, Jr. Twentieth Century–Fox Home Entertainment, Inc., 2002. DVD.

"I Was Made to Love You." 2001. *Buffy the Vampire Slayer.* Season 5. Episode 15. Written by Jane Espenson. Directed by James A. Contner. Twentieth Century–Fox Home Entertainment, Inc., 2003. DVD.

"I Will Remember You." 1999. *Angel.* Season 1. Episode 8. Written by David Greenwalt. Directed by David Grossman. Twentieth Century–Fox Home Entertainment, Inc., 2003. DVD.

"Jaynestown." 2007. *Firefly: The Official Companion.* Volume Two. Written by Ben Edlund. Directed by Marita Grabiak. London: Titan Books. Broadcast 2002.

Johnson, Mark. 1993. *Moral Imagination: Implications of Cognitive Science for Ethics.* Chicago: Chicago University Press.

Johnson, Mark. 2007. *The Meaning of the Body: Aesthetics of Human Understanding.* Chicago: Chicago University Press.

Kant, Immanuel. 1996. *Groundwork of the Metaphysics of Morals in Practical Philosophy.* Trans. and ed. Mary J. Gregor. Cambridge: Cambridge University Press. *Grundlegung zur Metaphysik der Sitten,* 1785.

Kaveney, Roz, ed. 2004. *Reading the Vampire*

Slayer: The New, Updated Unofficial Critical Companion to Buffy and Angel. Second Edition. London: I.B. Tauris.

Keller, J. Gregory. 2005. "The Moral Thinking of Macbeth." *Philosophy and Literature* 29.1: 41–56.

Kessenich, Laura. 2006. "'Wait Till You Have an Evil Twin': Jane Espenson's Contributions to *Buffy the Vampire Slayer.*" *Watcher Junior* 3.1, 18 pars. http://www.watcher junior.tv/03/kessenich.php

Kinney, Arthur F. 1993. "Editor's Note." In Richard Hillman *William Shakespeare: The Problem Plays.* New York: Twayne.

Knapp, James A. 2001. *Image Ethics in Shakespeare and Spenser.* New York: Palgrave Macmillan.

Kociemba, David. 2009. "Understanding the Espensode." In Lynne Y. Edwards, et al., eds. *Buffy Goes Dark: Essays on the Final Two Seasons of Buffy the Vampire Slayer on Television.* Jefferson, NC: McFarland, 23–39.

Koontz, K. Dale. 2010. "Czech Mate: Whedon, Čapek, and the Foundations of *Dollhouse.*" *Slayage: The Journal of the Whedon Studies Association* 8. 2 & 3 [30 & 31]. Accessed May 15, 2011. http://slayageonline. com/essays/slayage30_31/koontz.pdf.

Kowalski, Dean A., and S. Evan Kreider, eds. 2011. *The Philosophy of Joss Whedon.* Lexington: University Press of Kentucky.

Kramer, Heinrich, and James Sprenger. 1971. *The Malleus Maleficarum of Heinrich Kramer and James Sprenger.* Trans. Montague Summers. New York: Dover.

Kreider, S. Evan. 2011. "Dollhouse and Consensual Slavery." In Dean A. Kowalski and S. Evan Kreider, eds., *The Philosophy of Joss Whedon.* Lexington: University Press of Kentucky, 55–68.

Kreider, Jodie A., Meghan K. Winchell, eds. 2010. *Buffy in the Classroom: Essays on Teaching with the Vampire Slayer.* Jefferson, NC: McFarland.

Lackey, Mercedes. 2004. "*Serenity* and Bobby McGee: Freedom and the Illusion of Freedom in Joss Whedon's *Firefly.*" In Jane Espenson, ed., *Finding Serenity: Anti-Heroes, Lost Shepherds, and Space Hookers in Joss Whedon's "Firefly.*" Dallas: BenBella, 63–73.

Lakoff, George. 1987. *Women, Fire, and Dangerous Things: What Categories Reveal About the Mind.* Chicago: University of Chicago Press.

Lakoff, George. 1993. "The Contemporary Theory of Metaphor." In A. Ortony, ed., *Metaphor and Thought.* Second Edition.

Cambridge: Cambridge University Press, 202–251.

Lakoff, George. 2004. *Don't Think of an Elephant! Know Your Values and Frame the Debate—The Essential Guide for Progressives.* White River Junction, VT: Chelsea Green Publishing.

Lakoff, George. 2008. *The Political Mind: Why You Can't Understand 21st-Century Politics with an 18th-Century Brain.* New York: Viking.

Lakoff, George, and Mark Johnson. 1980. *Metaphors We Live By.* Chicago: University of Chicago Press.

Lakoff, George, and Mark Johnson. 1999. *Philosophy in the Flesh: The Embodied Mind and its Challenge to Western Thought.* New York: Basic Books.

Lakoff, George, et al. 1991. *Master Metaphor List.* Second Edition (First Edition 1989). Berkeley: Cognitive Linguistics Group. http://araw.mede.uic.edu/~alansz/meta phor/METAPHORLIST.pdf

Lametti, Daniel, et al. 2012. "Which Pop Culture Property Do Academics Study the Most?" *Slate: Browbeat, Slate's Culture Blog.* http://www.slate.com/blogs/browbeat/ 2012/06/11/pop_culture_studies_why_ do_academics_study_buffy_the_vampire_ slayer_more_than_the_wire_the_matrix_ alien_and_the_simpsons_.html. Accessed June 22, 2013.

Lanier, Douglas. 2013. "'There won't be puppets, will there?': 'Heroic' authorship and the cultural politics of *Anonymous.*" In Paul Edmondson and Stanley Wells, eds., *Shakespeare Beyond Doubt: Evidence, Argument, Controversy.* Cambridge: Cambridge University Press, 215–224.

Lavery, David. 2014. *Joss Whedon, a Creative Portrait: From* Buffy the Vampire Slayer *to Marvel's* The Avengers. London: I. B. Tauris.

Lavery, David, and Cynthia Burkhead, eds. 2011. *Joss Whedon: Conversations.* Jackson: University Press of Mississippi.

"Lessons." 2002. *Buffy the Vampire Slayer.* Season 7. Episode 1. Written by Joss Whedon. Directed by David Solomon and Joss Whedon. Twentieth Century–Fox Home Entertainment, Inc., 2004. DVD.

"Lie to Me." 1997. *Buffy the Vampire Slayer.* Season 2. Episode 7. Written and directed by Joss Whedon. Twentieth Century–Fox Home Entertainment, Inc., 2002. DVD.

"Lies My Parents Told Me." 2003. *Buffy the Vampire Slayer.* Season 7. Episode 17. Written by David Fury and Drew Goddard. Directed by David Fury. Twentieth Century–Fox Home Entertainment, Inc., 2004. DVD.

Listphoria. 2001. "Shakespeare's Contribution to the English Language." http://listphoria. blogspot.ca/2011/10/shakespeares-contribution-to-english.html.

Loftis, J. Robert. 2009. "Moral Complexity in the Buffyverse." *Slayage: The Journal of the Whedon Studies Association* 7.3 [27]. 34 pars. http://slayageonline.com/PDF/Loftis.pdf. Accessed January 18, 2014.

Lowenthal, David. 1997. *Shakespeare and the Good Life: Ethics and Politics in Dramatic Form*. Lanham, MD: Rowman and Littlefield.

Lucking, David. 2007/2008. "'To Tell My Story': Narrating Identity in Shakespeare." *The Upstart Crow* 27: 52–66.

Lumenick, Lou. 2012. "Toronto 2012: 'Much Ado About Nothing.'" http://www.nypost. com/p/blogs/movies/toronto_much_ado_about_nothing_kTk13M77hRZ3XwpTdy-kc7M#axzz2N0NCVfCR. Accessed March 26, 2013.

Mabillard, Amanda. 2000. *Richard Burbage*. Shakespeare Online. 21 November 2000. (accessed 22 March 2013). http://www.shakespeare-online.com/biography/richardbur bage.html.

MacNeil/Lehrer Productions. 2005. "Sez Who? Slayer Slang." PBS. http://pbs.org/speak/words/sezwho/buffy/. Accessed April 9, 2013.

Maguire, Laurie, and Emma Smith. 2013. *30 Great Myths About Shakespeare*. Chichester, West Sussex: Wiley-Blackwell.

"Making *Dollhouse* featurette." 2009. *Dollhouse*. Twentieth Century–Fox Home Entertainment, Inc. DVD. Season 1. Disc 4.

Marvel's The Avengers. 2012. Written and Directed by Joss Whedon. Walt Disney Studios Home Entertainment. 2012. DVD.

Maus, Katharine Eisaman. 1997. "Introduction" to *Richard II*. In *The Norton Shakespeare*, ed. Stephen Greenblatt, et al. New York: W.W. Norton, 943–951.

Maus, Katharine Eisaman. 1997. "Introduction" to *Titus Andronicus*. In *The Norton Shakespeare*, ed. Stephen Greenblatt, et al. New York: W.W. Norton, 371–378.

McGinn, Colin. 2006. *Shakespeare's Philosophy: Discovering the Meaning Behind the Plays*. New York: HarperCollins.

McPherson, Dennis. 1998. "A Definition of Culture: Canada and First Nations." In Jace Weaver, ed., *Native American Religious Identity: Unforgotten Gods*. Maryknoll, NY: Orbis Books, 77–98.

McPherson, Dennis H., and J. Douglas Rabb. 2001. "Indigeneity in Canada: Spirituality, the Sacred and Survival." *International Journal of Canadian Studies* 23: 57–79.

McPherson, Dennis H., and J. Douglas Rabb. 2003. "Restoring the Interpretive Circle: Community-Based Research and Education." *International Journal of Canadian Studies, Dedicated Issue: Health and Well-Being in Canada* 28: 133–161.

McPherson, Dennis H., and J. Douglas Rabb. 2011. *Indian from the Inside: Native American Philosophy and Cultural Renewal*. Jefferson, NC: McFarland.

Mealing, S. R., ed. 1990. *The Jesuit Relations and Allied Documents: A Selection*. Ottawa: Carleton University Press.

Mills, Anthony R., John W. Morehead, and J. Ryan Parker, eds. 2013. *Joss Whedon and Religion: Essays on an Angry Atheist's Explorations of the Sacred*. Jefferson, NC: McFarland.

Morison, Samuel Eliot. 1942. *Admiral of the Sea: A Life of Christopher Columbus*. Boston: Little, Brown.

Morris, David B. 2002. "Narrative Ethics and Pain: Thinking with Stories." In R. Charon and M. Montello, eds., *Stories Matter: The Role of Narrative in Medical Ethics*. New York: Routledge, 196–218.

Much Ado About Nothing. 2013. Screenplay by Joss Whedon. Directed by Joss Whedon. Bellwether Pictures and Lionsgate. DVD.

Nelson, Alan H. 2013. "The Life and Theatrical Interests of Edward de Vere, Seventeenth Earl of Oxford." In Paul Edmondson and Stanley Wells, eds., *Shakespeare Beyond Doubt: Evidence, Argument, Controversy*. Cambridge: Cambridge University Press, 39–48.

Neuman, W. Lawrence. 2000. *Social Research Methods: Quantitative and Qualitative Approaches*. Boston: Allyn and Bacon.

"A New Man." 2000. *Buffy the Vampire Slayer*. Season 4. Episode 12. Written by Jane Espenson. Directed by Michael Gershman. Twentieth Century–Fox Home Entertainment, Inc., 2003. DVD.

"New Rules, Part One." 2014. *Buffy the Vampire Slayer*. Season 10. Number 1. Script by Christos Gage. Art by Rebekah Isaacs. Executive producer Joss Whedon. Milwaukee: Dark Horse Comics.

"No Place Like Home." 2000. *Buffy the Vam-*

pire Slayer*. Season 5. Episode 5. Written by Douglas Petrie. Directed by David Solomon. Twentieth Century–Fox Home Entertainment, Inc., 2003. DVD.

"Normal Again." 2002. *Buffy the Vampire Slayer*. Season 6. Episode 17. Written by Rick Rosenthal. Directed by Diego Gutierrez. Twentieth Century–Fox Home Entertainment, Inc., 2004. DVD.

Nussbaum, Emily. 2011. "Must-See Metaphysics." In David Lavery and Cynthia Burkhead, eds., *Joss Whedon: Conversations*. Jackson: University Press of Mississippi, 64–70.

Nussbaum, Martha C. 1986. *The Fragility of Goodness: Luck and Ethics in Greek Tragedy and Philosophy*. Cambridge: Cambridge University Press.

Orr, Christopher. 2013. "Joss Whedon on the 'No Brainer' of Modernizing *Much Ado About Nothing*." *The Atlantic* 7 June. http://www.theatlantic.com/entertainment/archive/2013/06/joss-whedon-on-the-no-brainer-of-modernizing-i-much-ado-about-nothing-i/276409/.

"Out of Mind, Out of Sight." 1997. *Buffy the Vampire Slayer*. Season 1. Episode 11. Written by Ashley Gable, Thomas Swyden, and Joss Whedon. Directed by Reza Badiyi. Twentieth Century–Fox Home Entertainment, Inc., 2002. DVD.

Overbey, Karen Eileen, and Lahney Preston-Mattau. 2002. "Staking in Tongues: Speech Act as Weapon in *Buffy*." In Rhonda V. Wilcox and David Lavery, eds., *Fighting the Forces: What's at Stake in* Buffy the Vampire Slayer. Lanham, MD: Rowman and Littlefield.

Parfit, Derek. 1986. *Reasons and Persons*. Oxford: Oxford University Press.

Parfit, Derek. 2011. *On What Matters*. 2 vols. Oxford: Oxford University Press.

Pateman, Matthew. 2006. *The Aesthetics of Culture in* Buffy the Vampire Slayer. Jefferson, NC: McFarland.

"Peace Out." 2003. *Angel*. Season 4. Episode 21. Written by David Fury. Directed by Jefferson Kibbee. Twentieth Century–Fox Home Entertainment, Inc., 2004. DVD.

Peikoff, Leonard. 1996. The 1991 Introduction to *Atlas Shrugged,* by Ayn Rand, 1–8. New York: Signet.

Pinker, Steven. 2011. *The Better Angels of Our Nature: Why Violence Has Declined*. New York: Viking.

Pinker, Steven. 2002. *The Blank Slate: The Modern Denial of Human Nature*. New York: Viking.

"Primeval." 2000. *Buffy the Vampire Slayer*. Season 4. Episode 21. Written by David Fury. Directed by James A. Contner. Twentieth Century–Fox Home Entertainment, Inc., 2003. DVD.

"Prophecy Girl." 1997. *Buffy the Vampire Slayer*. Season 1. Episode 12. Written and directed by Joss Whedon. Twentieth Century–Fox Home Entertainment, Inc., 2002. DVD.

Rabb, J. Douglas. 1989. "The Silence of Thomas Carlyle." *English Language Notes* 26.3: 70–81.

Rabb, J. Douglas, and J. Michael Richardson. 2007. "Myth, Metaphor, Morality and Medicine: Finding the Care in Health Care Ethics." http://chce.lakeheadu.ca/events/?display=events&eventid=30&unitid=1)

Rabb, J. Douglas, and J. Michael Richardson. 2008a. "Reavers and Redskins: Creating the Frontier Savage." In Rhonda Wilcox and Tanya Cochrane, eds., *Investigating* Firefly *and* Serenity. London: I. B. Tauris, 127–138.

Rabb, J. Douglas, and J. Michael Richardson. 2008b. "Medical Ethics, Clinical Judgment, and Cognitive Science." *Theoretical Medicine and Bioethics* 29: 419–422.

Rabb, J. Douglas, and J. Michael Richardson. 2009. "Myth, Metaphor, Morality and Monsters: The Espenson Factor and Cognitive Science in Joss Whedon's Narrative Love Ethic." *Slayage: The Journal of the Whedon Studies Association*. 7.4 [28]. 30 pars. http://slayageonline.com/PDF/Rabb_Richardson.pdf

Rand, Ayn. 1943/1993. *The Fountainhead*. New York: Signet.

Rand, Ayn. 1968/1993. Introduction to the Twenty-fifth Anniversary Edition of *The Fountainhead*, v–xi. New York: Signet.

Rand, Ayn. 1957/1996. *Atlas Shrugged*. New York: Signet.

"The Replacement." 2000. *Buffy the Vampire Slayer*. Season 5. Episode 3. Written by Jane Espenson. Directed by James A. Contner. Twentieth Century–Fox Home Entertainment, Inc., 2003. DVD.

Richardson, J. Michael, and J. Douglas Rabb. 2007. *The Existential Joss Whedon: Evil and Human Freedom in* Buffy the Vampire Slayer, Angel, Firefly, and Serenity. Jefferson, NC: McFarland.

Riess, Jana. 2004. *What Would Buffy Do? The Vampire Slayer as Spiritual Guide*. San Francisco: John Wiley & Sons.

Risden, E.L. 2012. *Shakespeare and the Problem Play: Complex Forms, Crossed Genres and*

Moral Quandaries. Jefferson, NC: McFarland.

Rosch, Eleanor. 1973. "Natural Categories." *Cognitive Psychology* 4: 326–350.

Rosch, Eleanor. 1977. "Human Categorization." Neil Warren, ed., *Studies in Cross-cultural Psychology*. London: Academic Press. I, 1–49.

Rosch, Eleanor, and B.B. Lloyd, eds. 1978. *Cognition and Categorization*. Hillsdale, NJ: Lawrence Erlbaum.

Sartre, Jean-Paul. 1971. *Being and Nothingness: An Essay on Phenomenological Ontology*. Trans. Hazel E. Barnes. New York: Washington Square Press.

"School Hard." 1997. *Buffy the Vampire Slayer*. Season 2. Episode 3. Written by David Greenwalt. Directed by John Kretchmer. Twentieth Century–Fox Home Entertainment, Inc., 2002. DVD

Schudt, Karl. 2003. "Also Sprach Faith: The Problem of the Happy Rogue Vampire Slayer." In James B. South, ed., Buffy the Vampire Slayer *and Philosophy: Fear and Trembling in Sunnydale*. Chicago: Open Court, 20–34.

Schwartz, Terri. 2013. "WC13: *Much Ado About Nothing* Tackles the Bard the Whedon Way." http://spinoff.comicbookresources. com/2013/04/03/wc13-much-ado-about-nothing-tackles-the-bard-the-whedon-way/. Accessed April 4, 2013.

"Seeds." 2014. *Marvel's Agents of S.H.I.E.L.D.* Season 1. Episode 12. Written by Monica Owusu-Breen and Jed Whedon. Directed by Kenneth Fink. ABC Studios Production.

"Selfless." 2002. *Buffy the Vampire Slayer*. Season 7. Episode 5. Written by Drew Goddard. Directed by David Solomon. Twentieth Century–Fox Home Entertainment, Inc., 2004. DVD.

"Selfless." 2002. *Buffy the Vampire Slayer*. Season 7. Episode 5. Written by Drew Goddard. Directed by David Solomon. Shooting script. http://www.buffyworld.com/buffy/scripts/127_scri.html. Accessed May 27, 2013.

Serenity. 2005. Movie. Written and directed by Joss Whedon. Universal Studios. DVD.

"Serenity." 2006. In *Firefly: The Official Companion*. Volume 1. Written and directed by Joss Whedon. Broadcast 2003.

Serenity: The Official Visual Companion. 2005. London: Titan Books.

Serenity: Leaves on the Wind. 2014. Number 1. Script by Zack Whedon. Pencils by Georges Jeanty. Executive Producer, Joss Whedon. Milwaukee: Dark Horse Comics.

Serenity: Leaves on the Wind. 2014. Number 2. Script by Zack Whedon. Pencils by Georges Jeanty. Executive Producer, Joss Whedon. Milwaukee: Dark Horse Comics.

Shakespeare, William. 1997. *Hamlet*. In *The Riverside Shakespeare*. Second Edition. Edited by G. Blakemore Evans, et al.

Shakespeare, William. 1997. *1 Henry IV*. In *The Riverside Shakespeare*. Second Edition. Edited by G. Blakemore Evans, et al.

Shakespeare, William. 1997. *2 Henry IV*. In *The Riverside Shakespeare*. Second Edition. Edited by G. Blakemore Evans, et al.

Shakespeare, William. 1997. *Macbeth*. In *The Riverside Shakespeare*. Second Edition. Edited by G. Blakemore Evans, et al.

Shakespeare, William. 1997. *Measure for Measure*. In *The Riverside Shakespeare*. Second Edition. Edited by G. Blakemore Evans, et al.

Shakespeare, William. 1997. *The Merchant of Venice*. In *The Riverside Shakespeare*. Second Edition. Edited by G. Blakemore Evans, et al.

Shakespeare, William. 1997. *Much Ado About Nothing*. In *The Riverside Shakespeare*. Second Edition. Edited by G. Blakemore Evans, et al.

Shakespeare, William. 1997. *Othello*. In *The Riverside Shakespeare*. Second Edition. Edited by G. Blakemore Evans, et al.

Shakespeare, William. 1997. *Sonnets*. In *The Riverside Shakespeare*. Second Edition. Edited by G. Blakemore Evans, et al.

Shakespeare, William. 1997. *The Tempest*. In *The Riverside Shakespeare*. Second Edition. Edited by G. Blakemore Evans, et al.

Shakespeare, William. 1997. *Titus Andronicus*. In *The Riverside Shakespeare*. Second Edition. Edited by G. Blakemore Evans, et al.

Shakespeare, William. 1997. *Twelfth Night*. In *The Riverside Shakespeare*. Second Edition. Edited by G. Blakemore Evans, et al.

Shakespeare in Love. 1998. Directed by John Madden. Written by Tom Stoppard and Marc Norman. Miramax Films. DVD.

Sherman, Donovan. 2013. "Stages of Revision: Textuality, Performance, and History in *Anonymous*." *Literature/Film Quarterly* 41.2: 129–142.

Shoard, Catherine. 2012. "Much Ado About Nothing—Review." http://www.guardian.co.uk/film/2012/sep/13/much-ado-about-nothing-review. Accessed March 26, 2013.

Sidney, Sir Philip. 1595/1961. *An Apologie for Poetrie*. Edited by J. Churton Collins. Oxford: Clarendon Press.

Siegel, Paul N. 1953 "*Measure for Measure*: The Significance of the Title." *Shakespeare Quarterly* 4.3: 317–320.

Sinclair, Peter. 2009. "*Macbeth*: A Meditation Upon Meta-Theater." http://whatapieceof work.wordpress.com/2009/12/05/mac beth-a-meditation-upon-meta-theater/. Accessed April 4, 2013.

Somerville, Margaret. 2006. *The Ethical Imagination: Journeys of the Human Spirit*. Toronto: House of Anansi.

South, James B. 2001. "'All Torment, Trouble, Wonder, and Amazement Inhabits Here': The Vicissitudes of Technology in *Buffy the Vampire Slayer*." *Journal of American and Comparative Cultures* 24.1/2: 93–102.

South, James B., ed. 2003. Buffy the Vampire Slayer *and Philosophy: Fear and Trembling in Sunnydale*. Chicago: Open Court.

Spike: A Dark Place, Part Two. 2012. Season 9. No. 2. Script by Victor Gischler. Colors by Cris Peter. Executive Producer, Joss Whedon. Milwaukee: Dark Horse Comics.

Stafford, Nikki. 2007. *Bite Me! The Unofficial Guide to* Buffy the Vampire Slayer: *The Chosen Edition*. Toronto: ECW Press.

"Steven S. DeKnight." 2013. http://www.tv. com/people/steven-s-deknight/. Accessed June 6, 2013.

Stevenson, Gregory. 2003. *Televised Morality: The Case of* Buffy the Vampire Slayer. Lanham: Hampton Books.

Stillman, Robert E. 2002. "The Scope of Sidney's Defence of Poesy: The New Hermeneutic and Early Modern Poetics." *English Literary Renaissance* 32.3: 355–385.

Stroud, Scott R. 2003. "A Kantian Analysis of Moral Judgment in *Buffy the Vampire Slayer*." In James B. South, ed., Buffy the Vampire Slayer *and Philosophy: Fear and Trembling in Sunnydale*. Chicago: Open Court. 185–194.

Swinford, Susan. 2006. "Adapting *Serenity*: Genre, Myth, and Freedom." Popular Culture Association/American Culture Association Conference, Atlanta, GA, 12–15 April.

"Tabula Rasa." 2001. *Buffy the Vampire Slayer*. Season 6. Episode 8. Written by Rebecca Rand Kirshner. Directed by David Grossman. Twentieth Century–Fox Home Entertainment, Inc., 2004. DVD.

"The Target." 2009. *Dollhouse*. Season 1. Episode 2. Written and directed by Steven S. DeKnight. Twentieth Century–Fox Home Entertainment, Inc., 2009. DVD.

Thompson, Ann, and John O. Thompson. 1987. *Shakespeare: Meaning and Metaphor*. Iowa City: University of Iowa Press.

Thompson Evan. 2010. *Mind in Life: Biology, Phenomenology, and the Sciences of Mind*. Cambridge: Harvard University Press.

Thompson, Evan. 2014. *Waking, Dreaming, Being: New Light on the Self and Consciousness from Neuroscience, Meditation, and Philosophy*. New York: Columbia University Press.

Thompson, Gregory J., and Sally Emmons-Featherston. 2008. "'What Shall Cordelia Say?' Buffy as Morality Play for the Twenty-First Century's Therapeutic Ethos." In Emily Dial-Driver, et al., eds., *The Truth of Buffy: Essays on Fiction Illuminating Reality*. Jefferson, NC: McFarland, 158–172.

Thomson, Judith Jarvis. 1985. "The Trolley Problem." *Yale Law Journal* 94.6: 1395–1415.

Thomson, Peter. 1983. *Shakespeare's Theatre*. London: Routledge.

Tracy, Kathleen. 2003. *The Girl's Got Bite: The Original Unauthorized Guide to Buffy's World, Completely Revised and Updated*. New York: St. Martin's Griffin.

Tribble, Evelyn B. 2006. "'The Dark Backward and Abysm of Time': *The Tempest* and Memory." *College Literature* 33.1: 151–168.

"Twilight, Part Four." 2010. *Buffy the Vampire Slayer*. Season 8. Number 35. Script by Brad Meltzer. Pencils by George Jeanty. Executive producer Joss Whedon. Milwaukee: Dark Horse Comics.

Varela, Francisco, Evan Thompson, and Eleanor Rosch. 1991. *The Embodied Mind: Cognitive Science and Human Experience*. Cambridge: MIT Press.

Vyvyan, John. 2011. *The Shakespearean Ethic*. London: Shepheard-Walwyn.

Waggoner, Erin B. ed. 2010. *Sexual Rhetoric in the Works of Joss Whedon: New Essays*. Jefferson, NC: McFarland.

Wagner Katherine A. 2013/2014. "Haven't We Been Here Before? *The Cabin in the Woods*, the Horror Genre, and Placelessness." *Slayage: The Journal of the Whedon Studies Association* 10.2/11.1 [36–37]. 21 pars. http:// slayageonline.com/essays/slayage36/ Wagner.pdf. Accessed January 25, 2014.

"Welcome to the Hellmouth." 1997. *Buffy the Vampire Slayer*. Season 1. Episode 1. Written by Joss Whedon. Directed by Charles Martin Smith. Twentieth Century–Fox Home Entertainment, Inc., 2002. DVD.

Whedon, Joss. 1992. *Buffy the Vampire Slayer*. Original Film Script. http://buffy.wikia.

com/wiki/Buffy_the_Vampire_Slayer_ (film)/Original_Script. Accessed June 21, 2013.

Whedon, Joss. 2012a. Interview: Joss Whedon on What "Much Ado About Nothing" Has in Common with "The Avengers." http:// www.indiewire.com/article/joss-whedon- much-ado-toronto-the-avengers?page= 1#articleHeaderPanel. Accessed March 26, 2013.

Whedon, Joss. 2012b. Interview: Joss Whedon: "I want to make things that are small, pure and odd." http://www.indiewire.com/ article/joss-whedon-talks-cabin-avengers- much-ado-and-his-love-for-stephen- sondheim?page=1#articleHeaderPanel. Accessed March 26, 2013.

Whedon, Joss. 2012c. "Afterword." In *The Cabin in the Woods: The Official Visual Companion*. London: Titan Books, 172–173.

Whedon, Joss. 2013. *Much Ado About Nothing: A Film by Joss Whedon*. London: Titan Books.

Whedon, Joss, and Drew Goddard. 2012. "Into the Woods: Joss Whedon and Drew Goddard on the Making of the Film." In *The Cabin in the Woods: The Official Visual Companion*. London: Titan Books, 8–42.

White, Mark D., ed. 2012. *The Avengers and Philosophy: Earth's Mightiest Thinkers*. Hoboken, NJ: John Wiley and Sons.

Wilcox, Rhonda V. 2005. *Why* Buffy *Matters: The Art of* Buffy the Vampire Slayer. London and New York: I.B. Tauris.

Wilcox, Rhonda V. 2006. "In 'The Demon Section of the Card Catalog': *Buffy* Studies and Television Studies." *Slayage: The Journal of the Whedon Studies Association* 6.1 [21]. 27 pars. http://slayageonline.com/ PDF/wilcox4.pdf. Accessed March 26, 2013.

Wilcox, Rhonda V. 2008. "'I Do Not Hold to That': Joss Whedon and Original Sin." In Rhonda Wilcox and Tanya Cochrane, eds., *Investigating* Firefly *and* Serenity. London: I. B. Tauris, 155–166.

Wilcox, Rhonda V. 2011. "'Let it Simmer': Tone in 'Pangs.'" *Slayage: The Journal of the Whedon Studies Association* 9.1 [33]. 27 pars. http://slayageonline.com/essays/slayage33/ Wilcox.pdf. Accessed June 21, 2013.

Wilcox, Rhonda V. 2013. "Much Ado About Whedon: 'Better Than Reportingly.'" *Joss in June*, Cleveland Community College, Shelby, NC, 29 June.

Wilcox, Rhonda, and Tanya Cochrane, eds. 2008. *Investigating "Firefly" and "Serenity."* London: I. B. Tauris.

Winter, Steven L. 2001. *A Clearing in the Forest: Law, Life, and Mind*. Chicago: Chicago University Press.

"The Wish." 1998. *Buffy the Vampire Slayer*. Season 3. Episode 9. Written by Marti Noxon. Directed by David Greenwalt. Twentieth Century–Fox Home Entertainment, Inc., 2003. DVD.

Wright, H.G. 2007. *Means, Ends and Medical Care*. Philosophy and Medicine Series, edited by H. Tristram Engelhardt, Jr. Volume 92. Dordrecht, Netherlands: Springer.

Index